# THE VOICE OF THE POOR IN THE MIDDLE AGES

# THE VOICE OF THE POOR IN THE MIDDLE AGES

## AN ANTHOLOGY OF DOCUMENTS FROM THE CAIRO GENIZA

*Mark R. Cohen*

PRINCETON UNIVERSITY PRESS

PRINCETON AND OXFORD

PUBLISHED BY PRINCETON UNIVERSITY PRESS, 41 WILLIAM STREET,
PRINCETON, NEW JERSEY 08540
IN THE UNITED KINGDOM: PRINCETON UNIVERSITY PRESS, 3 MARKET PLACE,
WOODSTOCK, OXFORDSHIRE OX20 1SY


LIBRARY OF CONGRESS CATALOGING-IN-PUBLICATION DATA

THE VOICE OF THE POOR IN THE MIDDLE AGES : AN ANTHOLOGY OF DOCUMENTS FROM
THE CAIRO GENIZA / [EDITED BY] MARK R. COHEN.
P. CM.
INCLUDES BIBLIOGRAPHICAL REFERENCES (P. ) AND INDEX.
ISBN-13: 978-0-691-09262-1 (CL. : ALK. PAPER)—ISBN-13: 978-0-691-09271-3 (PB. : ALK. PAPER)
ISBN-10: 0-691-09262-1 (CL. : ALK. PAPER)—ISBN-10: 0-691-09271-0 (PB. : ALK. PAPER)
1. JEWS—EGYPT—CHARITIES—HISTORY. 2. POVERTY—RELIGIOUS ASPECTS—JUDAISM.
3. JUDAISM—CHARITIES—HISTORY. 4. JEWS—EGYPT—SOCIAL CONDITIONS.
5. POOR—EGYPT—HISTORY. I. COHEN, MARK R., 1943- II. POVERTY AND
CHARITY IN THE JEWISH COMMUNITY OF MEDIEVAL EGYPT.

HV17.V65 2005
363.5'089'924062—DC22 2004062827

BRITISH LIBRARY CATALOGING-IN-PUBLICATION DATA IS AVAILABLE

THIS BOOK HAS BEEN COMPOSED IN GOUDY

PRINTED ON ACID-FREE PAPER. ∞

PUP.PRINCETON.EDU

PRINTED IN THE UNITED STATES OF AMERICA

1 3 5 7 9 10 8 6 4 2

*For Hanan, Tamar, Uri, and Nina Sarah*

# CONTENTS

# LIST OF ILLUSTRATIONS

# ACKNOWLEDGMENTS

DURING THE many years I have worked on this book—a companion to my *Poverty and Charity in the Jewish Community of Medieval Egypt* (Princeton University Press 2005)—I have benefited from the assistance of many individuals and institutions. As with my previous projects I am particularly indebted to Cambridge University Library, to the Director of the Taylor-Schechter Geniza Research Unit, Professor Stefan C. Reif, and to the staff of the Manuscripts Reading Room. I am grateful also to the Reverend Dr. David Cornick, Principal of Westminster College, and to the Reverend Dr. Janet Tollington, former librarian, for their assistance with Geniza manuscripts in the nearby Westminster College Collection. Similarly, I thank the British Library in London and the staff of the Oriental and India Office Reading Room; the librarian of the Jewish Theological Seminary and library staff, particularly Rabbi Jerome Schwarzbard and David Wachtel; Dr. Avraham David, supervisor of the S. D. Goitein Laboratory for Geniza Research at the Institute for Microfilmed Hebrew Manuscripts, Jewish National and University Library in Jerusalem; and the S. D. Goitein Laboratory for Geniza Research in the Department of Near Eastern Studies at Princeton University. I thank the Syndics of Cambridge University Library and Professor Stefan C. Reif for permission to reproduce in this book eight facsimiles of Geniza documents from their library. I must add here my gratitude for another resource that facilitated my research immeasurably: the word processor Nota Bene, where I created a corpus of about 890 documents and used its marvelous index and search feature, Orbis, to retrieve data that otherwise would have lain buried and virtually inaccessible.

Support for the research and writing was provided over the years by the Princeton University Committee for Research in the Humanities; by the John Simon Guggenheim Foundation with a grant in 1996–97; by the Institute for Advanced Studies in Jerusalem, which generously gave this former Fellow a quiet office to work in that year; by the Center for the Study of Religion at Princeton University and its director, Professor Robert Wuthnow, for a grant in support of the project in 2001–2002; and finally, by the Wissenschaftskolleg zu Berlin, its rector Dieter Grimm and wonderful staff, which afforded me the luxury of a yearlong fellowship in 2002–2003, when I finished the book.

My graduate students over the years read many of these texts with me and I am grateful for what I learned from them. I make particular mention of Jessica Goldberg from Columbia University, and from Princeton, Nancy Khalek, Phillip Lieberman, and Uriel Simonsohn. My research assistant and former student Roxani Eleni Margariti, now teaching at Emory University, made my life immeasurably easier, and I benefited from comments of my former student Marina Rustow, also now at Emory.

I profited greatly from feedback I received over the years when delivering papers on my research-in-progress: at Ohio State Univerity, New York University, the University of California in Los Angeles, the University of Michigan, the Middle East Studies Association, the Association for Jewish Studies, Virginia Tech University, the Society for Judaeo-Arabic Studies, and in Berlin at the Freie Universität, the Humboldt Universität, and the Wissenschaftskolleg.

My longtime friend and colleague Professor Raymond P. Scheindlin of the Jewish Theological Seminary read the entire manuscript, bringing his literary expertise in medieval Hebrew and Judaeo-Arabic to bear in reviewing my translations of the texts. Errors that remain are my own.

A brief overview of some of the material in this book appeared as "The Voice of the Jewish Poor in the Cairo Genizah," in *Semitic Papyrology in Context,* ed. Lawrence Schiffman (Leiden and Boston: Brill, 2003), 239–55. A few of the texts were published by me in "Four Judaeo-Arabic Petitions of the Poor from the Cairo Geniza," in *Jerusalem Studies in Arabic and Islam* 24 (2000), 446–71. I thank the publishers for granting permission to reuse the material in the present volume.

Finally, I wish to thank my editor at Princeton University Press, Brigitta van Rheinberg, for her sage advice about this project, and the ever-so-diligent copyeditor, Marsha Kunin.

# NOTE

TRANSCRIPTIONS OF Arabic follow the *Encyclopaedia of Islam*, second edition, except that *dj* is replaced by *j* and *ḳ* by *q*. Transcriptions of Hebrew are simplified by the omission of the macron. In both Arabic and Hebrew, "ʿ" represents *ayn/ayin* and "ʾ" represents *alif/hamza/alef*. Following accepted conventions used in editing such texts, square brackets [ ] indicate a lacuna in the manuscript or letters or words that are difficult to decipher; double square brackets [[ ]] indicate something crossed out in the manuscript; slashes // // indicate something added above (sometimes below) the line; single slashes (/ /) are used when only a single letter is so added. A question mark indicates an uncertain reading or translation. In Judaeo-Arabic letters, words set in italics are in Hebrew or Aramaic in the text. Abbreviations of Geniza documents used in the notes are explained in the "List of Geniza Texts" at the end.

# PART ONE

## LETTERS ABOUT THE POOR AND ABOUT CHARITY

# INTRODUCTION

"THE VOICE OF the poor can generally be heard only through records and observations compiled by their literate social superiors, from the tax collector to the inquisitor's clerk, and from the judge of criminals to the benefactor of the helpless."[1] What the distinguished historian of poverty and charity, Brian Pullan, says about early modern Italy—an observation that holds true for most of premodern European history and for the Islamic world as well—makes the voices of the poor heard in this book almost unique. Though emanating from one of the marginal groups in world history, the documents translated here help close a much lamented gap in premodern social history, offering intimate insight into an important and central problem in human history. They present a vivid case study illustrating not only medieval Jewish life but also structural aspects of poverty and charity that are only vaguely visible in the Christian and Islamic pasts.

Compiled for the benefit of students, scholars, and the general reader, the anthology comprises a representative sample (94 in total) of the some 485 letters, 315 alms lists, donor lists, and other accounts used in the author's *Poverty and Charity in the Jewish Community of Medieval Egypt*.[2] That book presents a full analysis and interpretation of those documents, as well as of Maimonides' contemporaneous laws about charity. The vast majority of the documents are hitherto unpublished and most of them are herewith being made available for the first time in any format.

The letters of the poor, whether written in their own hand or dictated to a scribe or family member, recount a panoply of hardship, suffering, and strategies for obtaining relief. From a somewhat different angle of vision, letters of recommendation on behalf of the poor illustrate, in addition to the plight of the poor, the attitude of the more fortunate members of society toward poverty and its relief. The alms lists and donor lists show how benevolent Jews fulfilled a time-honored obligation, or *miṣva*, in Judaism through public charity. Seemingly

[1] Brian Pullan, "Support and Redeem: Charity and Poor Relief in Italian Cities from the Fourteenth to the Seventeenth Century," *Continuity and Change* 3 (1988), 179.

[2] Princeton University Press, 2005. References below to chapters in *Poverty and Charity* can usually be pinpointed with the aid of the "Index of Geniza Texts" there.

rather dry at first glance, these lists take on vibrant life when subjected to the kinds of questions that animate this study. They allow us to hear the voice of the poor, too, although it is a silent voice.

## The Cairo Geniza

An ancient Jewish custom with roots in the period of the Mishna (codified 200 C.E.) and Talmud (ca. 200–500 C.E.) prohibits the destruction of pieces of sacred writing—in theory, fragments of the Bible containing God's name but in practice anything copied or printed in the Hebrew script. These papers must be buried in a *geniza* (the word *geniza* means both "burial place" and the act of "burying"). Normally, a geniza is located in a cemetery. But the Cairo Geniza was special. For various reasons, not fully understood to this day,[3] it was situated behind a wall *inside* the synagogue, the so-called Ben Ezra Synagogue in Fustat (Old Cairo), which dates back to the Middle Ages and possibly even to pre-Islamic times.[4] This had two fortunate consequences. One, the contents of this Geniza were concentrated in one space and easily accessible, once it was discovered. Two, because Egypt is such an arid country, the pages buried there stood the test of centuries, without molding, so that even when a page is torn or riddled with holes, the ink can be read today almost as clearly as when it was copied, as long as a thousand years ago. Not well known, the Jewish custom of geniza has its parallel in Islam, mainly for Qur'ān fragments but also for other religious literature and even documents from everyday life.[5]

It has been estimated that the Cairo Geniza contains upward of 210,000 items (shelfmarked fragments) of handwritten text. When individual folios are counted the total rises to around three-quarters of a million. The vast majority are leaves from books, such as medieval Hebrew poetry, rabbinic fragments, midrashic texts, philosophical works, magical texts, and liturgical fragments (usually pages from prayer books). Surprisingly, the cache also includes a wide variety of individual documents from everyday life, many of which we would call "secular." They date mostly from the eleventh to thirteenth centuries and comprise letters, court records, marriage contracts, deeds of divorce, wills, accounts,

[3] See Mark R. Cohen and Yedida K. Stillman, "The Cairo Geniza and the Custom of Geniza among Oriental Jewry: A Historical and Ethnographic Study" (in Hebrew), *Peʿamim*, no. 24 (1985), 3–35.

[4] See Phyllis Lambert, ed., *Fortifications and the Synagogue: The Fortress of Babylon and the Ben Ezra Synagogue, Cairo* (London, 1994).

[5] See my "Jewish and Islamic Life in the Middle Ages: Through the Window of the Cairo Geniza," in a book on Jewish-Islamic creative coexistence to be edited by Joseph Montville. Also Joseph Sadan, "Genizah and Genizah-Like Practices in Islamic and Jewish Traditions," *Bibliotheca Orientalis* 43 (1986), 36–58 and my "Geniza for Islamicists, Islamic Geniza, and the 'New Cairo Geniza,'" lecture given at Harvard University's Center for Middle Eastern Studies, February 12, 2004, to be published in the *Harvard Middle Eastern and Islamic Review*.

book lists, lists of recipients of charity and of gifts for charitable purposes, as well as official documents, such as petitions to be submitted to Muslim authorities (and hence written in Arabic script). These individual fragments, which we call the "historical documents" (as opposed to the literary fragments mentioned above) constitute perhaps 5 percent of the Geniza as a whole. Though many are in Hebrew or Aramaic, most are written in Judaeo-Arabic, that is, Arabic in Hebrew characters and displaying grammatical and syntactic features differentiating it from the Arabic of the Qur'ān and all other medieval Arabic writings (classical Arabic). The Geniza also contains fragments from Islamic books, even pages of the Qur'ān in Hebrew transcription, signs of the well-known cultural embeddedness of the Jews in Arab-Muslim society of the Middle Ages. The Jewish documents from the Geniza confirm that the so-called classical Geniza period (eleventh to mid-thirteenth centuries) was one of relatively peaceful coexistence, especially compared to the high Middle Ages in northern Europe.[6]

Discovered at the end of the nineteenth century, the contents of the Geniza were dispersed among more than twenty libraries and private collections, from Cincinnati, Ohio, to St. Petersburg, Russia.[7] More than one hundred years of research on these fragments have produced more knowledge about Jewish life and literature in the Islamic Middle Ages than can easily be imagined. In particular, the historical documents have revealed aspects of economic, social, and family life, as well as of material culture and the mind of the individual, that were previously completely unknown.

## The Voice of the Poor in World History

The voice of the poor that we hear in the Geniza documents stands in bold relief on the canvas of the world history of poverty. Sources for antiquity, medieval Christendom, and medieval Islam largely lack it. Roger Bagnall notifies the readers of his lavishly detailed study *Egypt in Late Antiquity* that "almost all [of the Greek papyrological evidence] comes from the viewpoint of the propertied classes of the cities of Egypt," and that the Coptic papyri from everyday life, which do not become common until long after the Council of Chalcedon

[6] This comparison is explored in my *Under Crescent and Cross: The Jews in the Middle Ages* (Princeton, 1994).

[7] See the Introduction to S. D. Goitein's *A Mediterranean Society: The Jewish Communities of the Arab World as Portrayed in the Documents of the Cairo Geniza*, 6 vols. (Berkeley and Los Angeles, 1967–93), in volume 1 (1967) (hereafter *Med. Soc.*), as well as Stefan C. Reif, *A Jewish Archive from Old Cairo: The History of Cambridge University's Genizah Collection* (Richmond, Surrey, 2000). Microfilm copies of most or all of the Geniza manuscripts are held in the Institute of Hebrew Microfilmed Manuscripts in the Jewish National and University Library in Jerusalem, Cambridge University Library in England, at Yeshiva University, and the Jewish Theological Seminary in New York. Subsets of the entirety are available in photocopy or microfilm at other institutions, for instance, Tel Aviv University, Princeton University, and Emory University.

(451), emanate largely from the Christian monasteries. *"[T]his too is not the viewpoint of the poor."*[8] The situation does not improve for the period after late antiquity. Historians of poverty in medieval and early modern Europe like Brian Pullan have noted with regret that the materials at their disposal do not include the voices of the indigent masses. Assessing, for instance, "the complex attitudes and responses that poverty evoked" in medieval Europe, Michel Mollat—to cite one example from among many—laments that the evidence available to him "generally exhibits only one point of view, that of the non-poor casting their gaze upon the poor."[9]

Things are no better for the world of Islam. "Given the absence of sources for statements by the poor," Adam A. Sabra, author of a pioneering book on poverty and charity in Mamluk Cairo, laments, "the ideal task of determining how the poor saw their own fate is next to impossible."[10] In his masterful bibliographical survey of Middle Eastern historical studies, Stephen Humphreys cites the methodological obstacle with regard to the peasantry as a whole (who were not

[8] Bagnall, *Egypt in Late Antiquity* (Princeton, 1993), 5 (emphasis mine).

[9] Michel Mollat, *The Poor in the Middle Ages: An Essay in Social History*, trans. Arthur Goldhammer (New Haven and London, 1986), 2. In her study of poverty in medieval Cambridge, Miri Rubin writes "we are usually much better informed about the identity of the giver, the founder, donor or testator, than we are about the recipients." *Charity and Community in Medieval Cambridge* (Cambridge, 1987), 6. Sharon Farmer notes the same deficiency in *Surviving Poverty in Medieval Paris: Gender, Ideology and the Daily Lives of the Poor* (Ithaca and London, 2002), 3–4: "Historians who have focused on the actions and perspectives of propertied members of medieval society have produced numerous studies of hospitals and hospices . . . ; of charitable almsgiving in urban wills; of the attitudes toward the poor. Occasionally, but not often, studies of hospitals and confraternal charity offer a profile of the recipients of such charity, but the sources left behind by medieval hospitals and confraternities *reveal almost nothing about their daily lives*." Her book seeks partially to make up for this deficiency with evidence from "testimonies" of poor people claiming to have received a miraculous cure at the shrine of St. Louis. In her study of poverty and welfare in Habsburg Toledo, Linda Martz begins her chapter on the "recipients of relief" with a confession: "The bulk of the extant records have to do with the finances of charitable institutions or with the individual who was wealthy enough to make a last will and testament, while the recipients of poor relief remain colourless and vaguely defined individuals in among the mass of humanity known as the poor." *Poverty and Welfare in Habsburg Spain: The Example of Toledo* (Cambridge, 1983), 200. Paul Slack, discussing *Poverty and Policy in Tudor and Stuart England* (London and New York, 1988), notes (p. 7): "The sources seldom allow the poor to speak for themselves." The problem persists even at the beginning of the modern era. Gertrude Himmelfarb laments: "There is one kind of source the historian would dearly love to have: the direct testimony of the poor themselves. . . . What we do have, by way of working class sources, are documents more often addressed to the working class than originating with them." See *The Idea of Poverty: England in the Early Industrial Age* (New York, 1984), 14. Carlo Ginzburg reminds us that this is a general problem when writing about the non-elites in the European past: "[T]he thoughts, the beliefs, and the aspirations of the peasants and artisans of the past reach us (if and when they do) almost always through distorting viewpoints and intermediaries." *The Cheese and the Worms*, trans. John and Anne Tedeschi (Baltimore, 1980), xv.

[10] Adam Sabra, *Poverty and Charity in Medieval Islam: Mamluk Egypt, 1250–1517* (Cambridge, 2000), 8.

all poor) under the rubric "The Voiceless Classes of Islamic Society."[11] The tiny handful of letters from or on behalf of needy persons thus far discovered among the Arabic papyri and fragments on paper from Egypt and in the so-called archive (probably an Islamic geniza) of a thirteenth-century merchant from the Red Sea Port of Quseir al-Qadīm bear significant similarities to the Judaeo-Arabic letters from the Geniza, and it is to be hoped that the numbers of such Muslim letters will grow as research on the papyri and on Arabic letters on paper dating from even later than the papyri progresses.[12] Similar headway can be made now for European history thanks to research on recently discovered "pauper letters" from early industrial England and from the continent of Europe—an enterprise consciously aimed at making up for a lacuna in the sources for social history.[13]

[11] R. Stephen Humphreys, *Islamic History: A Framework for Inquiry*, rev. ed. (Princeton, 1991), 284–308.

[12] Yūsuf Rāġib, *Marchands d'étoffes du Fayyoum au IIIe/IXe siècle d'après leurs archives (actes et lettres), II La correspondance administrative et privée des Banū ʿAbd al-Muʾmin* (Cairo, 1985), 44–46. Werner Diem, *Arabische Briefe auf Papyrus und Papier aus der Heidelberger Papyrus-Sammlung. Textband* (Wiesbaden, 1991), 212–15 (12th century) (it is not certain that the recommendee of this letter was in financial need; he is a foreigner, being introduced to a dignitary, who is asked to "help him"); 227 (9th century) (an appeal for assistance, *laysa bi-yadī nafaq[a]*, "I have no sustenanc[e]"); 277 (11th century) (letter of appeal to fulfill a promise to give a gift for the writer's wedding, *fa-in tafaḍḍala sayyidī wa-mawlāya an yaʾmur . . . bi-qalīl qamḥ mā amkana ḥattā yakūn nafaqatan*, "please be so kind as to order . . . (for me) a little wheat, insofar as is possible, for my sustenance"; and idem, *Arabische Privatbriefe des 9. bis 15. Jarhunderts aus der Österreichischen Nationalbibliothek in Wien. Textband* (Wiesbaden, 1996), 183–84 (13th century or later) (letter of appeal for clothing); Li Guo, "Arabic Documents from the Red Sea Port of Quseir in the Seventh/Thirteenth Century, Part I: Business Letters," *Journal of Near Eastern Studies* 58 (1999), 186–90. The relevant letter, as I understand it, is a petition from a needy person seeking assistance for himself and his family. See my discussion of these documents in "Geniza for Islamicists, Islamic Geniza, and the 'New Cairo Geniza.'"

[13] Acknowledging the lacuna for England, a recent collection of essays attempts to find and exploit "the words of the poor" fortuitously preserved in parish records and so write the history of poverty "from below." *Chronicling Poverty: The Voices and Strategies of the English Poor, 1640–1840*, ed. Tim Hitchcock, Peter King, and Pamela Sharpe (New York, 1997), see esp. the editors' introduction and the essays by Pamela Sharpe, "'The Bowels of Compation': A Labouring Family and the Law, c. 1790–1834"; James Stephen Taylor, "Voices in the Crowd: The Kirkby Lonsdale Township Letters, 1809–36"; Thomas Sokoll, "Old Age in Poverty: The Record of Essex Pauper Letters, 1780–1834." See also Pamela Sharpe, "Survival Strategies and Stories: Poor Widows and Widowers in Early Industrial England," in *Widowhood in Medieval and Early Modern Europe*, eds. Sandra Cavallo and Lyndan Warner (Essex, 1999), 220–39. See also Thomas Sokoll, "Negotiating a Living: Essex Pauper Letters from London, 1800–1834," *International Review of Social History* 41 (2000), 19–46; the collection, *Essex Pauper Letters, 1731–1837*, ed. Thomas Sokoll (Oxford, 2001); the collection of letters, petitions, examinations, and depositions regarding the poor sojourning outside their parish of settlement at the end of the eighteenth and the beginning of the nineteenth centuries, James Stephen Taylor, *Poverty, Migration, and Settlement in the Industrial Revolution: Sojourners' Narratives* (Palo Alto, 1989). The same goal of writing history from below underlies a publication containing letters and appeals from "the common folk" in nineteenth-century Germany. Siegfried Grosse et al., eds., *"Denn das Schrieben gehört nicht zu meiner täglichen Beschäfti-*

## Geniza Letters and European "Pauper Letters"

The European "pauper letters" just mentioned play an important background role in the present collection. Though separated geographically, culturally, and chronologically from the Jewish material, they contain remarkable parallels to the Geniza letters and illustrate their value as evidence of structures of history shared across time and across societies with different religions. Moreover, they enable us to evaluate certain methodological problems that need to be addressed—with encouraging results. First comes the question of repetitiousness of language from letter to letter, especially as this relates to "facticity." Second, many of the personal letters of appeal, especially those of the women, may not actually have been written by the indigents themselves, similarly raising questions about the reliability of these documents as witnesses to social history. These issues do not, however, detract from the value of the letters as specimens of the voice of the poor. As Thomas Sokoll writes in his study of "pauper letters" from early industrial England in a comment that is applicable to our case: "It is obvious . . . that in interpreting a pauper letter we have to watch out for stereotypes, exaggerations or even literary make-ups which must not be taken literally. And yet, despite this, we may normally still regard it as a true record of the specific circumstances of an individual case, providing that the account is not grossly inconsistent or unlikely."[14]

Sokoll reminds us, too, that the definition of "author"or "writer" in premodern societies without universal literacy, and even in eighteenth- and early nineteenth-century England, was not sharp. "In the context of the social history of language, terms like 'author,' 'writer,' or 'scribe' are insufficient and inappropriate if understood in their conventional sense. . . . The power of writing is not confined to those who themselves were able to write. It also applies to anyone who *had* a piece being written in a given place at a given time."[15] Moreover, he adds, letters that other people wrote on behalf of the needy provide important, complementary information about their experience of poverty "in that they show to what extent certain attitudes, images and beliefs were shared across social groups, thus providing important insights into the social range of contemporary notions such as the nature of poverty."[16] These observations also hold true for the Geniza letters, as we shall point out.

*gung:" Der Alltag kleiner Leute in Bittschriften, Briefen und Berichten aus dem 19. Jahrhundert: Ein Lesebuch* (Bonn, 1989).

[14] Thomas Sokoll, "Old Age in Poverty," 131; idem, *Essex Pauper Letters*, 67–70.

[15] Idem, "Old Age in Poverty," 133–34; idem, *Essex Pauper Letters*, 62–67. James Stephen Taylor, writing about pauper letters addressed to the township of Kirkby Lonsdale, states: "Even if it were the pen of a neighbour or family member, writing out of charity or for a pittance, the voice would not be markedly altered, except in an obvious case"; "Voices in the Crowd," 116.

[16] Sokoll, "Old Age in Poverty," 135.

The attentive reader of the notes and commentaries to the letters below will find fascinating similarities and even stylistic parallels between letters of the Christian poor in late eighteenth- and early nineteenth-century England and Jewish letters from the eleventh to mid-thirteenth centuries. Contemporaneous Islamic ideas of poverty and its relief, and medieval Christian notions of poverty and charity also come into play. All of this illustrates structural features of the history of poverty that our study has confirmed from a previously unknown angle.

The "pauper letters" from England and from other places, it should be stated, while they originate from the poor, differ from the Geniza specimens in some important respects. They are "official" letters—appeals to parish overseers of charity by or on behalf of indigents living in another parish and seeking nonresident or "out-township" relief. By way of contrast, the Geniza specimens are addressed primarily to private individuals. This makes them doubly precious, insofar as they concern the elusive realm of *private charity*. Additionally, the Geniza letters stem from a religious age, and thus religious sentiments permeate their lines. The pauper letters are striking in the absence of religious content. This does not mean that the indigents of late eighteenth- and early nineteenth-century England lacked religious feeling. It means that the medieval people—poor and benefactor alike—lived and breathed religion in a much more fundamental way and believed that charity, as much a duty toward God as toward one's fellow man, made a difference to the Creator. By contrast, the English paupers knew that the handouts they requested were part of a legislated, mandatory, "secular" system—no longer part of a calculus of giving that would bring salvation. Promising to pray to God on behalf of poor law administrators charged by civil law to distribute tax revenues as charity would have sounded a bit out of place.[17]

There remains the question of repetitiveness—also a characteristic of the pauper letters—and what that says about the facticity of our sources. The Geniza letters do show a certain amount of formulaic repetitiousness "at the edges," as the letter writers, or those writing down their stories for them, "shaped narratives" to get results, to use Natalie Zemon Davis's term in *Fiction in the Archives*.[18] Nonetheless, the central core of their stories is believable enough. The kinds of fictional embellishments peppering the fascinating "pardon tales" in Davis's study are largely absent. The Geniza paupers, like Davis's characters, were certainly concerned about their future and that of their families, but the stakes were not so high. Their plight could be mitigated

[17] In a very rare exception, a widow closes her letter of appeal to a parish poor law administrator: "I hope God will bless You for doing good for the fatherless & Widow." Sokoll, *Essex Pauper Letters*, 519, and again on the same page, a similar blessing by the same widow writing another letter to the same official.

[18] *Fiction in the Archives: Pardon Tales and Their Tellers in Sixteenth-Century France* (Oxford, 1987).

by a simple gift of some cash, food, or an article of clothing. Moreover, even when they had an interesting "story" to tell to explain their indigence, when all is said and done, they had less need to justify themselves than Davis's sixteenth-century French murderers claiming extenuating circumstances before the authorities in order to save their lives. Even in rare instances in our material, such as that of the impoverished widow of the cantor Ben Naḥman—whose moving, dire, and fascinating tale of woe we shall read includes physical violence perpetrated against her—the facts of the cases seem credible enough.

Finally, as the greatest of all Geniza scholars, S. D. Goitein, pointed out, the Geniza is "the very opposite of an archive."[19] Unlike an archive, its contents were not stored for future retrieval, not housed in systematic fashion to enable people later on to find documentation of this or that fact or event. It is a waste bin for discarded papers. Largely uncensored and unmediated, however, and not meant to be read by future generations, the Geniza letters, side by side with the silent evidence of the alms lists and donor registers, allow us to hear the real voice of the poor and to study the strategies they employed to survive in the absence of a well-organized state poor-law mechanism and to avail themselves of the "entitlement" afforded them by the divine command to give charity.[20]

## Letters as Petitions

A large number of the letters (the first example is no. 1 below) display the stylistic conventions of the Arabic petition, particularly the classic structure of *arenga-expositio-dispositio*, the introduction, exposition of the case, and request clause characteristic of petitions in the Greco-Roman world and also found in the Jewish Aramaic papyri from Upper Egypt in the fifth century B.C.E.[21] We know a lot about petitions to Muslim rulers in Egypt thanks to medieval Arab authors like al-Qalqashandī, whose epistolographic manual sets forth the stylistic rules for writing petitions and gives examples. *Actual* petitions are to be found among the written remains of the minority communities—in the Monastery of St. Catherine in Sinai, where they were archived for future reference, and in the Cairo Geniza, where they were "buried" because they no longer had use—and among the Arabic papyri, which were dumped into the

[19] *Med. Soc.*, 1:7.

[20] On the usefulness of the concept of "strategies" in the analysis of letters of the poor, see Pamela Sharpe, "Survival Strategies and Stories," 230–32; Sokoll, "Negotiating a Living," 42–46.

[21] See one example in A. Cowley, ed. and trans., *Aramaic Papyri of the Fifth Century* B.C. (1923; reprinted Osnabrück, 1967), 108–122, a petition (two versions, probably drafts) from the Jewish colony in Elephantine to the Persian governor of Judaea; Bezalel Porten et al., eds., *The Elephantine Papyri in English: Three Millennia of Cross-Cultural Continuity and Change* (Leiden, 1996), 139–47.

garbage. The Arabic petitions preserved in the Geniza have been most thoroughly studied by Geoffrey Khan.[22]

The Jews were fully aware of the petition form. Many members of their community worked in the government chancery and so dealt directly and on a daily basis with what al-Qalqashandī describes. Jews also petitioned the Muslim authorities regularly, as the remains of such Arabic petitions (usually drafts) in the Geniza attest. Furthermore, within their own community, individuals addressed petitions in Judaeo-Arabic to *Jewish* communal officials and heads, as well as to private persons, seeking redress of grievances or, in our case, charity.[23] Even Hebrew letters sometimes betray the influence of the form and style of Arabic petitions.

Elsewhere I have argued that the Geniza letters of the poor should not be equated (as they often have been) with the "Schnorrerbriefe" that became common in central and eastern Europe after the middle of the seventeenth century, when pogroms in Poland caused an increase in Jewish mendicancy and vagabondage.[24] Sometimes known in Hebrew as *qibbuṣim* ("collection letters"), these European letters recommend indigents for charity and resemble in function the royal "beggars' licenses" in Christian society that served the same purpose for Christian captives.[25]

The Judaeo-Arabic petitions of the poor in the Geniza functioned, not as an instrument for begging, but as a respectable instrument for obtaining private charity. They were addressed to one person (or group of persons), and meant for a single use, not for repetitive begging from person to person or house to house. A preponderance of the petitioners wrote because they needed temporary assistance to overcome a temporary hardship. And they wished to do this

[22] Geoffrey Khan, *Arabic Legal and Administrative Documents in the Cambridge Genizah Collections* (Cambridge, 1993), chapter 12, 302–409. Petitions preserved among the early papyri from Egypt represent an early stage in the evolution of the document's form, prior to the Fatimid period. See Geoffrey Khan, "The Historical Development of the Structure of Medieval Arabic Petitions," *Bulletin of the School of Oriental and African Studies* 53 (1990), 8–30. Some Arabic petitions from everyday life have also been discovered among the "late papyri" (which include writings on paper), e.g., Diem, *Arabische Briefe auf Papyrus und Papier aus der Heidelberger Papyrus-Sammlung, Textband*, Index s.v. "Petition," e.g., 30–36 (14th century), and especially interesting, as it demonstrates the use of the petition form inside the other minority community in Egypt, 18–25 (a Christian petition to the Patriarch of Alexandria, 13th century).

[23] See Mark R. Cohen, "Four Judaeo-Arabic Petitions of the Poor from the Cairo Geniza," *Jerusalem Studies in Arabic and Islam* 24 (2000), 446–71.

[24] Cohen, "Four Judaeo-Arabic Petitions of the Poor," and Cohen, *Poverty and Charity*, chapter 7.

[25] Examples of the qibbuṣ letters are preserved in the epistles of Rabbi Judah Aryeh Modena (d. 1648 in Venice) (*Iggerot R. Yehuda Aryeh Mi-modena* [Letters of Rabbi Leon Modena], ed. Yacob Boksenboim [Tel Aviv, 1984], e.g., 209–12, 213–15, 224–25, 232–33, 293–94) and in pedagogical manuals like *Iggerot melammedim* (Letters of Jewish Teachers), ed. Yacob Boksenboim (Tel Aviv, 1985), 52, and index s.v. qibbuṣim. On Christian "begging licenses," see Jarbel Rodriguez, "Prisoners of Faith: Christian Captives in the Later Middle Ages" (Ph.D. diss., Princeton University, 2001), passim.

*privately*, "uncovering their faces" to a limited audience. For this purpose, the petition form was ideally suited.[26] It allowed these unfortunates to minimize their embarrassment and to retain some of their dignity by employing a known instrument of Muslim administration and following its diplomatic conventions.

These texts have additional social meaning. The relationship between petitioner and petitioned functioned very much like the ancient and gentlemanly system of patronage that pervaded Near Eastern society. That relationship was characterized by bonding between the benefactor and the recipient of his protection, who prayed to God on behalf of his or her patron in gratitude for a gift bestowed (or anticipated) and would praise him publicly for his generosity. The petition form of Jewish letters of appeal also confirms and is in turn confirmed by patterns of an earlier period in the history of Christian charity. Peter Brown has suggested that the ancient Near Eastern model of petitioning for justice, which entered Christianity through the Hebrew Bible, suffused the new charity of the later Roman Empire, and also led to what he calls an "'upward slippage' of the notion of the 'poor' in Christian texts of the time."[27] His insight about early Christianity—including his claim, among others, that the ancient Near Eastern model was that of plaintiff, rather than beggar—accords with the practice of the later period in the Near East as represented in the Judaeo-Arabic petitions of the poor from the Cairo Geniza.

## Society and Culture of the Non-Elite

Incidental to its main focus, this collection has broader significance for medieval social and cultural history. It offers insight into the society and culture of the underclass, normally hidden from the historian's gaze. We hear about their personal hardships, about their debts, about illness and unemployment, about the anxiety produced by being "cut off" (in their language) from income or from family assistance—subjects often omitted from chronicles and other literary sources. The collection also introduces the normally mute voice of women, describing their adversities and sometimes the travails of their marriages, while at the same time revealing the strategies they employed, taking

[26] "Pauper letters" (Christian, not Jewish) in Germany in the nineteenth century had a formal structure similar to the diplomatic scheme of the petition of antiquity. They were "official" written appeals, addressed to public authorities, following the prohibition of begging in Prussia at the beginning of the nineteenth century. See Siegfried Grosse et al., eds., "*Denn das Schrieben gehört nicht zu meiner täglichen Beschäftigung*," 29–30, and Sokoll, *Essex Pauper Letters*, 57. For the petition form in pauper letters from England, see Taylor, "Voices in the Crowd," 111, 115. The Geniza letters, it must be reiterated, display features of the classical and Arabic petition, but most of them are requests for *private* charity. They offer an opportunity to respond to Sokoll's lament about the dearth of "comparative research into the social history of petitioning." Ibid, 60.

[27] Peter Brown, *Poverty and Leadership in the Later Roman Empire* (Hanover, NH, and London, 2002), 69–73.

charge of their lives when they could, to protect themselves and their children from privation. Our letters are peppered, further, with unmediated access to family relationships as well as to relationships between the common folk and the Jewish officialdom. Everywhere, whether it be in the letters or in the alms lists, we encounter the mobile society of the Islamic Mediterranean, especially what we call here the foreign poor, and we even meet people, sometimes as refugees, coming from Europe into the Islamic orbit. This perspective complements the better known life of the merchants of the Geniza portrayed so fascinatingly by Goitein.[28]

On the cultural side, the letters accurately reflect the religiosity of the average Jew, from the religious motivation to give charity, based on biblical and rabbinic instruction, to ideas of poverty centered in traditional Jewish texts or echoing concepts floating around in the Muslim environment. We sense the mentality of the *Homo religiosus*, always offering prayers and frequently expressing hopes for divine redemption. We hear, further, about relations between the Jews of Egypt and the community in Palestine, which held a special place in Jewish religious consciousness. This was enhanced by close geographical and political affiliation, as Palestine belonged then to the Muslim empire centered in Cairo (except when occupied by the conquering Christian Crusaders). As a cultural artifact, the letters themselves represent prize examples of the Arabic and Hebrew epistolography of people from the non-elite of society, differing from though in some ways based upon the letter-writing of Arab high society, exemplified in the many Arabic epistolographic manuals from the Middle Ages. The Judaeo-Arabic petitions themselves constitute another genre of Arabic literature that Jews adopted from their surroundings during the great Judaeo-Arabic acculturation of the Middle Ages, an aspect of the topic that remains to be systematically investigated. The society and culture of the non-elite and their mentality, often missing from medieval literary sources (Muslim and Jewish alike), shine brightly in the letters of and about the poor originating in the Cairo Geniza.

By way of introduction we present in chapter 1 several letters that illustrate basic themes about poverty and charity in the Geniza. Many of these themes are then revisited in a more focused way in subsequent chapters, as we apply the cases at hand to illuminate larger questions in the history of the poor and poor relief. The chapters that follow deal with the taxonomy of the poor (chapter 2), the foreign poor (chapter 3), indigent captives and refugees (chapter 4), debt and the poll tax (chapter 5), women and poverty (chapter 6), and public charity (chapter 7). They focus mainly on the poor and their plight and the strategies they employed to obtain assistance, but they pertain to charity as well. Part 2 deals with public charity as reflected in alms lists and

[28] S. D. Goitein, *Letters of Medieval Jewish Traders* (Princeton, 1973).

donor accounts (chapters 8 and 9). Part 3, the epilogue (chapter 10), contains a set of letters emanating from the office of the head of the Jews Joshua Nagid (d. 1355), the great-great grandson of Maimonides, illustrating poverty and charity in the fourteenth century, a period of decline in the Jewish as well as the general economy in Egypt.

In the nature of things, a single document often speaks to more than one theme. The general index will enable readers to locate information in the book no matter where it may be.

## Chapter One

# BASIC THEMES

PRIVATE CHARITY, by its very nature, is not easily observed in other periods and societies in premodern times.[1] In the Islamic case, it can be tracked mainly for rulers and other members of the elite, whose beneficence toward the poor was often recorded in Arabic chronicles.[2] But the letters of the Geniza open a wide window on this subject and for a much broader range of society. Private charity was sought by people of means who "fell from their wealth" (*yored mi-nekhasav*, a rabbinic expression found frequently in the Geniza letters) as well as by the working poor who temporarily slipped below the poverty line. These people normally kept themselves *mastūr*, "concealed" from public exposure by living lives of self-sufficiency. The Arabic term with this connotation can be found in medieval Islamic sources and in modern Egyptian colloquial Arabic.[3] When a crisis hit—a general economic emergency, loss of a job, loss of a husband, illness, debt, or frustration as a newcomer without work or local means of familial support—these people wrote private appeals for help, in order to limit their shame and avoid "uncovering their face" in public by standing in line alongside the chronic poor who collected bread and other alms from the community.

The best way to avoid "uncovering the face" was to turn to family. Jewish law puts care of family before charity for all others.[4] But family charity was (and is) the most private of private sources of charity and so we observe it only obliquely in the documents. That is because what was taken for granted and offered with grace normally did not need to be mentioned. Nonetheless, we get occasional glimpses of family charity in the letters when it is absent, denied, or otherwise problematic. We may surmise, too, that the extremely large number of widows on the alms lists (see the lists below) simply had parents who were too old to assist them, or had died. But there is no reason to doubt

[1] For instance, Sharon Farmer writes in *Surviving Poverty in Medieval Paris*, 6: "Because of the limitations of the sources . . . medieval historians have thus far uncovered only fragmentary information about poor people's noninstitutional social networks and forms of support."

[2] Sabra, *Poverty and Charity in Medieval Egypt*, 50–58, a section that begins with the lament, "Unfortunately, we know little about the charitable acts of the common people . . . [for they left] no written record for the historian to use as documentation."

[3] See Cohen, *Poverty and Charity*, chapter 1, notes 31, 57, and 58.

[4] See below, chapter 3, and Cohen, *Poverty and Charity*, chapter 2.

the important role that family (first, the immediate, nuclear family, then the extended kinship circle), along with neighbors, played as benefactors of the poor in the Geniza world. This can be asserted despite the multitude of well documented extra-familial avenues for Jewish poor relief, the very kind of "mixed economy" of charity that is proposed by some revisionist scholars as a substitute for the "golden age" of predominantly family-based welfare in the premodern world.[5]

## 1. "I remained in hiding, unable to appear in public"

We begin with a letter from Yaḥyā b. ʿAmmār of Alexandria, a man of the working poor who took care of members of his immediate and extended family. The letter exhibits many of the themes and strategies of the poor. We find Yaḥyā hiding out in Fustat from Muslim creditors. Unable to show himself in public, lest his creditors catch up with him, he sends a letter of appeal to ʿUlla ha-Levi b. Joseph (Arabic name: Ṣāʿid b. Munajjā), *parnas* (social welfare official) and trustee of the court in Fustat (dated documents: 1084–1117).[6] The handwriting is that of the well-known scribe and court clerk Ḥalfon b. Menasse ibn al-Qaṭāʾif (dated documents 1100–38).

Formally, the letter deploys seven of the eight structural features of the Arabic petition as described by Geoffrey Khan.[7] It begins with (1) a *tarjama* in the upper left corner, in which the suppliant's name is given (in the translation, the tarjama is placed in the upper right corner). This opening formula is normally followed, in the Arabic petition, by (2) the Islamic *basmala* ("in the name of God the Merciful and Compassionate"), but here, by a Jewish equivalent. In the Arabic petition, next comes (3) a blessing on the ruler to whom the petition is addressed—here, a verse from Psalms praising charity and other blessings for the parnas, ʿUlla ha-Levi. The Arabic petition is followed at this point by (4) an expression of obeisance ("the slave kisses the ground"). Though missing here, it is found in most of the petitions of the Jewish poor. (Sections 1–4 parallel the Latin *arenga*). The formula introducing the exposition (5), beginning with the term "the slave reports"/"informs" [*yunhī*]) follows. The actual request or "disposition" (6) in the language of diplomatic,

[5] Peregrine Horden, "Household Care and Informal Networks: Comparisons and Continuities from Antiquity to the Present," in *The Locus of Care: Families, Communities, Institutions and the Provision of Welfare since Antiquity*, eds. Peregrine Horden and Richard Smith (London and New York, 1998), 53. Though elusive, evidence of the (continued) role of family in care for the needy is being uncovered—indeed, even for the post "golden age" period—in pauper letters from early industrial England; Sokoll, "Old Age in Poverty," 135–39.

[6] On the parnas, see Cohen, *Poverty and Charity*, chapter 8. See also *Med. Soc.*, 2:78.

[7] See Intro., note 22 above.

often containing motivational rhetoric, comes next. The following section (7) constitutes what Khan calls the *raʾy* formula ("to our lord belongs the lofty decision,[8] raʾy, in this," etc.). The petition ends with (8) closing formulas, less elaborate here than in Islamic petitions, and typically Jewish.

Some Geniza petitions are perfect in their structure (having all eight parts), but many more are less complete than this one, as is true also of petitions to Muslim authorities.[9] Rabbinic Judaism frowned upon unstructured begging. This explains, on the one hand, the mass of letters seeking *private* charity and adopting the Islamic petition form, with its social construction of patronage rather than begging. It also explains the organized system of alms collections and distributions that are represented in the Geniza lists.

When Yaḥyā fled to Fustat from his Muslim creditors he left behind a large family, including an elderly, blind mother. When he mentions his burden of family, he adds between the lines (marked here by double slashes) the names of several relatives from his extended clan. This afterthought was meant to play on the sympathy of his would-be benefactor. Mentioning the burden of family is also part of the strategy of the poor depicted in English and German pauper letters from the period of the early Industrial Revolution.[10]

The biblical verse from Psalms, "Happy is he who is thoughtful of the wretched; in bad times may (the Lord) keep him from harm," used as an epigraph and introducing the blessing for the addressee, was popular with the Geniza people. It served as part of the rhetorical strategy of the poor and their advocates. So does the description of the illness of Yaḥyā's aged mother. These and other themes, like the "large family" motif, though common, even commonplace, do not detract from the facticity of the letter any more so than they do for the English pauper letters. The writer's wish for his would-be benefactor, "May the Creator . . . make you always one of the besought rather than a beseecher," appears frequently in the Geniza, sometimes in Hebrew in a form that has an antecedent in the midrash "the giver should give thanks [that he is] among the givers and not the takers."[11] The sentiment parallels similar expressions in early Christianity and in Islam,[12] though some forms of Christian

[8] Khan translates "resolution."

[9] See Cohen, "Four Judaeo-Arabic Petitions of the Poor," 448.

[10] See for instance Sokoll, *Essex Pauper Letters*, index, 712, s.v. "family, large (more than three children)."

[11] Midrash Zuṭa, Shir ha-Shirim, ed. Buber (Berlin, 1894), 20 (par. 1:15). See below several times.

[12] See Cohen, "Four Judaeo-Arabic Petitions of the Poor," 453. In Christianity: "It is better to give than to receive" (the apostle Paul in Acts 20:35). In Islam: "The hand on top is better than the hand below. The hand on top gives, and the one below begs" (a famous Islamic ḥadīth quoting the words of the Prophet). Cf. the continuation of the above-mentioned midrash: "There are two hands, one above and one below. The hand of the poor is below and the hand of the rich (lit: "householder," *baʿal ha-bayit*) is above. One must give thanks that his hand is above and not below." Midrash Zuṭa, Shir ha-Shirim, ed. Buber, 20 (par. 1:15).

and Islamic asceticism also admired ascetic poverty, whereas rabbinic Judaism did not. The refrain reflects not only an ideal in rabbinic culture but also, I think, a society in which the unpredictable forces of an individualistic, commercial economy could easily reduce even the rich to penury. One precaution against this was to give charity in the expectation that God would reward the giver by guarding him from a similar fate. Yaḥyā plays upon that theme.

When Yaḥyā tells his would-be benefactor that his generosity will bring him close to God, ("do with me what will bring you close to God"), he may also be echoing the Islamic idea that charity results in *qurba*, or nearness to God, one of the chief incentives in Islam for being charitable. For a Jew, this concept resembled, linguistically and in meaning, a rabbinic dictum that charity substitutes for the burnt sacrifices (*qorban*) that were offered up in the Temple in Jerusalem to thank God or to atone for sin, a motif that, we shall see below, crops up regularly in the Geniza letters. This doctrine was enunciated shortly after the destruction of the Second Temple in 70 C.E., when Jews despaired at the loss of their chief means of worshiping the divine.

This petition illustrates the constant anxiety of the working poor, cast into temporary poverty by a sudden crisis, ashamed to "uncover his face." By seeking private charity he hopes to get back on his feet and return home, without exposing his temporary financial plight openly. He pleads: "furnish me something to eat and something to bring back to my family . . . and to pay some of my debts." Once he pays back his creditors he will be able to return to the public sphere, go back to work in Alexandria, and take care once again of his large family.

Another notion in this letter that is common throughout the Geniza has important religious significance. Yaḥyā humbles himself before God and his would-be earthly benefactor: "I throw myself before God and you to help me." The phrase "before God and you" is formulaic in the "request" clauses in Jewish petitions of the poor. The combination is also found in medieval Muslim letters on papyrus and paper.[13] Jewish petitioners invariably appeal to both God and man. In Judaism, of course, the dual appeal echoes biblical concepts. God is the ultimate ruler, from whom one seeks and expects help. He is also, according to one view, the possessor of all that is in the world ("The earth is the Lord's and all that it holds, the world and all its inhabitants," Psalm

[13] For an example of the Muslim case, see Diem, *Arabische Briefe auf Papyrus und Papier aus der Heidelberger Papyrus-Sammlung, Textband*, 95–96n5: *wa'l-mamlūk mā lahu illā allāh taʿālā wa-mawlānā*, and many other examples cited there. A colorful version of the formula is found in a Hebrew petition, employing rhymed prose: "I prostrate myself with a request, petition, and supplication (*teḥina*) before Him who dwells in the heavenly habitation (*meʿona*) and before our lord, the Nasi of the community—who can count it? (*mi mana*)" (ENA 2808.31, lines 5–7), an allusion to a passage at the end of the Passover Haggadah: *ḥasal siddur pesaḥ ke-hilkhato . . . zakh shokhen meʿona qomem qehal mi mana*. My thanks to David Wachtel for pointing this out to me. Cf. also *Med. Soc.*, 5:328–29.

24:1). But according to another view, God made man the proprietor of the material world ("The heavens belong to the Lord, but the earth he gave over to man," Psalm 115:16). Moreover, human beings should imitate God in their material beneficence, for which God will, in return, reward them.

The idea that one must rely upon the Creator as well as upon his fellow man has the effect, therefore, of equating man and God in the act of charity. Imitation of God through charity is an idea inherited from ancient Judaism by Christianity.[14] Though the privileging of God as source of succor has its roots in talmudic ethics, it might have been reinforced by the Sufi ascetic ideal of *tawakkul*, or absolute trust that God will provide for all of one's needs.

Finally, Yaḥyā's complaints about hunger, lack of food (bread), and imminent starvation in his family similarly anticipate a major theme in the letters of the poor. The diet of the poor, even those who received public food distributions, was below nutritional sufficiency.[15] Exaggerations to the contrary notwithstanding, their cries of hunger ring true and should not be dismissed as meaningless rhetoric.

The numbers in parentheses below correspond to the sections of the Arabic petition.

TS 13 J 18.14[16] (Judaeo-Arabic)

(1)[17] Your slave Yaḥyā the Alexandrian
b. ʿAmmār

(2) *In (your) name O M[e]rc(iful)*[18]

[14] For rabbinic concepts of charity and their relationship to Christianity, see E. E. Urbach, "Political and Social Tendencies in Talmudic Concepts of Charity" (Hebrew) *Zion* 16 (1951), 1–27.

[15] Cohen, *Poverty and Charity*, chapter 6.

[16] Ed. and trans., Cohen, *Jerusalem Studies in Arabic and Islam* 24 (2000), 449–56; I have made a few small changes in the translation here. Cf. Cohen, *Poverty and Charity*, chapter 7. I wish to thank Professor Sasson Somekh for his help in understanding several difficult idiomatic expressions in this document.

[17] The tarjama, situated in the upper left-hand corner (here, placed in the right-hand corner), as expected in petitions from the Fatimid period.

[18] Jewish petitions and other types of letters characteristically employ a Jewish counterpart of the Islamic basmala, in Aramaic, as here: *bi-shmakh raḥmana'*, abbreviated, *b-sh-m r-ḥ-m*. Jews, of course, knew the *complete* Islamic religious formula and sometimes wrote it out, usually in Arabic script but sometimes in Hebrew characters. See TS Misc. Box 8.25r, right side, *Med. Soc.*, 2:443–44, App. B 24 (1100–40), a fragment from the beginning of a letter in Arabic characters. Some lists of alms recipients written in Arabic characters include the Islamic basmala, e.g., ENA 2591.8 (upper part) + f.11 (lower part), *Med. Soc.*, 2:504–505, App. C 126 (ca. 1180), but see also TS NS J 293 (a) verso, left side, line 1, where the Islamic basmala appears in Hebrew letters (!) at the beginning of a list of clothes for the poor (1139–40 C.E.). Elsewhere in the same list the basmala is abbreviated in Arabic, *b-m*. See additional discussion in chapter 10, no. 87.

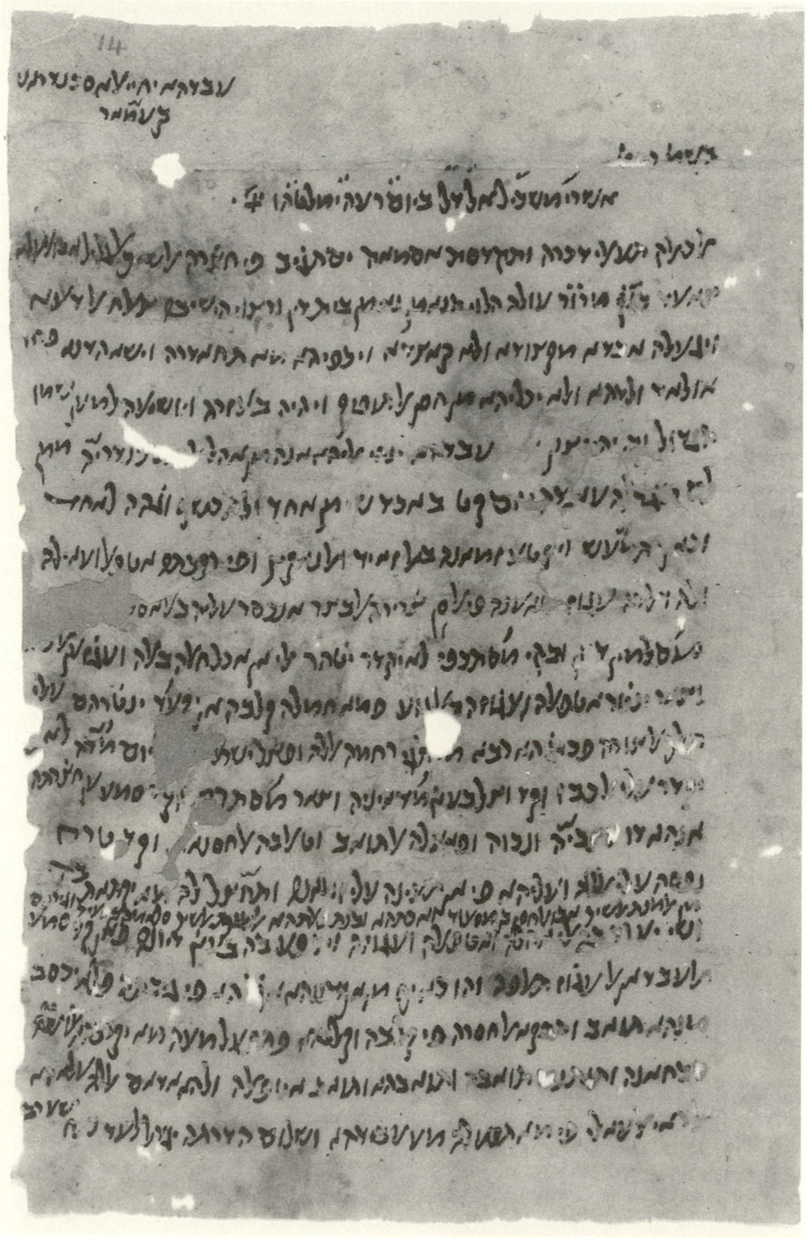

Fig. 1. Petition from Yaḥyā ibn ʿAmmār of Alexandria, (no. 1) TS 13 J 18.14

(3) *"Happy is he who is thoughtful of the wretched; in bad times may (the Lord) keep him from harm"* (Psalm 41:2).[19]

May the Creator, may His mention be exalted and His names be sanctified, answer the pious prayer for your excellency the illustrious elder Abu'l-ʿAlā Ṣāʿid, *(your) h(onor,) g(reatness), ho(liness), (our) ma(ster) and t(eacher)* ʿUlla ha-Levi *the Trustee, Trustee of the Court and Favorite to the Yeshiva,*[20] and make you always one of the besought rather than a beseecher and protect you from what you fear. May He grant that we witness the joy of seeing children of your children, may He not deprive you of good success, *and may He be your help and salvation, for the sake of His great name, and s[o] may it be His will.*

(5) Your slave informs you[21] that I am an [A]l[ex]andrian who has never [b]een in the habit of taking from anyone[22] nor of uncovering his face[23] to anyone. I have been earning a livelihood, just managing to get by.[24] I have responsibility for children and a family and an old mother, [a]dvanced in years and blind. I incurred losses because of d[e]bts owed to Muslims in Alexa[ndria].[25] I remained in hiding, unable to appear in public, to the point that my mind became racked by the situation.[26] Unable to [go out], I began watching my children and old mother starve. My heart could not bear to let me sit and watch them in this state. So I fled, seeking re[f]uge in God's mercy and the kindness of the Jewish community (lit. "Israel").[27] [As of to]day it has been a (long) time since I have been able to get any bread.[28] One of my creditors arrived and I went back into hiding.

[19] Quoting biblical verses formed part of the literary strategy in petitions of widows in early industrial England, too; see Sharpe, "Survival Strategies and Stories," 236. Where relevant in Jewish petitions, as here, titles of the addressee would also be included; this was general practice in correspondence, for titles were highly valued (a general phenomenon of Arab society).

[20] Two titles, the first, *ne'eman bet din,* commonly given to parnasim, or social welfare officials, who also doubled as functionaries of the court; the second, *reṣuy ha-yeshiva,* a title granted by the Palestinian yeshiva to loyal notables.

[21] Arabic: *yunhī ilayhā.* Beginning of the exposition in the petition form. The fourth part, the expression of obeisance, is omitted here. According to Khan, the obeisance clause, *yuqabbil al-arḍ,* did not come into regular use in Fatimid petitions to the ruler until the reign of al-Āmīr (1101–30); *Arabic Legal and Administrative Documents,* 310–12. Our petition probably dates from between 1084 and 1117. See also Khan, "The Historical Development of the Structure of Medieval Arabic Petitions," 25–26. The formula was also omitted in some Arabic petitions to dignitaries below the rank of caliph or vizier; Khan, *Arabic Legal and Administrative Documents,* 310 (no. 97).

[22] See above.

[23] Arabic, *lā kashf wajhihi,* i.e., exposing his misfortune.

[24] Arabic: *wa-kāna yatamaʿʿashu wa-yaqṭaʿu zamānahu bi'l-zā'id wa'l-nāqiṣ* ("now gaining, now losing"), altogether a precise description of the "working poor." On the unusual denominative verb, *yatamaʿʿashu,* see Cohen, "Four Judaeo-Arabic Petitions of the Poor," 451n18.

[25] On debt as a factor in impoverishment, see below, chapter 5.

[26] Arabic: *akala ḥāluhu bālahu* (translation suggested by Professor Sasson Somekh).

[27] On flight to evade debt, including the poll tax obligation, see below, chapter 5.

[28] Bread is the subsistence food in the English pauper letters and we sometimes hear such laments as "I really stand in Need of support. And find great difficulty to get a piece of Bread." Sokoll, *Essex Pauper Letters,* 567. The complaint is entirely regular in the Geniza letters; *Med. Soc.,* 5:88–89.

(6) I heard[29] that your excellency has a heart for his fellows Jews[30] and is a generous person,[31] who acts to receive reward (from God) and seeks to do good work[s], so I throw myself before God and you to help me[32] against the vicissitudes of Time and furnish me something to eat and something to bring back to my family, // including the widow of the elder Abu'l-Ḥasan b. Masʿūd and her sister and the daughter of her maternal aunt, the widow of the elder Salāma b. [S]aʿīd, and others, // and my children and old mother, and to pay some of my debts. In fact, your slave has just heard that his old mother has been injured and I fear that her t[im]e has come near because of me and that I will not be rewarded by seeing her; rather, an unrequited desire will remain in my heart and in hers. So do with me what will bring you close to God, be [p]raised, and ear[n] reward (for helping) me and her and my children.
(7) To you, may God perpetuate your high rank, belongs the lofty decision[33] concerning what to do for your humble slave.[34]
(8) *And may the welfare of your excellency increase forever.*[35] *Great salvation.*[36]

[29] Khan explains that in most extant Fatimid petitions the "request" section opens with a phrase incorporating the verb "ask" (*sa'ala*) or one that is semantically equivalent, like *ḍariʿa*, and that these two are frequently combined, e.g., *yas'al wa-yaḍraʿ*, "asks and implores." *Arabic Legal and Administrative Documents*, 312. The introduction to the request clause using the word "ask" occurs only once in the petitions I have studied: "Your slave Joseph kisses the ground before . . . and informs you that . . . Your slave's request (*wa-su'āl āl-mamlūk*) . . ." TS 8 J 21.20, line 9 (no. 4 below). In the present document the petitioner uses motivational rhetoric before going on to employ a more intensified verb of asking in the second part of this sentence, where he "throws himself" before God and the addressee for help.
[30] Arabic: *dhū ʿaṣabiyya*, using the Arabic historian Ibn Khaldūn's term hundreds of years later for the ésprit de corps that unites Arab tribesmen. On *ʿaṣabiyya* in Geniza letters, see *Med. Soc.*, 2:64. In the absence of a single word in English I have adopted this expression suggested by Raymond P. Scheindlin.
[31] Arabic: *nakhwa*. See *Med. Soc.*, 5:193–94.
[32] Arabic: *wa-qad ṭaraḥa nafsahu ʿalā allāh wa-ʿalayhā fī an tuʿīnahu*).
[33] Arabic: *al-ra'y al-ʿālī*, cf. Khan, *Arabic Legal and Administrative Documents*, 314–16. The ra'y clause, coming at the end of Arabic petitions, found its way into only a few Judaeo-Arabic petitions of the poor. The addressee here was one of the chief parnasim of Fustat, and indeed played a major role deciding on the distribution of charity.
[34] "Humble slave": *ʿubaydihā*. Or: "your slaves": *ʿabīdihā*.
[35] The Jewish closing formula in this petition consists of a blessing for the addressee, whereas the closing formulas in Arabic petitions addressed to Muslim rulers focus on God or on the Prophet and his family. It included the *ḥamdala (al-ḥamd lillāh waḥdahu*, "praise be to God alone") followed by the *taṣliya* (e.g., *ṣalawāt allāh ʿalā sayyidinā Muḥammad nabiyyihi wa-ālihi wa-sallama*, "blessings of God be upon our lord Muḥammad, his prophet, and his family, and save them" or *wa-salāmuhu*, "and his [God's] peace." Sometimes also the *ḥasbala* (e.g., *ḥasbunā allāh wa-niʿma al-wakīl*, "Our sufficiency is God. What an excellent keeper is he") appears. See Khan, *Arabic Legal and Administrative Documents*, 317, and D. S. Richards, "A Fāṭimid Petition and 'Small Decree' from Sinai," *Israel Oriental Studies* 3 (1973), 143. In our petitions, as well as in Jewish letters, generally, the Hebrew closing formula usually contains the word *shalom*, "welfare, peace." Frequently, as here, one also finds a messianic prayer.
[36] Hebrew: *yeshaʿ rav*, one of many short phrases, sometimes a messianic hope, that serve the same function as the ʿalāma, or authenticating "signature" motto in Arabic official letters.

## 2. "Kindly assist me with anything that God provides"

Yaḥyā ibn ʿAmmār's petition is longer than most of the letters of the poor. The second example is more characteristic in its brevity. A notation on the back indicates that the petitioner dictated the letter to a scribe. The scribe's hand is beautiful. Perhaps the plaintiff's was not very legible. He requests help so that he may remain in Jerusalem, called Har-El, "God's mountain," alluding to the Temple mount. Making the pilgrimage to the Holy City was highly valued, and the needy there or on their way there could expect extra attention to their pleas. In a Hebrew epistle to the Egyptian nagid Samuel b. Ḥananya, the poet Judah ha-Levi, on his way from Spain to the Holy Land, goes out of his way to state that (unlike other such suppliants) he does not need charity![37]

The writer of our letter employs typical rhetoric, including the prayer that God will cover his would-be benefactor "with the cover (*be-seter*) of His wings." This biblical phrase (Psalm 61:5) echoes in Hebrew the Arabic notion we will encounter in letters below (and that we mentioned above) of being "concealed" from poverty and especially from having to disclose it in public by resorting to communal alms. The Hebrew root *s-t-r* of *seter* is cognate with the root of the Arabic *mastūr*. Also typical, he asks his would-be benefactor to "assist me with anything that God provides," espousing the idea that God is ultimately the provider of all, so that a gift to the poor actually constitutes a kind of regifting of divine beneficence to another worthy person.

The beginning of the letter, which would have contained the opening section of the petition form, is torn away.

TS 8 J 18.28[38] (Judaeo-Arabic)

[ . . . ] I turn to you and ask you that you kindly assist me with anything that God provides so that I might remain in *Har-El*, the noble place. I ask God the ex(alted) to increase your well-being and add to it and multiply among our people the likes of you. May He favor us with your long life. *May God cover you with the cover of His wings and save you from all evil and distress and may you merit to see the goodness of the Lord and to visit his sanctuary. The Lord grants strength to His people and blesses His people with peace.* I am [l]ooking forward to what my master sends me. I ask God to reward you and grant that we see your face in this place in a state of well-being and good [h]ealth. *Amen.*

Verso: "*Those who love Your teaching enjoy well-being; they encounter no adversity*" (Psalm 119:165). Dictated by Saadya b. Futūḥ.

[37] See the fragment of the letter published and discussed (not this matter) by Shraga Abramson, "Judah ha-Levi's Letter on His Emigration to the Land of Israel" (Hebrew), *Kiryat Sefer* 29 (1953–54), 141 (my thanks to Professor Raymond Scheindlin for pointing this letter and this passage out to me).

[38] Cf. *Med. Soc.*, 5:35 and Cohen, *Poverty and Charity*, chapter 1.

## 3. "I was left *naked and bare*"

A needy person, clearly a man of some learning, asks for charity. His letter alludes to inadequate clothing and lack of a place to sleep, part of the universal and cross-cultural triad of "food, clothing, and shelter" that crops up time and time again, in part or in its entirety, in the Geniza, as it does in the English pauper letters. Sometimes illness is also mentioned, as in the letter that follows this one (no. 4). Our writer had worked as the beadle in a synagogue, an important though financially unrewarding position in the community, but had left his job. Another typical theme (not less believable because it occurs so frequently), is his complaint that he has three children and a wife to support ("especially in these difficult times . . . less than this would have been enough," he adds). Perhaps exaggerating, however, he claims that he had lost an item worth 5,000 (dirhems?).

Endeavoring to cloak his appeal and perhaps thereby his shame in more respectable garb, as an afterthought (in a postscript in the margin after the close of the letter), he offers to give the addressee something in return, to make a copy of the Hebrew liturgy of the Prayer for Rain that is recited in the synagogue on the Eighth Day of Assembly, at the end of the Feast of Tabernacles (usually October). By suggesting to transform charity into a form of employment, he appeals to his would-be benefactor to put into action the highest form of giving recommended in rabbinic midrash and codified by Maimonides in his well-known "ladder of charity" in the Mishneh Torah.[39]

One other comment of his, not fully clear because some of the writing is effaced, may be significant: It refers to "a collection in *the synagogue* of something for which your [slave] will be glad, and if not, may [ . . . ] me the pious trust and may *our lord* ask the community of the *p(recious) el[de]rs* for something of the sort." The writer may be asking here for a special variance allowing him to receive direct charity from an endowment, which may not have been part of the stipulation of the founder of the trust. In general, only a small percentage of the income from pious foundations went for direct relief of the poor.[40]

[39] Hilkhot mattenot ʿaniyyim (Gifts for the Poor), 10:7, English translation in *The Code of Maimonides*, book 7, trans. Isaac Klein (New Haven and London, 1979), 91. The third century (?) midrash Avot de-Rabbi Nathan (ed. Schechter, version A, chapter 41) states: "Three things were said of men: one gives charity, may blessing come upon him; superior to him is one who lends his funds; superior to all is one (who forms a partnership with the poor) on terms of one half the profits (for each) or on terms of sharing what remains"; trans. Judah Goldin, *The Fathers According to Rabbi Nathan* (New Haven, 1955), 171.

[40] Cohen, *Poverty and Charity*, chapter 8.

TS 8 J 37.11[41] (Judaeo-Arabic)

[ . . . ] your slave does not know what to do [ . . . ] I sold and pawned the [ . . . ] the [ . . . ] *the synagogue* when I was *beadle*. I was left *naked and bare*, with [nothing] upon me and nothing beneath me. Your sl(ave) lost an item worth 5,000 [ . . . *bles]sed be God who decrees what is right*. Your sl(ave) rejoices in serving *our lord, may (your) R(ock protect you)* [ . . . ] may you keep watching over your sl(ave). Whatever *our lord* does for your sl(ave) will be [ . . . ] by our master.[42] Your sl(ave) seeks from your abundant charity that you [ . . . ] request a collection in *the synagogue* of something for which your [slave] will be happy, and if not, may [ . . . ] me the pious trust and may *our lord* ask the community of the *p(recious) el[de]rs* for something of the sort. *May our [l]ord lift up his horn (?)*[43] so they execute a collection, for your sl(ave) is poo[r]. Your sl(ave) has nothing to rely on but our lord's charity and the charity of the noble community, *(may) G(od) b(e) t(heir succor)*. Do not t[u]rn your sl(ave) away disappointed. Because I depended[44] on the charity of *our lord, the [e]lder (who) r(ests in) E(den)*, may *our lord* not turn people away from his presence disappointed. The community knows about your sl(ave's) situation, especially in these difficult times, your sl(ave) having in his compass three children and a wife, when less than this would have been enough. *May your welfare increase, and peace*.

(Margin bottom): *Our lord* should [i]nform your sl(ave) if he [has] the (prayer for) *the time for rain* and if not, your sl(ave) will write it for you. *And peace. Our lord [ . . . ] Eighth Day of Assembly [ . . . ] rain [ . . . ]* the palm branc[h][45] [ . . . ] *Your young slav[e]* [J]acob b. Aaron [ . . . ].

(Margin right side): *[Our] lord* knows that your s[l](ave) does not have words enough to (torn off).

## 4. "Your slave is being killed by the cold and by hunger"

This letter also has the structure and technical terminology of the Arabic petition and voices some of the common complaints and needs of the poor. The writer was suffering from cold and hunger and asks for assistance to buy a robe. He exhorts his would-be benefactor with the perfectly pertinent verse from the Book of Isaiah, "When you see the naked, clothe him and do not ignore

[41] Cf. *Med. Soc.*, 5:90 and Cohen, *Poverty and Charity*, chapter 8.

[42] Arabic: *mawlānā*, referring evidently to a different person.

[43] Arabic: *ṣ-w-r*. Meaning uncertain.

[44] For *ikhlāl* in the sense of being dependent upon someone else, see A. de Biberstein Kazmirski, *Dictionnaire arabe-français*, 2 vols. (Paris, 1860), 1:606.

[45] Arabic: *al-jarīd[a]*, used in the ceremony of the lulav during the Sukkot holiday, which is followed immediately by the Eighth Day of Assembly.

your own kin." There the prophet means, not blood relatives, but the kinship of all of Israel, which is the sense intended by our writer.

TS 8 J 21.20[46] (Judaeo-Arabic)

In (your) na(me, O Merciful)[47]　　Your slave Joseph

kisses the ground[48] before *(your) ex(cellency), hono(r), gr(eatness), ho(liness), pr(ecious), el(evated), pe(arl), wr(eath), cr(own), gl(ory), (our) ma(ster) and te(acher),* Yeshuʿa *the great Dignitary*[49] *among the Jews, may God his Rock protect him and be his succor,* and informs you[50] that your slave is being killed by the cold and by hunger. Your slave cannot face asking anything from anyone.[51] Your slave's request[52] from our merciful and charitable master is for help with money for a robe. You will earn a reward that [is written], *"When you se[e the naked], clothe him [and] do not ignore [your own kin]"* (Isaiah 58:7).[53] Your slave in[f]orms you about this. *And peace.*

## 5. "I have not even one fals with which to buy anything"

Like other letters above, this next missive, addressed to a notable by a penurious person, follows the petition form. It is torn off at the upper left corner where the writer's name would have appeared in the tarjama. Like many other letters, it was composed at the time of a holiday, a particularly propitious time for giving charity, as in the surrounding Muslim society. The triad "naked," ill, and hungry appears in the suppliant's self-description, again, not less believable because formulaic. Persons deprived of adequate food and short on adequate clothing were often vulnerable to illness. The man was also out of work, not surprising in the light of his illness.

[46] Cf. *Med. Soc.* 5:102.

[47] The abbreviation for the Aramaic blessing, *bi-shmakh raḥmanaʾ*, is written in Arabic characters, *b-sh-m*, with three dots over the Arabic letter *shin*.

[48] Here we have the Arabic formula *yuqabbil al-arḍ*, the "obeisance clause" in the Arabic petition.

[49] As elsewhere, the Hebrew *sar* denotes a person having connections with the Muslim government. See Mark R. Cohen, *Jewish Self-Government in Medieval Egypt: The Origins of the Office of Head of the Jews, ca. 1065–1126* (Princeton, 1980), 167–68. In that book I translated *sar* as "prince."

[50] Arabic: *wa-yunhī*, the Arabic word introducing the "exposition" in the Arabic petition.

[51] Arabic: *mā liʾl-mamlūk wajh*. I take this as an allusion to the notion of "uncovering the face."

[52] Arabic: *suʾāl al-mamlūk*, the proper formula introducing the "request clause" in the Arabic petition.

[53] The prophet exhorts Israel to ethical duty as being more meritorious than meaningless fasts, "to share your bread with the hungry, and to take the wretched poor into your home; when you see the naked, to clothe him, and not to ignore your own kin." Our letter-writer uses the second half of the verse standing alone (though he knew the rest, and so did his addressee), and so I have translated it as an independent statement.

TS 8 J 41.1 (Judaeo-Arabic)

[ . . . k]isses the ground and informs the most illustrious [ . . . ] "*the Precious Chosen One*," *(may your) e(nd be) g(ood)*, the beneficent, who acts kindly toward his slave and [his] servan[t] at all times. Your slave[54] is grateful for [ . . . ] for [ . . . f]or your beneficence and for [ . . . ]. May God the e[xal]ted make constant your high rank give you a *peaceful end // and a loyal house // and grant that you live* to see the *redeemer*, you *and the whole house of Israel.*[55] Your slave is [experiencing] adversity[56] on account of his being naked and ill and lacking food during the upcoming holiday. I have not even one fals (a copper coin of low value) with which to buy anything. I have earned nothing this year. Your charitable deeds toward your slave are many. Do not turn your slave away disappointed. *And peace.*

## 6. "I am burdened with a family and am out of work"

A brief letter of appeal from a man in straits, out of work, burdened with a family, and hungry. His plea for a handout so he can avoid "uncovering his face" again is de rigueur. The verse from Psalms he quotes at the top of the letter, "Happy is he who is thoughtful of the wretched; in bad times (may the Lord) keep him from harm," which we have already encountered, is one of the favorites in these letters, reflecting the notion, common to the three monotheistic religions, that giving to the poor will be rewarded by God. The idea is made explicit at the end of the letter.

TS 13 J 20.4[57] (Judaeo-Arabic)

*In (your) n(ame, O) Me(rciful)*

"*For the work of charity*[58] *shall be peace, and the effect of ch(arity, calm and confidence forever)*" (Isaiah 32:17).

[54] The writer uses three different words to express his subservience, *ʿabd, ghulām, mamlūk*, in that order.
[55] An example of the messianic wishes so often encountered in Geniza letters.
[56] *Shidda*, found commonly in letters of appeal and evocative of the Arabic literary genre *Al-Faraj baʿd al-shidda*, "relief after adversity," known to Jews in the Jewish version of such a book written by the Qayrawanese rabbinic scholar Nissim b. Jacob ibn Shahīn (d. 1062). See the English edition, *An Elegant Composition concerning Relief after Adversity*, trans. by William M. Brinner (New Haven and London, 1977), and Cohen, *Poverty and Charity*, chapter 6. Also *Med. Soc.*, 5:51–53.
[57] Cf. *Med. Soc.*, 5:525n125.
[58] Hebrew: *ṣedaqa*, which means "righteousness" in most places in the Bible but which came to mean "charity" in postbiblical Hebrew, and so it was understood by the Geniza people when they quoted such verses. Throughout I translate the word as "charity" when rendering biblical verses quoted in the documents.

*"Happy is he who is thoughtful of the wretched; in bad times (may the Lord) keep him from harm"* (Psalm 41:2).

May God, may His mention be exalted, answer (my) pious prayers on behalf of my master the most illustrious elder *and lengthen your days with goodness and your years with favor.* Your slave turns to God, may He be praised, and to your noble excellency for help against Fate. I am burdened with a family and am out of work,[59] unable to get a hold of anything for expenses, even for bread to satisfy them. The Creator knows how I desire to find that which would free me from the need to uncover my face.[60] May God the exalted never keep your excellency from doing charity and may He make it stand in your favor when you are experiencing adversity. *May your peace increase forever and ever. Selah.*

*May salvation come.*

## 7. "The bearer of this letter is a poor, down-and-out man"

This is our first example of a letter of recommendation on behalf of the poor. It is a tiny fragment, preserving the words "the bearer of this letter is a poor, down-and-out man." The missive is probably addressed to Isaac b. Samuel the Spaniard, a learned scholar, author, and judge in Fustat at the end of the eleventh and during the first three decades of the twelfth century.[61] Discovered by the present writer among some unconserved, tiny fragments in the Geniza collection of the Jewish Theological Seminary in New York, its interpretation might easily have been missed, save for the author's familiarity with dozens of such letters of recommendation, readily identifiable by the Arabic word "letter-bearer" (*mūṣil*). Though the rest of the letter is missing, the addressee was doubtless asked to help the poor man out.

This fragment is characteristic of some of the smaller pieces in the Geniza, which often have significance despite their size and poor state of preservation.

ENA NS 77.36 (Judaeo-Arabic)

[Isaa]c *the gr[eat] Rav, "the [He]lp of the Nesiut," "Head [of the Scholar]s" may his diadem blossom, son of* Sam[u]el *the pious the Sefaradi (Spaniard) of (blessed) m(emory)* [ . . . tha]t the bearer of this letter is a poor, down-and-out man[62] who was [ . . . ].

[59] Arabic: *baṭṭāl*, cf. *Med. Soc.*, 5:525n125.

[60] Arabic: *taksīf al-wajh*, possibly a spelling error for *takshīf al-wajh*, an unattested variant of *kashf al-wajh*. The word *taksīf* can mean "cut into pieces" (Kazimirski, *Dictionnaire arabe-français*, 2:898). Two words follow at the beginning of the next line, *mā wajada*. If we imagine that originally the suppliant wrote *taksīf mā wajada*, "free me from the need to cut (the meager food) I found into pieces," then inserted *al-wajh* after *taksīf* to form the standard idiom (the word *al-wajh* is in fact written above the word *taksīf* at the end of the line), we would have a neat solution to the anomaly.

[61] On whom see Cohen, *Jewish Self-Government*, 119–21.

[62] Hebrew and Arabic: *ʿani ṣuʿlūk*.

## 8. "The reason for [th]is note is to ask my master for a [k]indness to be sent to me"

A brief letter from a person in need requesting assistance forms our next example. The times are "stressful," he says. The intimate though formulaic expression of "longing" for the addressee, whom the writer had not seen for some time, suggests a familiar relationship between the two, a solid foundation for seeking and giving private charity.

JTS Krengel 5.123 (Judaeo-Arabic)

*[In] your na[me]*

May God [make eter]nal the nights of my master the elder and prolong your life [ . . . ] and your good will. [I have not s]een my master for a long time and I miss [you]. You are aware of this stressful time. I need [ . . . ] my needs. My need calls out [ . . . ]. The reason for [th]is note[63] is to ask my master for a [k]indness[64] to be sent to me with Abu['l- . . . ] the bearer of this petition[65] [ . . . ] with this, God w[i]lling [ . . . ] God [ . . . ].

## 9. "Far be it from the generosity of my master that he should neglect someone in this great *trouble*"

A schoolmaster, who had not earned anything during the week of the holidays, a vacation period, requests half a wayba of wheat or its cash equivalent for his hungry children. He describes the utter dearth in his household with the ascending image: no wheat, or flour, or loaf of bread, or any other food.

TS Arabic Box 18 (1).33[66] (Judaeo-Arabic)

Moses, who thanks you

I honor R. Amram ha-Levi, *the precious, the honored, the scholar, may the Guardian of the souls of the pious guard you and make prosper your works*, with best regards and a thousand greetings and the respect of Moses, who thanks you, without intending any ill-will. I sent your excellency a petition,[67] which

[63] Arabic: *jarīda*, a word more often used for "list," but there, too, the basic idea is a notation of something.

[64] Arabic: *[f]aḍl*.

[65] Arabic: *ruqʿa*, more generally "note."

[66] Cf. *Med. Soc.*, 2:188; partial Hebrew translation in S. D. Goitien, *Sidrei ḥinnukh bi-mei ha-geonim u-veit ha-Rambam* (Jewish Education in Muslim Countries, Based on Records from the Cairo Geniza) (Jerusalem, 1962), 107.

[67] Arabic: *khidma*. *Khidma* in the Geniza normally means "service" to the community or "service"

includes some of my complaints about my situation and the severe and ever-increasing straits in which I suff[er]. But I have not received an an[s]wer.[68] As God is my witness, today I am in even greater straits, and facing the greatest adversity yet. Far be it from the virtuous generosity[69] of my master that he should neglect someone in this great *trouble*, who turns to him for help. In fact, you should favor me without my having to turn to you. As God is my witness, in my house there is no [ . . . ][70] wheat or flour or loaf of bread or any other food, as God is witness to its (exhorbitant) price. I asked your excellency for half a wayba of wheat, or money to buy it, so I can make my young ones happy this week. After the break for the *holiday* I tried to get a quarter of a dirhem, and couldn't. As God sees what's best, I am describing only part of my complaint to God the exalted [ . . . ] *His name. And may your welfare increase.*

## 10. "During the entire eight months the man gave me only [f]ifteen dirhems"

This letter holds interest not only for its insights into poverty and charity, but also for what it reveals about family solidarity and the politics of a prominent group of Jewish merchants in medieval Egypt. A needy man from Qayrawan had applied for assistance from his relative, the esteemed Tunisian merchant and scholar Nahray b. Nissim, who lived in Fustat during the second half of the eleventh century.[71] Nahray had given his relative handouts for eight months. Now the man describes a delicate problem and asks for help from others. Before turning to Nahray he had already received donations from another prominent Tunisian merchant, Abū Zikrī (Judah b. Moses ibn Sighmār). Nahray had become annoyed. It is not clear whether he was angry because he

in government. Reverberating with the more general usage in that society (and corresponding to a subsidiary meaning of the word "service" in English), it means something to be given, an act of assistance, a kind of service done for (or owed to) the needy (as in the duty to give charity), or an offer of reciprocal service in the form of gratitude from the petitioner, or both. In the letters it reflects the relationship of patronage between petitioner and petitioned. See Cohen, *Poverty and Charity*, chapter 7, note 51.

[68] This comment, ubiquitous in Geniza letters, no matter what the subject, gives expression to the anxiety people felt at absence of communication. Merchants write this because correspondence was their main means of keeping tabs on their investments and on the welfare of their business associates. Others simply show concern for the health and well-being of family and friends.

[69] Arabic: *muruwwa*. On this ancient Arabic (Bedouin) term for "manliness, bravery" transformed into the meaning of "generosity," see *Med. Soc.*, 5:192.

[70] I cannot determine what the word preceding "wheat" says.

[71] Much has been written about the North African merchant and scholar, Nahray b. Nissim, who settled in Fustat in the middle of the eleventh century. For instance, see Goitein, *Letters of Medieval Jewish Traders*, 145–74. There is even a historical novel in French with Nahray as the central character. Sylvie Crossman and Michel Gabrysiak, *La guéniza* (Paris, 1987).

felt that people might have thought he was neglecting his relative or became peeved for some other reason, such as competition over patronage—or perhaps both. Our needy writer seems to have gotten caught up in the politics of the Maghrebi merchant network in Fustat, when all he wanted was assistance, as he says, out of "dire necessity."

Westminster College, Misc. 34[72] (Judaeo-Arabic)

*"You love righteousness and hate wickedness; rightly [has God, your God, chosen to] a[noint you] with oil of gladness over all your peers"* (Psalm 45:8). *"And decree and it will be fulfilled, and light will shine [upon your affairs]"* (Job 22:28).

My elder, the head, my master, may He (God) perpetuate your honor. I am from Qayrawan, one of the merchants. I am writing you this petition out of dire necessity.[73] I came to Fustat and turned to a man called Nahray, who is my relative, my flesh and blood, and whom I respect. I have been with him now for eight months. Before that, when my master the elder Abū Zikrī,[74] may God grant him long life, arrived, I went to him and greeted him. Some people told him about my situation, and he was not stingy with charitable gifts for me, may God requite him with go[o]d on my behalf and watch over his son. Nahray became very annoyed over this and [asked me, "W]hy did you do this?" So I swore to him that I would not take anythin[g] from anyone [ . . . ] with you.[75] Now, during the entire eight months the man gave me only [f]ifteen dirhems. When I told the Maghrebis about this they were troubled and were not stingy with me. I am embarrassed about speaking to the elder Abū Zikrī, may God protect him from harm, so I am writing this petition to my master the elder asking from God and you to favor your slave and protégé by doing for me what you can. *And may the welfare of my master increase forever.*

72 Ed. and trans. into Hebrew in Moshe Gil, *Be-malkhut yishmael bi-tequfat ha-geonim* (In the Kingdom of Ishmael: Studies in Jewish History in Islamic Lands in the Early Middle Ages) 4 vols. (Tel Aviv and Jerusalem, 1997), 4:430–31, discussed 1:713 (bottom). My transcription, made directly from the manuscript at Westminster College, yielded a few improvements and my interpretation differs substantially from Gil's.

73 A regular motif also in the English pauper letters. Indigents excuse themselves for imposing on parish poor law administrators to send them their allowance, e.g., "I hope you Will Excuse Me for Troubleing you with Another Letter But I am Oblige to It for Necisity forces me to It for We are at A Very Low Ebb I Dont know where to get Another Weeks Bread Without Some Assistance." Sokoll, *Essex Pauper Letters*, 311 (I retain the original spelling, punctuation, and capitalizations of the original letters, so carefully reproduced by Sokoll in his masterful edition).

74 On Abū Zikrī Judah b. Moses ibn Sighmār, a contemporary of Nahray b. Nissim's and another of the important Maghrebi merchants who settled in Fustat in the middle of the eleventh century, see, for instance, my article, "A Partnership Gone Bad: A Letter and a Power of Attorney from the Cairo Geniza, 1085," in Sasson Somekh Festschrift, eds. David Wasserstein and Mahmud Ghanaim, forthcoming.

75 Gil translates "musk," in Arabic *m-s-k*, though he transcribes correctly *m-ʿ-k*. He interprets the letter incorrectly as having to do with money owed the writer by Nahray for a shipment of musk.

## Chapter Two

# TAXONOMY: STRUCTURE AND CONJUNCTURE[1]

MEDIEVAL AND early modern European historians of the Annales school like to draw a distinction between two general categories of indigence. One is "structural poverty," the other "conjunctural poverty." The former pertains to those who live in permanent or chronic destitution, a "structural" state of deprivation in which, for one reason or another, such as ill-health, physical disability, widowhood, or old age, they cannot find work or other dependable means of sustenance. Most beggars fall into this category.

The second type encompasses those for whom poverty or need arises under specific, intermittent circumstances, the result of what the Annalistes call a "conjuncture."[2] Some of these people earn enough through their labors to support their families (the "working poor," a class well known from early modern Europe but actually as old as the *penēs* of ancient Greece). Others derive income from property or commercial enterprises that provide for their daily needs and those of their dependents. Poverty in these cases results from a particular convergence of circumstances that changes their economic situation for the worse. Sudden impoverishment is also a source of shame. The "shamefaced poor," as they are called in medieval and early modern European texts, resist turning to others for help, let alone resorting to the embarrassment of the public dole or to beggary.[3]

Features of the Geniza letters that we have already begun to see show the same taxonomy of structural and conjunctural poverty. Popular conception actually distinguished between the two.[4] As in the Christian European case,

[1] See Cohen, *Poverty and Charity*, chapter 1.

[2] Mollat, *The Poor in the Middle Ages*, 26: "An inelegant but useful terminology distinguishes between 'structural' and 'conjunctural' poverty according as the primary cause of distress was institutional or circumstantial." See also the use of the distinction in Yannick Fouquet, *Pauvreté et assistance au XVIIe siècle: le cas exemplaire de Chambery* (Chambery, 1986), 49. "Those who do not have the strength to work or are incapable of working form the large battalions of structural poverty. Conjunctural poverty recruits from all social milieus."

[3] Bronislaw Geremek, *Poverty: A History*, trans. Agnieszka Kolakowska (Oxford, 1994), 39, 60.

[4] I prefer the original terminology of the Annalistes to the alternative "deep/shallow," which Paul

conjunctural poverty was associated by Jews with shame. To be sure, as already mentioned, rabbinic sources from much earlier times are aware of the plight of the conjuncturally poor, those who "fall from their wealth" (*yored mi-nekhasav*), and even of their accompanying shame.[5] However, it is only with the Geniza and its rich documentary remains that we are able to observe these phenomena in such detail and even to understand their significance for the earlier period.[6]

## 11. "He is ashamed, for this has never been his habit"

The concepts of structure, conjuncture, and shame are nicely illustrated by this letter. The writer invites relatives (the letter is addressed to his father and father-in-law) in Qalyūb, a town northeast of Fustat, to attend a family celebration at upcoming holiday time. He entrusts delivery of the letter to someone he knows. At the beginning of the letter, as if to compensate the man for the favor (or perform the much praised charitable act of inducing others to give to the needy), he relates the latter's tale of woe and asks his relatives to give him succor.

The man had been "healthy, working strenuously in order to 'conceal' himself and his family." "Conceal" renders the verb *satara*, which, as we have seen, describes a person getting by financially, even if just barely. Like Yaḥyā ibn ʿAmmār of Alexandria (no. 1 above), the letter-bearer was one of the "working poor," living just above the poverty line. What reduced him to indigence was typical in our period: illness, debt, and the annual poll tax (another kind of debt; more on this below). The recommender bids his family in Qalyūb to assist the man and exhorts them by invoking the ancient Jewish notion that a gift to the poor will stand in place of a sacrifice to God (a qorban). As we noted above in connection with the petition of Yaḥyā ibn ʿAmmār (no. 1), this ancient rabbinic idea, that charity substitutes for the sacrifices brought to the holy temple in Jerusalem before it was destroyed by the Romans, may have

Slack finds more suitable to England in the sixteenth and seventeenth centuries (*Poverty and Policy in Tudor and Stuart England*, 39, and passim) and which others have begun to adopt as well. While "deep poverty" describes the chronic nature of structural poverty and could be used as an equivalent term, "shallow poverty" fails to encompass the precipitous fall into temporary deprivation that often affected the well-to-do when struck by an unexpected crisis (conjuncture); nor does it adequately convey the self-perception of those of the working poor in my sources who prided themselves in their normal self-sufficiency (bare bones as it was) and wished not to be thought of as indigent. This latter sentiment, of course, may be specifc to the case of Judaism, in which poverty was always considered a misfortune and never (or rarely) a virtue, as in Christianity or Sufi Islam.

[5] See Cohen, *Poverty and Charity*, chapter 1, note 23.

[6] Ibid., chapter 1.

been reinforced by the Islamic belief that charity creates a nearness (qurba) to God.

The letter-bearer, finally, is said to be experiencing shame. Normally self-sufficient ("concealed"), it is not his habit to seek charity. Independently, at the end of the letter, discussing family matters, the letter-writer mentions a young girl whom they are trying to match in marriage. She is described as "not a poor girl," but "concealed" (*mastūra*).

TS 13 J 20.20[7] (Judaeo-Arabic)

*In the n(ame of the)* Me*(rciful)*

*"Say as follows: 'To life! Greetings to you,'" etc.* (1 Samuel 25:6).
*May your [h(onor)] g(reatness and) h(oliness), (our) ma(ster) and t(eacher)* Solomon ha-Kohen *the precious elder have many blessings and imminent salvation, pity, and compassion and the fulfillment of every request, much luck, and all available blessings. May God bless you and grant life to your son and let you see his joyous occasion and wedding canopy; and (your) h(onor), g(reatness), and h(oliness) (our) ma(ster) and te(acher)* Yeshuʿa *the precious elder, may God open before you the gates of mercy and grant life to your son and let you see his joyous occasion and wedding canopy, Amen forever.*

I am dispatching this letter to the most illustrious elders, may God preserve them, to inform them that the bearer of this (letter) is a man who was healthy, working strenuously in order to "conceal"[8] himself and his family, when Fate betrayed him and he became weak,[9] such that anyone looking at him needs no explanation about his condition. In addition, debt and the poll tax caught up with him. Whoever assists him with something with which he can maintain his way of life[10] shall be deemed to have made an offering (to God). He is ashamed, for this has never been his habit. Whoever does him a good turn[11] shall be deemed to have done so for the sake of God, and the Creator will magnify his reward. *And peace.*

In addition to this, your son Maʿānī and his children ask about Father, the elder Abu'l-Rabīʿ Sulaymān, and Ibrāhīm, and want them to grace us by coming on the holiday, may God bring it to us and you for many years to come and let us see the joyous occasion of the sons of Ibrahīm in your lifetime. I want you to come and grace us in the joyous occasion we are making for Abu'l-Khayr. All our lives we have come to you for the holidays. By God, O [my] brother Ibrahīm,

[7] Edition of the text to be published by the author in the Proceedings of the Seventh International Conference of the Society for Judaeo-Arabic Studies held at the University of Strasbourg, Strasbourg, France, July 1995, ed. by Paul Fenton. Cf. also *Med. Soc.* 3:55, 438n31; 5:15.
[8] Arabic: *li-yastura*.
[9] On the synonym "weak" for "poor," see Cohen, *Poverty and Charity*, chapter 1, note 3.
[10] Arabic: *madhhab*.
[11] Arabic: *khayr*, lit. "good," which can also mean "charity."

come visit your daughter so that her heart may take pleasure during t[h]is holiday. Also (the writer is now addressing his mother-in-law), have regard for Abuʾl-Khayr and let her (her daughter) be fulfilled through you (your presence). May you not need to be commanded. Unlimited greetings especially to you and greetings to Umm Ibrahīm and to Abuʾl-Faraj and to (verso) Umm ʿImrān, may I not be deprived of her favor, and to all those who are in Qalyūb. (We) have saved the girl for Abuʾl-ʿAlāʾ. If he is coming, have him send a message and inform us. If not, don't let him detain her. *And Peace*. She is not a poor girl.[12] She is "concealed."[13] *And Peace*. The scribe who wrote this letter, the teacher[14] of Abuʾl-Khayr, sends you greetings. He asks for a little [ . . . ].

## 12. "Count me among the *'poor of your household'*"

This man was driven to seek charity because he was under house arrest for failure to pay three poll-tax payments: his own, his eldest son's, and his younger son's. In addition he owes three hundred dirhems that he borrowed at interest to marry off his son. The poll tax and other kinds of debt figure prominently in the sudden impoverishment of the normally self-sufficient (more on this in chapter 5). Victim of "conjunctural poverty," he refers to himself as having "fallen from his wealth," using the standard rabbinic locution for this kind of sudden impoverishment. He states, too, "I only buy bread sold in the market." I interpret these words to mean that he avoids going on the community dole, the weekly distributions of bread to the chronically ("structurally") poor. Ashamed of his poverty, like the "shamefaced poor" of late medieval and early modern Europe, he asks the addressee not to tell one of his relatives about his misfortune.

Another theme here, anticipating the main topic of chapter 3, is based on the *halakha* that privileges the poor of one's family household or place of residence over the foreign poor. Writing from abroad and knowing the prioritization that could work in his disfavor, our writer asks his would-be benefactor: "count me among the *'poor of your household.'*"

As is common, the letter is prefaced with biblical verses commending doers of charity (*ṣaddiqim*, from the word *ṣedaqa*, "charity"). Addressed to a notable with connections to the government (that is the usual meaning of *sar*, "Dignitary," in the Geniza letters),[15] another particularly pertinent biblical verse is quoted: "You shall find grace and good favor in the sight of God and man" (Proverbs 3:4).

[12] Arabic: *ṣuʿlūka* written *ṣuʿlūkhā* by mistake.

[13] Arabic: *mastūra*, that is, "not needy."

[14] If the word is *muʿalli[m]*, otherwise it could be a name like Maʿ[ā]lī.

[15] See above, chapter 1, note 49.

BNUS 4038.9[16] (Judaeo-Arabic)

*"Salvation of the righteous comes from the Lord, He is their stronghold in time of trouble"* (Psalm 37:39).
*"Be glad in the Lord and rejoice, you just ones, and shout for joy, all you upright in heart"* (Psalm 32:11).
*"Rejoice in the Lord, you righteous, in lauding, O upright, the Glorious One"* (Psalm 33:1).

I inform *your gl(orious) ma(jesty), our master and teacher Yefet the honored Dignitary, the benefactor and generous one, "Benefactor of the Communities" and "Generous One of the Congregations," may your glory be exalted and your honor increased. May God give you fame and glory and raise your prominence higher and higher. May you be granted grace and good favor in the sight of Go[d and m]an, as the Bible says: "You shall find grace and good favor in the sight of God and man"* (Proverbs 3:4).

Our lord is aware of the situation of your slave and what happened to him. Every year my master has urged the elder, "the Nafīs" ("the Precious One"), every year, with regard to (my) poll-tax payment. Now I am in *big trouble* because of it. The collector came and said that I must remain under house arrest,[17] since I owe for three poll-tax payments. Ever since my eldest son has been with me I have been unable (to pay) for him as well as for myself and the younger one. By the Torah, I owe three hundred dirhems which I borrowed at interest to marry off my son. I cannot sit another day in the house; otherwise every one here will die of hunger. I only buy bread sold in the market. My master knows that "*the poor of your household come before the poor of your town, and the poor of your town come before the poor of another town.*"[18] Count me among the "*poor of your household*" and may I never cease to receive my master's favor. May [Go]d make you a refuge for those [seek]ing refuge.[19] Yo[u] know the lot (?)[20] of the person who *falls from his wealth.*[21] I ask [my master] please do not inform my son-

[16] To be published by M. Cohen in the Proceedings of the Seventh International Conference of the Society for Judaeo-Arabic Studies; see above, note 7.

[17] Arabic: *murassam* (so vocalized in the text), from tarsīm, a form of punishment in which the detained person was required to pay the wages of the policeman assigned to prevent him from leaving his home, or, more generally, in which a debtor (including someone who had failed to meet his poll-tax obligation) was fined a certain sum each day he remained in arrears. See *Med. Soc.*, 2:372. Here actual house arrest is clearly meant.

[18] Quotation from the Babylonian Talmud, Bava Meṣiʿa 71a, and elsewhere, and also incorporated into the laws of charity in Maimonides' Code, the Mishneh Torah, Hilkhot mattenot ʿaniyyim 7:13. For further discussion see Cohen, *Poverty and Charity*, chapter 2.

[19] A phrase, in Arabic, reflecting the Jewish (perhaps general Arabic) version of the cross-cultural notion that it is better to give charity than to receive it: *maqṣūd liʾl-muqāṣid.*

[20] Arabic: *m-q-ʾ-r* (perhaps: "measure," meaning how to measure the difference between someone who is temporarily impoverished and someone who is chronically destitute). This translation requires an emendation of the text (*m-q-d-ʾ-r = miqdār*), normally not done with original documents like the Geniza letters. For a discussion of this problematic word, see my above-mentioned article.

[21] Hebrew: *yored mi-nekhasav.*

in-law (or: brother-in-law)[22] about any of this. *May your welfare increase and not abate, and may your reward from heaven be twofold, for I have spoken hitherto out of the greatness of my complaint and my vexation* (I Samuel 1:16).

Verso (a kind of docket): A petition[23] *laid before the Dignitary of the Levites (sar ha-leviim), whose fame is known on the farthest shores, may the living God grant you long life*. For my master is beyond all description.[24]

From your slave, *who th[ank]s you for your generosity.*

## 13. "He never sought anything from anybody, nor was this his habit"

This brief letter recommending a man from "the notables of Sunbāṭ" for charity echoes the plight of the writer of the previous letter, for this man, too, was burdened with debt and multiple poll-tax obligations (his own and his son's). We are apparently dealing here with someone from a normally well-off family, whose "house was (open) to all wayfarers," we read, and who "never sought anything from anybody," another refrain of the conjunctural poor. His personal economic troubles stemmed, as well, from general conditions ("these difficult times that befell everyone," the writer says). Sunbāṭ is a small town in Lower Egypt.

TS 6 J 3.28[25] (Judaeo-Arabic)

*In the n(ame of the) M(erciful)*

Your slave [who thanks you]
for your kindness,
Judah

I inform your excellency my master the most illustrious lord, the judge, *(may your) R(ock) p(rotect you)*, that the bearer of this (letter) was one of the notables[26] of Sunbāṭ. Their house was *(open) to all wayfarers*. He never sought anything from anybody, nor was this his habit. During these difficult times that befell everyone all was lost, and he is being sought for two poll-tax payments, his own and that of his son, as well as for another debt. I ask, please, that you take

[22] The Arabic word *ṣihr* means both.

[23] Arabic: *khidma*. See chapter 1, note 67.

[24] A rhetorical topos used particularly of dignitaries when writers felt their correspondents might have expected more adulatory phrases than they gave.

[25] Cf. Eliyahu Ashtor, "The Number of the Jews in Medieval Egypt," *Journal of Jewish Studies* 18 (1967), 36; Norman Golb, "The Topography of the Jews of Medieval Egypt," *Journal of Near Eastern Studies* 33 (1974), 142. Cohen, "Poverty and Charity," n54.

[26] Arabic: *aʿyān*.

care of his situation and strive in his regard. And may the welfare of your excellency increase forever and ever.

## 14. "God . . . commanded us to turn toward the 'common poor' among us and to those from good families who have fallen from their wealth"

This very interesting letter of appeal, written in Hebrew, reflects the realities of the "conjunctural" poor. The writer recommends the letter-bearer, Solomon b. Benjamin, a scholar from a "good family of noteworthy householders." In the past this Solomon had been a benefactor of the poor himself, but had "fallen from his wealth," alluding, as in the case of the notable from Sunbāṭ in the previous letter, to "many troubles that befell them." This, the conjunctural poverty of the normally nonpoor, is distinguished by the writer from the structural poverty of the masses of the underclass when he says, "God, may His praise be exalted, commanded us to turn toward the 'common poor' (quoting from the prophet Isaiah) among us and to those from good families who have fallen from their wealth."

Solomon was a refugee from war and wished to "go up," that is, make the pilgrimage to the holy city of Jerusalem, but sudden impoverishment had forced him to seek charity first. Then he would proceed to his destination. The information about his pilgrimage as well as about his temporary detour is inscribed above the line (marked here by double slashes), an afterthought added to enhance Solomon's worthiness for assistance. Pilgrimage to Jerusalem was a particularly commendable religious act and an added motivation for a would-be benefactor.

The recommender is the well-known Nathan ha-Kohen b. Mevorakh, judge, cantor, and scribe (here serving in his latter capacity) in Ascalon, Palestine, who was active during the last two decades of the eleventh century. He was in close touch with the leadership of the Jewish community of Egypt residing in the Egyptian capital, as well as with the prominent parnas Eli ha-Kohen b. Yaḥyā (Ḥayyim in Hebrew), to whom the present letter is addressed.[27] He urges Eli both to exhort others and to give himself, quoting a relevant rabbinic text. The letter begins (after biblical verses exhorting to charity) with several lines in rhymed Hebrew prose, marked here with slashes where rhyme words appear.

The letter is a learned one, commensurate with the fact that both the writer and the intended recipient of charity were learned men. Our Solomon might have come from Europe, like many other European Jewish pilgrims at the

[27] On Nathan, see Cohen, *Jewish Self-Government*, index s.v.

time,[28] so Nathan writes in Hebrew. Jerusalem contained a relatively small Jewish settlement that was not particularly wealthy, whereas Egypt, especially Fustat, was prosperous. Thus needy foreigners often went or were sent there for help. Solomon turned south for Egypt after reaching the Palestinian coastal city of Ascalon, armed with this letter from the leading Jewish notable of that community.

It is unlikely that Solomon would have been planning a pilgrimage to Jerusalem after the Crusader conquest, so this letter probably dates from before 1099. It is conceivable that he was in flight from the massacres, martyrdoms, and forced conversions of 1096 in the Rhineland and farther along the Crusaders' route and that he was seeking safety in the far more secure Muslim East before the slower-moving Crusader forces reached the Holy Land. Maybe he hoped they would never make it or would fail militarily to dislodge the Muslims!

TS 18 J 4.4[29] (Hebrew)

In your name, O Merciful

"Happy is he who is thoughtful of the wretched; in bad times may the Lord keep him (from harm)" (Psalm 41:2). "Happy is he who lends generously, who conducts his affairs with equity" (Psalm 112:5). "He who is generous to the poor makes a loan to the Lord, etc." (Proverbs 19:17). "It is to share your bread with the hungry, and to take the wretched poor into your home; when you see the naked, to clothe him, and not to ignore your own kin" (Isaiah 58:7). "Wealth is of no avail on the day of wrath, but charity saves from death" (Proverbs 11:4). "For the work of charity shall be peace, and the effect of charity, calm and confidence forever" (Isaiah 32:17).

I send peace and salvation / as a blessing and delight / to rescue from all evil / and all affliction and harm / to protect you always with mercy / to appear at every moment and hour, / great blessings / abundant success / compassion and favor / kindness and mercy along with all the other blessings that have been heralded / and words of comfort that have been spoken / to his honor, gre(atness and) hol(iness our) m(aster) and t(eacher) Eli ha-Kohen the parnas, the trustee,[30] / sweet as the (desert) manna[31] / may the steadfast God bless you / and establish your fame among the unbereft nation. / May He grant you an auspicious end / and may you have vigor in good old age, / son of Ḥayyim the

[28] Alexandra Cuffel, "Call and Response: European Jewish Emigration to Egypt and Palestine in the Middle Ages," *Jewish Quarterly Review* 90 (1999–2000), 61–102.

[29] Ed. Alexander Scheiber, *Geniza Studies* (Hildesheim, 1981), Hebrew section, 79–81.

[30] Abbreviation of his other title, "Trustee of the Court."

[31] The story is in Exodus 17.

"Expert,"[32] (may his) m(emory be) b(lessed). May you have abundant peace from the Lord of peace, and a blessing from God, your salvation, Who will give you salvation, and also from the one beloved by you and beloved friend, who prays at all times for you, and from your venerable brethren, for we dwell in peace and give thanks to the Rock, our salvation, as for all the kindness He has done for us.

I inform you,[33] may your Rock protect you and shield you from trouble, that God, may His praise be exalted, commanded us to turn toward the "common poor"[34] among us and to those from good families who have fallen from their wealth, in order to favor them and expend upon them blessing from the bounty of the Lord that He has given us, so that He will bless us in whatever we do,[35] all the more so in the case of scholars of the Torah, who are called such and who apply themselves diligently at its doors, guarding the doorposts of its entrances. Happy is he who wins merit for fulfilling this commandment, for the entirety of expressions of comfort and good tidings were spoken precisely with regard to those who benefit scholars of the Torah out of their own wealth, feed them, give them drink, and clothe them.

The bearer of these lines is Solomon b. Benjamin. He is a good and deserving man,[36] crowned with humility, a modest person, from a good family of noteworthy householders whose table was always set and whose houses were always wide open. However, on account of the many troubles that befell them they fell from their wealth, became poor,[37] and were forced to turn in their need to others. This man left as a war refugee, // wishing to go up to Jerusalem the Holy City, may God sustain it forever. // Because of his poverty, he has been forced to travel around in search of sustenance for himself, // and will go [t]here later. // He asked to have these two lines[38] written on his behalf to be an intercessor for

[32] Hebrew: *mumḥe*, a title often given to extremely well-trained cantors.

[33] Hebrew: *odiʿo*, seemingly a translation of the technical term in Arabic, *yunhī*, opening the "exposition" clause in formal petitions.

[34] Hebrew: *evyonei adam*, cf. Isaiah 29:19.

[35] I translate the phrase *u-le-hafiq lahem berakha mi-ṭuv ha-shem* "expend upon them blessing from the bounty of the Lord." I think the Hebrew here is reinforced by wording associated in the Qurʾān and later Islamic literature with giving charity to the poor, e.g., in Sura 2:273, *wa-mā tunfiqū min khayr fa-inna allāh bihi ʿalīm*, "whatever charity you expend, surely God knows it well." The Hebrew verb *le-hafiq* is a derivative from the root *p-w-q*, like the Aramaic verb *n-f-q*, meaning "bring, take out." It is cognate with Arabic *n-f-q* and appears ubiquitously in the word *nafaqa*, "expenditure," especially in Islamic law as maintenance payments for needy family members and also handouts to the poor. This term was known and used by the Jews, as attested in the Geniza (search *nafaqa* in the Princeton Geniza Browser, www.princeton.edu/~geniza).

[36] Hebrew: *hagun*.

[37] Hebrew: *niddaldelu mi-nikhseihem u-maṭṭa yadam*, the first words being a synonym for *yaredu mi-nikhseihem*, also found in rabbinic literature, e.g., Vayiqra Rabba (Vilna), 34, s.v. *ve-khi*; Midrash Mishlei, ed. Salomon Buber (Vilna, 1893), 22:22 (s.v. *al tigzol*), 92; Seder Eliyahu Zuṭa, ed. Friedman, 5, s.v. *dal*.

[38] A common figure of speech found also in Arabic letters and meaning "a short letter." Writers used this expression to humble themselves, much like calling themselves "your slave." The same

him,[39] because, on account of many sins, he is not bold enough to do this. I ask your excellency, (may your) R(ock) p(rotect you), when he approaches you, to be as diligent as you can and act with him as is your good habit with all wayfarers, and do not delay so that he must stay longer. "Let not the downtrodden turn away disappointed" (Psalm 74:21).[40] In return the Lord will give blessing. "If one says he will give and does give, he receives a reward both for saying and for doing. If one says he will give but does not manage to do so, he receives a reward for the commandment just as for the doing. If one does not say he will give but tells others to give he receives a reward for this, as it is written, 'for in return the Lord your God will bless you in all your efforts and in all your undertakings'" (Deuteronomy 15:10).[41]

These lines are being written with urgency because time is pressing and this Solomon is anxious to go. So I have not been able to write at greater length. May the King of the universe in His abundant mercy protect you and your son and cover you both with the cover of His wings and send His blessing in your barns that are hidden from the eye and make you dwell safely and tranquilly without fear of evil, and may He turn toward us and toward you in His abundant mercy, and announce to us peace from the mouth of peace, in the biblical verse that says, "How welcome on the mountain are the footsteps of the herald announcing peace (or: happiness), heralding good fortune, announcing victory, telling Zion, 'Your God is King'" (Isaiah 52:7).

May your welfare and the welfare of those who love you increase forever. Greetings to your son Ephraim, may he increase like the (swarms of) locusts[42] forever and ever. Selah. May salvation be near and peace and mercy in the end.

Your beloved friend Nathan ha-Kohen b. Mevorakh

---

language is found in letters of the humble poor in early industrial England beseeching dues from poor law administrators back in their home parish. See Sokoll, *Essex Pauper Letters*, 116 ("I Humbly Beg you to Show this Line or two to the Gentlemen"), 633 ("Sir I take Liborty in writing a few Lines"), and elsewhere.

[39] Intercession to induce others to give charity was as meritorious in Judaism as giving itself. See the end of the paragraph.

[40] A verse frequently quoted in the letters of appeal. The continuation in the psalm would not have been lost on potential donors, "let the poor and needy praise Your name," referring, of course, to God in the Bible, but alluding in context to the giver of charity. The verse is cited by Maimonides in his laws of charity, Hilkhot mattenot ʿaniyyim 7:7. The source of the formulation of this law and the rationale for citing a verse from outside the Torah are not clear; cf. Bar-Ilan, *Niqdash be-ṣedaqa*, 63–65. The commentators connect it with a tannaitic statement in Bava Batra 9a. We may surmise that Maimonides' formulation, particularly the verse quoted, was influenced by the rhetoric of the Geniza letters of the poor.

[41] This passage, from rabbinic literature, is found in Tosefta, vol. 1. Seder Zeraʿim, ed. Saul Lieberman (New York, 1955), 59–60, where the edition reads, "he receives a reward *for the saying* just as for the doing."

[42] A common allusion to the swarms of locusts in one of the ten plagues.

(Address on verso)
Deliver in joy and gladness to (his) h(onor) g(reatness and) h(oliness) Eli ha-Kohen the parnas and Trustee b. Ḥayyim ha-Kohen the "Expert," (may his) m(emory be) b(lessed).

(From) His "son" Nathan ha-Kohen b. Mevorakh (may his) e(nd be) g(ood). May great salvation be near.

(In Arabic characters)
To Fustat, God great and exalted willing. Deliver it, may God have mercy on you.[43]

## 15. "The highest and noblest form of charity is credited to the one who bestows charity upon someone anonymously"

A needy person from a "good family" had this letter written on his behalf to Abraham "the Elder of the Community" (a title) during the high holy days. The letter-bearer is "deserving . . . and he is unable to face asking t[he community.]" Quoting the crux verse in the Bible, "A gift in secret subdues (God's) anger" (Proverbs 21:14), the writer requests assistance from Abraham (privately). By keeping his case discreet, he could avoid the shame that the normally self-sufficient (let alone those from "good families" like him) felt when temporary (conjunctural) poverty struck and became known. Anonymous charity was the form of philanthropy highly praised by Maimonides in his famous "ladder of charity" (and also put into practice by ancient rabbis) to avoid embarrassing the recipient. Since the benefactor in this instance probably did not know the petitioner personally (and vice versa), the ethical principle had concrete relevance. A small gift sent by mail would have preserved the anonymity.

TS NS J 399[44] (Judaeo-Arabic)

[Calligraphic Arabic heading][45]
*To Abraham the Elder of the Community, (may) G(od) b(e your succor) and provide as [your] successor a good son, living [and strong].* Your slave brings to your noble

[43] Arabic: *balligh raḥimaka allāh*. The expression *raḥimahu allāh* is used of the living as well as the dead in medieval Arabic letters by Muslims; see Diem, *Arabische Briefe auf Papyrus und Papier aus der Heidelberger Papyrus-Sammlung, Textband*, 73, and for an example in an address of a letter, as here in our Judaeo-Arabic letter, see idem, *Arabische Briefe des 7. bis 13. Jahrhunderts aus den Staatlichen Museen Berlin, Textband* (Wiesbaden, 1997), 151. I am grateful to Petra Sijpesteijn for bringing this particular variation on the one Goitein noted, *balligh tu'jar* ("deliver [the letter] and be rewarded [by God]"; see *Med. Soc.*, 1:284), to my attention, along with the Diem references. For more variants with *balligh*, see Diem, *Arabische Briefe auf Papyrus und Papier aus der Heidelberger Papyrus-Sammlung*, 153.

[44] Verso has the word *al-qāʿa* in Judaeo-Arabic (the main floor in a house or other building), some other scribbling, and the name [A]braham, the latter in a different hand.

[45] I have not been able to decipher this.

knowledge [that the letter-bearer is] *from a good family*. He is deserving [ . . . ]. He cannot face asking t[he community]. He requests, therefore, that his matter [ . . . s]o that he does not experience *shame*[46] from anyone. As you know, the highest and noblest form of charity is credited to the one who bestows charity upon someone anonymously, rather than that he take.[47] As Solomon *the (king), p(eace be) u(pon him) said in the proverb: "A gift in secret [s]ub[dues] anger"* (Proverbs 21:14).[48] We prefer this kind of charity for the distresse(d)[49] on these *High Holidays*. May God the ex(alted) give you from His full treasury, and may all who [open wid]e their hands in giving *be blessed. "It will be to your merit as an act of righteousness (charity)*," etc. (Deuteronomy 24:13).

## 16. "You can tell from his demeanor that he comes from *a good family*"

Yefet is recommended for charity. He is described as someone for whom "it is not his habit to debase himself," using an Arabic expression similar to "uncovering the face," and as being *bayshan*, a Hebrew word that can mean either "bashful/humble/modest," or "ashamed." Here it has the latter sense.[50] Like others we have already encountered, Yefet was ashamed because he came from a "good family" that was not usually poor and had fallen into debt. Trying not to debase himself by going on the public dole, he wished to minimize his shame by appealing to an individual to arrange an ad hoc collection on his behalf from the community. We have here, then, a classic example of the Jewish "shamefaced poor."

Another point worth noting is that Yefet is said to be "from Fustat" (literally, in Arabic, "one of the people of Fustat"). I take this to be a notice to the addressee and, in turn, to the community, that the poor man is not a foreigner, hence should not be given the low priority assigned to foreigners by the halakha, on which see below in chapter 3 and above, no. 12.

The Arabic portion of the letter is preceded, as often (see also above), by a preface in rhymed Hebrew prose, a favorite literary device of Jews in the Arab world, which was transferred to Europe as well. The rhyme, nearly impossible to imitate in translation, is signaled by slashes.

Like the letter to Qalyūb (no. 11), the recommendation in this letter was incidental to the main purpose, namely, family matters. Many needy travelers

[46] The Hebrew word *busha*.

[47] Translation of last phrase uncertain.

[48] The Book of Proverbs is put into the mouth of King Solomon, the wise king (Proverbs 1:1).

[49] The text has the abbreviation *al-makrū*, which could stand for *al-makrū(bīn)* or *makrū(thīn)*, which have a similar meaning.

[50] See discussion in Cohen, *Poverty and Charity*, chapter 1.

like these doubled as letter-bearers. They met local Jews in the synagogue, who asked them to deliver a letter to family in Fustat and, in return, offered to recommend them for assistance when they delivered the written message. This procedure was part of the charity system itself.

TS 10 J 13.13[51] (Judaeo-Arabic)

*I send peace unbounded and infinite / and multitude of blessings like sand and dus[t] / , and everlasting covenant which will not be broken, / glorious favor, / splendor and luster, / crown of desire, / joy and delight, / long life and time extended, to his honor, greatness and holiness, our master and teacher Levi, may He grant life to his sons and ful(fill) through their life "May the Lord bless you from Zion; may you share the prosperity of Jerusalem all the days of your life and live to see your children's children. May all be well with Israel" (Psalm 128:5–6).*

I inform our lord, may God perpetuate your happiness, that the bearer of these lines, [(our) ma(ster)] and t(eacher) Yefet, is from Fustat. He is *ashamed.* God the ex(alted) used to favor him, but it stopped, by the will of the Creator, and debts came to burden him. He has family dependents, but it is not his habit to expose his face to indignity.[52] You can tell from his demeanor that he comes from *a good family*. I ask you kindly to do for him the same well-known kindness that you do for others, and to bid the community to take care of him, since it is not comfortable for him to speak. Accept my personal greetings and forgive us on account of the misfortune that has stricken us by the departure of our brother, *(who) r(ests in) E(den)*, and Sitt ʿAbd a[l- . . . ], may God perpetuate her life, on account of her setback. I am preoccupied with caring for her, for those who came (to be) with her have left, and we see them no more. I greet your sons, and also the elder Ibrahīm, with good wishes. Good wishes, too, to Isḥaq and his brothers, and to Saʿd al-Kohen and his son Joseph. To the elder [ . . . ] and the family, good wishes. *And peace.*

## 17. "I ask God and you to 'cover' me with a robe so I can enter the synagogue to hear *'Kadosh' and 'Barukh'*"

Joseph b. ʿAllān of Alexandria, the son of "good people" who are India traders, addresses Ḥananel b. Samuel, chief judge (*dayyan*) in Fustat and father-in-law of Abraham Maimonides. The letter was written when Ḥananel was still without children but already a dayyan (his dated documents are 1223 to ca. 1249). The writer wanted to collect his share of the estate of his brother,

[51] Cf. *Med. Soc.*, 3:2; 5:198–99 and 563n74. Verso, in different hands: some unrelated Hebrew writing and three lines from a letter in Arabic script.

[52] Arabic: *ibdhāl wajh*. Cf. *badhala wajhahu*, "prostituer son honneur, sa dignité"; R. Dozy, *Supplément aux dictionnaires arabes*, 3rd ed. (Leiden and Paris, 1967), 1:60.

who had died at sea on the way from Yemen to India, and whose money had been sent to the heirs in Alexandria by Maḍmūn, a member of one of the Jewish first families of Aden. Joseph's brother had promised the writer a share of the estate during a drinking party, but they had not formalized this in a legal document. Joseph had "gone up" (i.e., from Alexandria to Fustat) to appeal to the nagid (Abraham Maimonides). The nagid had written a number of letters to the community hoping to elicit some charitable aid for Joseph and his family (of nine persons!), apparently without result. Now, destitute, he asks for money for a robe (*thawb*, which could cost from one to two dinars) so he could cover himself and attend the synagogue. In the past he had been used to wearing elegant clothing, he says.

The letter follows the petition form.

TS 10 J 17.4[53] (Judaeo-Arabic)

*I(n the name of the)* M(*erciful*)[54] Your slave Joseph b. ʿAllān the Alexandrian

kisses the ground before the [l]ofty, most illustrious seat of the master R. Ḥananel *the wise and discerning, son of his honor, greatness and holiness (our) ma(ster) and t(eacher) Samuel the precious elder, the munificent benefactor, may his end be better than his beginning and may he live a long life to see living offspring from you*, and may He make your own reputation a good one in this world and the next.

I inform you that I am from a *good family*. My father is one of the India traders, and God favored us. Your father knows my father and brother, Futūḥ, who recently went on a journey to Yemen and died on shipboard. The elder Maḍmūn[55] took his money and transferred it to his heirs in the port (Alexandria).[56] When he (my brother) was setting out on his travels he made a bequest of something to me, if his time should come, namely, that I should be paid something out of his estate. But no docum[ent] to t[h]is effect was properly executed and recorded, for we were drinking at the time.[57] Your slave went up (to Fustat) to appeal to his excellency our lord, *may his glory be exalted*.[58] The latter wrote a number of letters to the community on my account, hoping I would be provided with something to take back to support my family, which consists of nine souls.

[53] Discussed *Med. Soc.*, 5:39, and mentioned in Goitein, *Letters of Medieval Jewish Traders*, 57. To be published in Goitein's posthumous book on the India trade. Trans. into Hebrew, Goitein, *Tarbiz* 50 (1980–81), 377–78.

[54] The letters are *b-r*, abbreviating the standard opening blessing in Aramaic, *bi-shmakh raḥmanaʾ*. Not noted by Goitein in *Tarbiz*.

[55] Maḍmūn (alias Shemarya) II b. David.

[56] Arabic: *al-thaghr*.

[57] Another example of promises made while drinking, in Goitein, *Letters of Medieval Jewish Traders*, 256.

[58] The head of the Jews, the nagid Abraham Maimonides.

Now that I am *starving and thirsty and without clothing or anything else*, I ask God and you to "cover" me with a robe so I can enter the synagogue to hear "*Kadosh*" *and* "*Barukh*"[59] in the presence of the noble God, having in the past been used to wearing "niṣāfī"[60] and "ṣābūrī"[61] and "mutakhkhat."[62] *May He save me from a cycle (of misfortune). And may your welfare increase.*

[59] Evidently a reference to the Kedusha prayer in the Eighteen Benedictions, that can only be recited in a quorum of ten men, usually in the synagogue. The word *barukh*, "blessed," may refer to the Barekhu prayer, which similarly can only be recited in a quorum. Or it may refer to a part of the Kedusha itself that begins with the word *barukh*.

[60] *Med. Soc.*, 5:547–48n138 mentions *niṣāfī*, usually designating silk and cotton woven together; cf. also 4:415n294.

[61] R. B. Serjeant, *Islamic Textiles: Material for a History up to the Mongol Conquest* (Beirut, 1972), 56–57: *ṣābūrī* cloth, perhaps from the district of Bishāpūr.

[62] Yedida Kalfon Stillman, *Arab Dress: A Short History from the Dawn of Islam to Modern Times* (Leiden, 2000), 59: *mutakhkhat*, a checked pattern.

# Chapter Three

## THE FOREIGN POOR[1]

MANY OF THE previous letters emanate from foreigners. Jews from outside of Fustat, wayfarers passing through and immigrants, regularly wrote for assistance. Their numbers included refugees from war or other depredations elsewhere, captives ransomed at the port of Alexandria or other cities in the country, proselytes from Christian lands, and simply down-and-outs attracted to Egypt and especially Fustat because of its community's renown for generosity and its responsive system of public poor relief.

In the nature of things, most of these people had left families back home and lacked in their new locale the succor of the kinship group. To be separated from home and family meant to be vulnerable to destitution. As an impoverished Jew, who had been sojourning in an Egyptian locale for two years seeking repayment of a debt, put it colorfully: "You know that I am alone and poor, here in the land of my exile, with neither relative nor friend—alone am I among them, 'like a tamarisk in the desert'" (Jeremiah 17.6).[2]

As we have noted already, an ancient halakha potentially impinged upon the acceptance of foreign, that is, nonlocal Jews, as worthy recipients of assistance. It rules that the poor of one's family take precedence in charity over the poor of one's town, and both take precedence over the poor of another town.[3] "The poor of another town" could, of course, apply either to indigents writing from "another town" to request assistance from a benefactor in the Egyptian capital, or to foreigners from "another town" sojourning in Fustat. As we shall see, alms lists in the Geniza are peppered with the names of poor people who had come to Fustat from another place. The letters of appeal presented in this chapter come from both: foreigners writing from outside the capital and foreigners already living there. For the latter, their "outsider" origins could continue to affect adversely their success collecting charity even after their arrival

[1] A full discussion of the foreign poor is to be found in my article "The Foreign Jewish Poor in Medieval Egypt," in *Poverty and Charity in Middle Eastern Contexts*, eds. Michael Bonner, Mine Ener, and Amy Singer (Albany, 2003), 53–72, and in expanded form in Cohen, *Poverty and Charity*, chapter 2.

[2] Dropsie 386, lines 2–3, ed. Mann, *Texts and Studies*, 1:459–60.

[3] Declarations of the priority of family over strangers can be found in early Christian writings as well. See Natalie Zemon Davis's essay concluding the volume *Poverty and Charity in Middle Eastern Contexts*, ed. Michael Bonner et al., 321.

in their new place. Determining the deservedness of foreigners (as well as others, to be sure) occupied the community as well as individual private contributors. Letters and alms lists, alike, attest to these concerns.[4] Some of them refer to or contain outside confirmation of their neediness. This resembles the comparative case of pauper letters from England in the early nineteenth century. Even though applicants for poor relief writing from outside their parish of settlement were eligible by law to continue to receive their allocation, they often sought and obtained confirmation of their continuing need, and these attestations appear noted on their letters back home.[5]

## 18. "I came to this city empty-handed"

We begin with a fascinating plaintive letter from a man from Persia (*balad al-ʿajam*) living in Fustat, addressed to a local man who was known for his beneficence. Following the common motif that we have seen many times, the writer insists that he has never before had to apply for charity and that he does not want to "uncover himself." He had left home impoverished, after having been self-sufficient, and had planned to get a job in Egypt as a communal functionary. But he had taken ill with smallpox and so could not work. He resides in the synagogue, probably a room there or a separate building in the synagogue compound, where the community provided shelter for the needy. In this he resembled the itinerant "foreigner" of the ancient world who found shelter in the "inn," the pagan Greek *pandocheion* (*pundaq* in pre-Islamic, rabbinic Hebrew), or, in early Christian times, the *xenodocheion* or *xenon* (Greek), or *hospitium* (Latin), and in Islamic times, in the mosque or the *funduq*. Needy Jews in the Geniza found shelter in both the synagogue and the Jewish funduq.[6]

CUL Or 1080 J 31[7] (Judaeo-Arabic)

*"For the Lord will be your trust; He will keep your feet from being caught"* (Proverbs 3:26).
*"The Lord will guard you from all harm; He will guard your life"* (Psalm 121:7).

O my master, may God sustain your might and strength and not depose you from your high rank. I am from the land of Persia and I live in the synagogue. I had enough to live on (lit., "to cover myself with"), but I lost it, and I remain without a pittance.[8] I came to this city empty-handed, intending that I would

[4] See nos. 24, 26, 29, 40, 69, and Cohen, *Poverty and Charity*, chapter 2 at notes 98–113.
[5] Some examples in Sokoll, *Essex Pauper Letters*, 99, 270, 284, 299, 300.
[6] See Cohen, *Poverty and Charity*, chapter 2.
[7] Cf. Ashtor, *Zion* 30 (1965), 66; *Med. Soc.*, 2:154; Cohen, *Poverty and Charity*, chapter 8.
[8] Arabic: *ḥabba*, "granule," also the name of a coin of tiny value.

support myself by serving the people,[9] but I fell sick with smallpox. Now I cannot function and I possess nothing. So I have written this petition[10] to your excellency my master, hoping you would help me out with something. I am singling you out with this request and no one else because of your renown and repute (for generosity). May God never terminate your position. By my brother,[11] I have never uncovered myself and would not have had to had not necessity brought this about.[12] I am looking forward to the favor of God the exalted and to the favor of my master. May God never put my master in need or humble him.[13] O master, do not turn me away disappointed but do for me as you do with others and "*let not the downtrodden turn away disappointed*," *etc*. (Psalm 74:21). *May the welfare of our lord increase forever, Amen*.

## 19. "To eke out a living"

The second letter from a foreigner, much longer than most (seventy-five lines) and much more colorful in its detail, was addressed to a Jewish government official named Ya'ir b. Elʿazar. The writer, who had been living in Egypt for just over a year and had possibly been a cantor in former times, chronicles his failed attempts to make it on his own in Fustat.

Wishing to prove himself deserving of financial assistance, like his counterpart in the previous missive and in numerous other letters of the conjunctural poor, he tries to convince his would-be benefactor that he did not intend to become a burden on anybody. Unlike less competent foreigners, he could take care of himself and, rather than outright charity, desired gainful employment. Here he echoes the midrashic idea, codified by Maimonides in the famous "ladder of charity" at the end of the laws of charity in the Mishneh Torah, where he recommends offering the poor a partnership or gainful employment or a loan or a gift that could be used to build economic security as the highest form of philanthropy.[14] The writer had not been able to find employment, not even the poorly paid work of a teacher. Then, luckless, he lost money in a commercial enterprise. Now desperate, he finally has had to ask for help.

[9] Arabic: *nakhdum al-nās*. On the expression *khidmat al-nās*, see *Med. Soc.*, 2:87, 541n104.

[10] Arabic: *ruqʿa*.

[11] A typical oath, similar to saying "by God."

[12] The last phrase, a common sentiment in these letters, occurs in similar form in the English pauper letters, e.g., "I have no wish to be burdensome to the Parish and therefore will never trouble them but when absolute necessity Compels me." Sokoll, *Essex Pauper Letters*, 226.

[13] A thought commonly expressed in these letters, in keeping with the notion that poverty is a misfortune and somewhat more prevalent in Jewish thinking than in some forms of Christian and Islamic asceticism.

[14] Mishneh Torah, Hilkhot mattenot ʿaniyyim, 10:7. See Cohen, *Poverty and Charity*, chapter 1, note 53, for the midrashic reference.

TS 24.46[15] (Judaeo-Arabic)

I[16] tried hard for the year and three months that I have been in Fustat to eke out a living[17] through teaching or something else, so that I could get two or three dirhems (a week) to improve my situation [ . . . ]. I turned to various people[18] to set me up with a livelihood, so that I wouldn't reach the point I have come to. Among the people I turned to to set me up with a livelihood was my master the illustrious elder, may God perpetuate his honor, but he told me, "I have no work." It was my intention thereby not to have to appeal to anyone, for the *sages, may their memory be blessed*, said: "*One should die before becoming dependent upon other people*."[19] As God is my witness, I did not intend to talk to a single being in this city about this. When I was on the way here I prayed, "O Lord, I shall not appeal in need another time." The proof of what I say is that I did not talk about it and did not conduct myself the way *cantors and scholars* do to get the maximum possible contribution. God knows that in my first year, *on the Ninth of Av*, the elder Abu'l-Faraj the banker, may God remember him for good, gave me a bag of dirhems but I threw it back at him immediately, saying: "I can take care of my own livelihood." He took it back and felt bad. Another proof is that my master // the illustrious // elder, your son, may God make his honor permanent, said to me that day or a few days later, "I have put something aside for you," to which I answered, "May you always be there for me. By God, you also promised me something another time." In sum, I did not intend to burden anyone and all I was hoping to do was to eke out a living.

(The next lines, partly damaged, describe an investment he made in a quantity of mercury [*zaybaq*], which resulted in financial loss and also allude to the writer's debts, rent he owed, and his liability to the poll-tax collector.)

I have told (you), my master the illustrious elder—*may the Rock protect you and help you and may you be enveloped by the will of God*—about my situation and my straitened circumstances and my loss, // for he who has no livelihood has no life [ . . . ]. (The writer goes on to ask the addressee to help him out with the investment, which, had he had luck, would have yielded a profit of six dinars.)

My master the illustrious elder, may God lengthen your days, knows that people redeem *captives* and they get out of *prison* and accomplish in this world what they can to do good, and a great deal more. May you, may God perpetuate

[15] Cf. *Med. Soc.*, 1:202, 2:123, 222.

[16] Translation as of line 40. I wish to thank Raymond P. Scheindlin and Sasson Somekh for their help in understanding this difficult letter.

[17] Arabic: *maʿīsha*.

[18] Arabic: *jamāʿāt*.

[19] A less severe version of this statement is found in Maimonides' Mishneh Torah, Hilkhot mattenot ʿaniyyim 10:18: "One should always restrain oneself and submit to privation rather than be dependent upon other people or cast himself upon public charity," citing a talmudic utterance, "Make the Sabbath a weekday rather than be dependent upon other people."

your honor, expend double that which people pray for from you and also give double to *scholars*.

My intention by this request is to eke out a living with the proceeds so that I can improve my situation and not have to ask anyone to support me. Dependent upon me are family members upon whom this is very hard, and besides, they give me no peace. I swear I have not provided them the taste (of food)[20] since the time I arrived here until today. I hope my rescue will come from God, may He be praised, and from my illustrious master, may God perpetuate your authority. To you, may God destroy your enemies, belongs the lofty decision about what to do for me.

(The last four lines are partly damaged.)

## 20. "I was one of the givers"

Foreigners from European countries not (or not yet) familiar with Arabic often wrote in Hebrew, as here. The man was formerly "among the givers," that is, a benefactor, but had lost his wealth: one of the conjunctural poor, we would say. He asks for assistance from the addressee.

TS 8 J 13.5 (Hebrew)

In the name of God, the Merciful the Compassionate[21]
[To] my lord the honored and p[recious] elder [ . . . ] and may He lengthen your days with goodness and [your] years [with pleasantness and grant you] good things and bless all [your] deeds [and all] your actions. May you merit to see [male] child[ren] and may He also grant you long life and guard and protect and make flourish [ . . . ] and lengthen your days and multiply your years [ . . . ].

I inform[22] my lord the [honored] elder that I came her[e][23] from a distant place. I was one of the givers and of those who do k[indness with] all my affluence and wealth, but [I] was left [ . . . ][24] My lord the good elder [knows] that [ . . . ]. Now, have mercy on me as is in keeping with your [good] habit [before] the Lord. I put [my] trust in you [ . . . ]. Therefore [ . . . ] with what the Lord [your God] gave to you and may the Lord, God of Abra[ham Isaac and Jacob] double your wealth and give [you your reward].

[20] The first form of the verb *dhāqa* is used, rather than the needed fourth form. In Judaeo-Arabic, forms I and IV of this kind of verb are often interchanged.
[21] The Hebrew, *be-shem el raḥum ve-ḥanun*, is a calque of the Muslim prayer *bismi llāh al-raḥmān al-raḥīm*. Occasionally Jewish letters use the Arabic Muslim phrase itself. The nagid Joshua Maimonides employed a shortened, Judaized version. See chapter 10.
[22] See above, chapter 1, note 21.
[23] Hebrew: *ʿad hen[ah]*. Completion could be: *ʿad ha-m[aqom ha-zeh]*, "to this place."
[24] Presumably something like [*req*] or [*be-ḥoser kol*], "[empty-handed]" or "[lacking everything]," respectively, followed by a verb meaning "knows," hence, "my lord [knows] that."

## 21. "I wander about like a lonesome bird on a rooftop"

Also in Hebrew, this letter, addressed to the Egyptian head of the Jews, David (b. Daniel) Nasi and "head of the diasporas of all Israel" (in office 1082–94),[25] is particularly fascinating as it emanates from a woman and gives us her own voice, something only rarely heard in other societies in a comparable time period. The letter preserves her first-person speech as dictated to a scribe. In one place the man inadvertently wrote *paneha*, "her face," then corrected it to *panay*, "my face," in conformity with the autobiographical voice of the rest of the letter. Her description of her body is itself unusual, not to speak of the fact that she describes it to a man who was not her husband (the copyist) and, at a distance, to the head of the Jews. She reports that she is alone, without husband, children, or siblings, and suffers from a degenerative skin disease, perhaps leprosy (she calls it, literally, "this plague," using the biblical word for the ten plagues in Egypt, one of which was a disease of the skin). She asks the head of the Jews to order that a *pesiqa* be arranged for her "whether in Cairo or in the city." (The spelling of Cairo, in Arabic, reflects that the writer did not know Arabic well; both he and the woman were doubtless foreigners. "The city," in Arabic *al-madīna*, probably means Fustat.) The pesiqa was a pledge drive, one of the common methods of raising donations for charity, usually done in the synagogue. More on this in chapter 7.

TS 13 J 13.16[26] (Hebrew)

"May the Lord answer you in time of trouble, the name of Jacob's God keep you safe" (Psalm 20:2).
"May He send you help from the sanctuary, and sustain you from Zion" (Psalm 20:3).
"He cares about the poor and the needy; He brings the needy deliverance" (Psalm 72:13).
To your honor, greatness, and holiness, the excellent diadem and crown and good name from on high. To our master and teacher our lord David the great nasi, head of the diasporas of all Israel,[27] may God protect you and grant long life to our lord and may our Creator guard you and may God grant that you see sons from your loins taking your place and the place of your righteous fathers, and may He lengthen your days and years with pleasantness, amen.[28]

[25] See Cohen, *Jewish Self-Government*, chapter 5.
[26] Cf. *Med. Soc.*, 5:194; Cohen, "The Voice of the Jewish Poor," in *Semitic Papyrology in Context*, ed. Lawrence Schiffman (Leiden and Boston, 2003), 251–52.
[27] He took on the title "head of the diaspora," normally reserved for the exilarch in Baghdad, only in 1090 or 1091; see Cohen, *Jewish Self-Government*, 190–93.
[28] The scribe left a space of several lines between the introduction and the body of the letter.

Your slave woman, poor, wretched, woeful, worried, and afflicted on account of my sins—I cast my entrea[t]y [ . . . ] before you, so that you heed the words of your slave, for many are my sighs and my he[ar]t is sick. I am on my own. I have neither husband nor son nor daughter nor brother nor sister, and I wander about like a lonesome bird on a rooftop. Because my sins and iniquities multiplied I became afflicted on my nose, then the malady[29] spread and my face[30] became wasted and eaten away. The disease gets worse and worse and I cannot work.[31] Meanwhile I am naked, thirsty, destitute,[32] and have no means of sustenance. Nobody takes care of me, even if I were to die.[33] Therefore, I cast myself down before the Lord and before my lord, so that you might take pity on me in your kindness and act toward me for the sake of the Lord and for the sake of the merit of your righteous and pious fathers, "and d[ecr]ee and it will be fulfilled, and light will shine upon your affairs" (Job 22:28). May my lord order a pe[s]iqa in every place our lord[34] wishes, whether in Cairo or in "the city,"[35] so that I may be given compassion and respite by the Lord and by you. Do not turn me away empty-hande[d . . . and d]isappointed by you. I shall pray to [the Lord] and for your generou[s . . . ] name. [ . . . May] Almighty God bless you and make you flourish and great, so that you become a congregation of peoples, and may He give [y]ou and your descendants the blessing of Abraham, and may your welfare grow and in[cr]ease and [may your] hono[r] grow great, and for everything, may it become great foreve[r and] ever. Amen.

## 22. "Inform the community about the power of chari[t]y"

This letter, similarly in Hebrew, recommends a formerly rich man who had come upon hard times. The addressee appears to be the ḥaver Ephraim b. Shemarya, head of the Palestinian congregation in Fustat during the first half of the eleventh century (ca. 1007–1055). Having lost all his wealth, the subject of the letter is heading for Egypt from his previous stop, Jerusalem, looking for assistance to finance his trip home (where that is, we are not told). The recommender asks the addressee to make an appeal for the man to elders of the community, both by approaching those gathered in the synagogue and by visiting private homes. "May the ḥaver inform the community about the power

[29] Hebrew: *ha-makka ha-zot*, literally "this plague."

[30] *Paneha*, "her face," corrected to *panay*, "my face."

[31] She probably refers to the spinning and weaving that women typically did at home, rather than going out to work in the marketplace.

[32] Hebrew: *be-ḥoser kol*, literally, "lacking everything."

[33] She means, no one to pay for her burial expenses.

[34] Meaning the head of the Jews.

[35] The names of the two cities are given in Arabic; the second probably refers to Fustat.

of chari[t]y given to those who regularly stretch forth their hands, all the more so to those who have f[allen] from their [w]ealth." These words echo the distinction between those who are chronically (or "structurally") poor and must beg or collect alms from the community, and those who fall from a position of self-sufficiency, whether the working poor or the well-off, as a result of a crisis (the "conjunctural poor").

Golb relates this letter to another, written on behalf of Reuben b. Isaac from France (RDWM, Rouen), who fled after an assault on his family in which his son was killed and his property stolen. Gil rejects this and believes on the basis of handwriting comparison that the letter was written by Abraham the son of the Palestinian gaon Solomon b. Judah. The needy man, Gil says, was probably from Byzantium and the letter was perhaps sent to Alexandria, since regards are sent to a cantor, which is not normal (he says) in letters to Fustat. Goitein thinks the letter was written by Solomon b. Judah himself.

The date given given at the bottom corresponds to 1034–35.

TS 10 J 10.9[36] (Hebrew)

This man was one of the notables of his community in his place, and he was rich. The ruler of his land imposed a punishment upon him, so he fled from there to Damascus. Then he left Damascus for the Land of Israel, but brigands attacked him, looting all (he had) and injuring him. He is in p[a]in. When he reached the Holy City, he said, "I shall go to Egypt where they will perhaps give me [s]omething for the road so I can I return to my place." It is the ḥaver's habit, (may your) R(ock) p(rotect you), to be good to all who come to Egypt, so may you be so with this man. Be his intercessor and advocate and speak to our elders in the holy community, those who are in the synagogue and those who are at home. May the ḥaver give him proper advice so that he may return to his home. May the honored King reward you. May the ḥaver inform the community about the power of chari[t]y that is given to those who regularly stretch forth their hands, all the more so to those who have f[allen] from their [w]ealth. I await the arrival of your letter about what is being done for him and also about your situation and every affair and every need (cf. Daniel 3:16). May your welfare increase, and regards to all the admirers and benefactors, the e[lders] and the cantor and the entire community [ . . . 4]795 [1034–35].

[36] Ed. Jacob Mann, *The Jews in Egypt and in Palestine under the Fāṭimid Caliphs*, 2:111; reprinted in Norman Golb, *Toledot ha-yehudim ba-ʿir Rouen* (History of the Jews of Rouen), 11–12, and partially translated in the English version, *The Jews in Medieval Normandy: A Social and Intellectual History* (Cambridge, 1998), 25–26; rev. ed. by Moshe Gil, *Ereṣ yisrael ba-tequfa ha-muslemit ha-rishona* (Palestine during the First Muslim Period [634–1099]) 3 vols. (Tel Aviv, 1983), 2:224; discussed in English in Gil, *A History of Palestine, 634–1099*, trans. Ethel Broido (Cambridge, 1992), 550. Cf. *Med. Soc.*, 2:544n18.

## 23. "Do not disappoint his hope"

The first part of this fragment (the right margin and top and bottom are cut off, which makes some of the translation uncertain) discusses the plight of a "humble" cantor and schoolmaster, a teacher of young (usually poor) children in a *kuttāb*, an elementary school for teaching recitation of the Bible. He had spent all his money and needed assistance, which the writer requests on his behalf. In the second matter, the writer asks the addressee to help the letter-bearer, a foreigner who is "from a good family." The man had arrived "in this country" from another place after great effort, apparently escaping something untoward, only to find another kind of difficulty. For this the writer uses a Hebrew word and an allusion to a biblical verse that has the meaning of the English, "out of the frying pan into the fire." On verso is found a fragment of a poetic text in Aramaic, in a different hand.

TS 8 J 24.6 (Judaeo-Arabic)

(Begins in mid-sentence) [ . . . ] the *blessin[g]* and remain [ . . . ] surprised that you did not take pity on him for a day, as befits [him] [ . . . ] you never sent him any gift. The humble cantor does not want [ . . . ] work that you have provided him. He wants his wages for (teaching in) the Bible school.[37] He has toiled much [ . . . ] especially in a year like this one, during which we ate [ . . . ] the yoke of being cantor, he suffered and will die from it and will not live [ . . . ] neither a dinar nor a dirhem. Rather he spent it all. Your son [ . . . ] assist him and send them something, for th[ey . . . ] more than that, for you know [he] is sick [ . . . ] relief comes only from God the exalted. Whatever you wish for this [ . . . ] I shall not again mediate between you, for I am tired [ . . . ] perhaps relief will come from God.

Concerning the bear[er of this letter, he asked me] to write to your excellency telling you about his situation [ . . . ] something, so that he will be treated munificently by you. Do not disappoint his hope, but occupy yourself [with] his [n]eed, for [he] is from a good family. God had [ . . . ] against him in his land on account of the affair of the supplier of metal to the mint.[38] He [ . . . ] that [ . . . ] would not befall him [ . . . ] arrived in this country after undergoing hardship and entered the [ . . . th]is *dispute*,[39] "*as when a man flees from a lion (and is attacked by a bear)*," (Amos 5:19). [He is] alone,[40] short on words, and very ashamed, and he has [ . . . ].

[37] Arabic: *fiḍḍat al-kuttāb* (*fiḍḍa* is a silver coin).

[38] Arabic: *mūrid*.

[39] Hebrew: *sikhsukh*.

[40] Arabic: *insān qaṭīʿ*.

## 24. "Help the poor, especially when [foreign origin] and utter poverty are combined"

Atypically replete with rabbinic quotations, this letter was composed on behalf of Abraham of Baghdad in the summer of 1229 by Solomon b. Elijah in Fustat and addressed "to the holy communities in Egypt." The indigent requested the letter so he could make the rounds of other Jewish communities in search of charity. As a foreigner, he might have known, or been made to know, that, especially in the capital, competition over limited resources between needy locals, including family, and newcomers was stiff. The recommendation is endorsed on the back by the judge Yeḥiel b. Eliakim of Aleppo. As an immigrant to Egypt himself, he could be expected to exert his influence on behalf of other newcomers. Foreigners usually needed more testimony of their deservedness than locals.

The midrashic excursus in this letter is highly unusual. It is a mini-sermon on the deservedness of the poor and reflects the extra effort sometimes needed to convince people to give to the foreigner, especially in the light of potential resistance supported by the halakha of "the poor of another town." Son of a learned judge, the writer, Solomon b. Elijah, was himself an elementary school teacher, cantor, and court clerk, from whose hand we have a plethora of administrative documents as well as some letters relating to poor relief. One wonders whether he was "showing off" some of the learning he did not normally get to exercise.

TS Arabic Box 46.253[41] (Judaeo-Arabic)

*To the holy communities in Egypt, may they be saved and guarded and protected against all evil and fear surrounding them.* May *He fulfill through them the verse "Then my people shall dwell in peaceful homes, [in] s[e]cu[r]e [dwe]llings"* (Isaiah 32:18) [ . . . ]. Their noble teaching obliges people to help the poor, especially when [foreign origin] and utter poverty are combined. One of their sayings is: *"Repentance and good works are a shield against r[etr]ibu[t]ion"* (Mishna Avot 4:11) [ . . . ] *repentance.* I call this charitable acts, because a man does not recover from ill[nes]s [ . . . ] eliminated because of this mixture of bodily illness. Thus said lord Daniel to Nebuchadnezzar *"Redeem your sins by beneficence," etc.* (Daniel 4:24), especially for the deserving poor.[42] Because charity was not done in the (right) places, namely, for those who deserved to receive it—considering that it saves from unnatural death, as is written, *"but charity saves from death," etc.* (Proverbs 10:2)—the prophet, lord Jeremiah, peace be upon him, for everything that *Israel* did to him and to themselves, prayed against them a terrible prayer, saying to the

[41] Cf. *Med. Soc.*, 2:509, App. C 140.
[42] Arabic: *al-maḥqūq min al-fuqarāʾ*.

Master of Heaven and his Benefactor, "*[Let them be made] to stumble before you, act against them in Your hour of wrath*" (Jeremiah 18:23). *The sa(ges), (may their) m(emory be) b(lessed)*, interpreted this to mean that he called out to God the ex(alted) not to bring their way a man deserving of charity, considering that *charity* has the benefit that would result from it. The *sa(ges), (may their) m(emory be) b(lessed)* therefore decided that whoever can should give to whomever asks, be he deserving or undeserving.

The bearer of this petition[43] to you illustrious persons is a man called Ibrahīm b. Ḥasan. He said he is of the people of al-Q[ . . . ]ān,[44] a foreigner and poor, incapable of anything. He requested that a letter be written to *the holy communities* with which he could invoke their pity. Whatever kindness, charity, or beneficence you can do for him and others who are deserving or not will be considered as a ray of light in front of you. *It will fulfill the verse, "Your charity shall march before you, the Lord's honor shall be your rear guard"* (Isaiah 58:8).[45] (margin:) *I wrote this* in the middle *of the month of Av (1)540 of (the Era of) D(ocuments) [1229], may its mourning be turned into joy. Much peace to you.*

Verso (endorsement)

*We know this poor man* Abraham al-Baghdādī *has nothing and is wandering in search of bread. Whoever takes pity on him, his reward from heaven will be double.*
Yeḥiel b. Eliakim[46]

## 25. "Do not forget a piece of meat or something else as charity for me"

Goitein writes about this foreigner: "A man whose use of both Arabic and Hebrew reveals that he had seen better days . . . [written] in irregular script and marred by misspellings which can readily be attributed not to ignorance but to what he himself describes." Abū Sahl b. Moses, the addressee, was a cantor. Since cantors also acted as court clerks, "keeping the lists of the beneficiaries of the communal distribution of bread, he was probably the first person contacted by the writer of our letter. Strangers not yet registered got only one loaf of bread. . . . Thus, our letter might reflect the specific plight of a newcomer." At the end, in a third (!) postscript, he requests some food should the ad-

[43] Arabic: *khidma*. See chapter 1, note 67.

[44] I am unable to decipher the name of the place written here. It may be al-Qirmisān, correctly spelled al-Qirmīsīn, the Arabic name of the Persian city of Kirmānshāh.

[45] The original Hebrew is better translated, "Your Vindicator (*ṣidqekha*) shall march before you, the Presence of the Lord shall be your rear guard," but here the Hebrew word is taken to mean charity (*ṣadaqa*) and the idea is that God protects the benevolent giver.

[46] Some letters following his name are overlined, meaning an abbreviation. Possibly *h-ṣ-w-m*, standing for *ha-ṣur yeraḥem*, "may the Rock have mercy." One would expect a prayer for his father in his patronymic.

dressee have a Jewish celebration (a wedding or circumcision or the like). As in the surrounding Muslim society, distributions of food on festive occasions, especially holidays, formed a popular means of giving charity. Meat rarely appeared on the tables of the poor.

TS 8 J 16.7[47] (Judaeo-Arabic)

"*[Say] as follows: '[To life!] Greetings to [you],'" etc.* (1 Samuel 25:6).
"*Those who love Your teaching enjoy well-being*" (Psalm 119:165).
"*Peace (well-being), peace to the far and the near*" (Isaiah 57:19).
The reason for this petition *to his honor (our) m(aster) and t(eacher)* the elder Abū Sahl *the ḥaver, the great Dignitary,*[48] *the wise and discerning one, who excels in everything, may his Rock protect him and grant long life to his three sons, the great Dignitaries, and the venerable holy men, first and foremost* Yefet the scholar, *may the Lord grant him favor and mercy and health from heaven, as well as to all his wise and discerning sons, may He protect them and help them, amen sela.* O my master the *ḥaver* the elder Abū Sahl, God in heaven knows the charity[49] you have done for me. You have saturated me with God's favor and your own. I rely on the highborn status[50] and generosity.[51] By the grave of your father "*the Ahuv*" (beloved, i.e., of the yeshiva) Moses *(may) the m(emory of) the r(ighteous be) b(lessed)*, do not fail to provide me with an evening meal, may it come from God and from you. I have not had anything to dine on except for half a loaf at night and a half loaf in the day. For whatever I have eaten and invoked a blessing I have offered prayers for you, may God never cut you off (from nourishment). *And peace.* Do not abandon
(Margin) Do not abandon me.[52] I rely on your patronage, may God not abandon you.
(Verso) By the religion *of the Jews,*[53] on account of great hunger and fasting a veil has come across my eyes and a blot over my heart such that I do not know what I am writing. Forgive me and do not [ . . . ] me that I cut short your honorific titles, for you are abo[v]e all need for such description. May God not cut you off (from support). I trust in God and in you to give me sustenance and to act *kindly* and with charity. *And peace.* By the religion of God's unity, I have benefited only from a nightly loaf, half of which I eat at night [an]d half for lunch. May God never lead you to bad times, *amen sela.*

[47] Cf. *Med. Soc.*, 5:87 and 530n205.
[48] See chapter 1, note 49.
[49] Arabic: *al-khayr.*
[50] Arabic: *ḥasab.*
[51] Arabic: *nakhwa.*
[52] Repeating the previous words.
[53] Hebrew: *benei yisrael.* An oath.

If you have a Jewish celebration including ritual slaughter for distribution do not forget a piece of meat or something else as charity for me, because I am a foreigner and know nobody. Whatever you do for me, God will produce for you in return.

## 26. "The people of al-Maḥalla know how weakened my situation is and how very poor I am"

Foreigners included those who arrived in the capital from other parts of Egypt. After being in Fustat a month, this poor, blind woman petitions the head of the Jews, Maṣliaḥ ha-Kohen Gaon b. Solomon (in office 1127–39), requesting help for herself and her blind child. Like so many others living on the margin, her sudden need resulted from the appearance of the government poll-tax collector. In a postscript she informs the gaon that the people of the town of al-Maḥalla in the Delta are aware of (and presumably can verify) her poverty. The letter was probably scribed by a man, who knew the correct form of the petition.

TS 12.303[54] (Judaeo-Arabic)

The sl[ave . . . ]

*In (your) n(ame) O Me(rciful)*

The slave of *your e[x]cellency our lord and Gaon* Maṣliaḥ ha-Kohen, *head of the Academy of the Pride (Gaon) of Jacob, may your glory be exalted and your greatness increase, and may He compensate you with a male child for the sake of His name, and fulfill in him the verse "In place of your fathers will be your sons, you will app[oint them] Dignitaries throughout the land" (Psalm 45:17), and may He grant him favor and [kindness] and mercy, fulfilling the saying, ("and you will) [find favor] and a[pprobation in the eyes] of God and man" (Proverbs 3:4).*

I inform your excellency and great[n]ess that I am a b[lind] woman with a blind child [ . . . ]. They dem[anded from me] the p[oll ta]x and we two do not even have br[e]ad [ . . . ]. I ask God and your kindness [to give me] something to help me and my child against the troubles of [the time]. You will earn your reward and recompense. I have never imposed on your generosity, even though your kindness, which everyone seeks, is like the sea. Your slav[e] is known as the wife of Samu(e)l.

*And [p]e[a]ce from* your s[lave].

[54] Ed. and trans. Cohen, *Jerusalem Studies in Arabic and Islam* 24 (2000), 457–58. Cf. *Med. Soc.*, 5:236, 257–58.

(Postscript in the margin): The people of al-Maḥalla know how weakened my situation is and how very poor I am. I have been in Fustat a month and have no[t] burdened anyone. Were it not for my exigency I would not [need to turn t]o you. May God the exalte[d make your h]igh [excellency] one of the besought [not a be]s[eecher], a refuge for the wretched[55] and down and out and the needy p[oo]r. *Amen, great salvation. And peace.*

## 27. "Fate snared him in its net and forced him to resort to human beings"

We have here a very interesting pair of letters on either side of the same sheet of paper. On one side, a Cairene notable is asked by one Nethanel to help, discreetly and instantly, a scholarly man from Europe, "whom Fate had caught in its net" and who had traveled to Cairo specifically because he had heard of the generosity of the addressee's father. The man is "modest and ashamed, having fallen from his wealth and having formerly been a doer of charitable deeds and kindness," a common combination of motifs of the conjunctural poor. The visitor wished to be on the high seas homeward by Passover, which was rapidly approaching. As was common, he was ashamed to make his sudden impoverishment known publicly and so appeals here for private charity.

The letter on the other side is by the foreigner himself and addressed to a different notable in Fustat. Evidently the first letter had been returned to the suppliant, who then used it to draft the second, and this draft along with the first letter was later discarded in the Geniza. Interestingly, at the end he asks help in divorcing the (second) wife he had taken in Egypt. Returning to Europe, where by that time polygyny had been forbidden by the rabbis, he had no choice. It was also necessary for the sake of the local wife he was planning to leave behind, so she could remarry.

TS 13 J 20.28[56] (Hebrew)

In (Your) name, O Mer(ciful). "The name of the Lord is a tower of strength to which the righteous man runs and is safe" (Proverbs 18:10).

"The mouth of the righteous utters wisdom and his tongue speaks," etc. (Psalm 37:30).

[55] *Li'l-ṣuʿlūk*, a term from the pre-Islamic vocabulary of poverty, denoting then, in the words of C. E. Bosworth, "restless characters who cut themselves off from their tribes and gave themselves up to a penniless but independent life of violence and adventure." *The Mediaeval Islamic Underworld: The Banū Sāsān in Arabic Society and Literature* (Leiden, 1976), 17. In the Geniza documents about the poor, *ṣuʿlūk* denotes extreme poverty, minus the other connotations. See Cohen, "Four Judaeo-Arabic Petitions of the Poor," 458n35.

[56] Cf. *Med. Soc.*, 2: 499, App. C 85; 3:48 and 437n3; 3:20; 5:330.

"But the lowly shall inherit the land, and delight in abundant we(ll-being)" (Psalm 37:11).

I inform your precious excellency, his honor, greatness and holiness, (ou)r maste(r) and teache(r) Obadaiah the wise and discerning, the scholar, son of his honor, greatness and holiness our master and teacher Benayahu the elder, the precious, the benefactor and generous one, "the Crown of the Elders," may his Rock protect him and be his succor, that the bearer of these lines is his honor, greatness and holiness our master and teacher Maṣliaḥ the honored elder, the scholar, the wise and the discerning, son of our master and teacher Jacob the honored elder (who) r(ests in) E(den). He is modest and ashamed, having fallen from his wealth and having formerly been a doer of charitable deeds and kindness. Fate ("Time") snared him in its net and forced him to resort to human beings. He came to Fustat trusting in your kindness, for he had heard the reputation of the beneficent elder, your father. When he comes to you, do with him as is in keeping with your good habit and your upright nature, per chance t(he) h(oly one) b(lessed be) H(e) will provide for him through your good hands, "for good things are brought about through the agency of good men." What you do should be done discreetly and swiftly, because he must be on shipboard for Passover. May the Lord of Hosts double your reward and be your succor and cover you with the cover of His wings and save you from every enemy and adversary. Accept greetings of drops of water, first from Him who dwells on high and then from your slave Nethanel b. Ḥalfon, who asks after your welfare and prays for your great prosperity, that God make it permanent, Selah.

Verso

I inform your honor my honored and pre[ci]ous lord, "the Crown of the El[ders"], the benefactor and generous one, "the Glory among Men," "the Diadem of the Speakers," may God protect you "and cover you in the cover of [His] tent and raise you high upon a rock" (Psalms 27:5) our master and teacher Maym[ū]n of the good name, whose reputation is renowned throughout the world and whose fragrance carries farther than all the powders of the merchants like clean myrrh. May God save you from the judgment of de[ath] and from its decrees and snares. I inform my lord that were it not for your good reputation and worthy [ . . . ] I would not have come to Fustat. I hope that you, my lord, will not [abandon me] and that God, in His mercy, will not forget me. I also wish that your honor would [ask] your friends who are like you, per chance God will make [t]h[em] have pity on me and they will help me. For I am in need and pressed [ . . . ] from His full hand. May He never put you in need of gifts from human beings. [I pray] to the Creator and to you, for I want to go on my way home in peace tomorrow or the day after, because I want to be on shi[pboard] for Passover. I cannot lift my voice or my head because of the shame. [I] come not [as a w]arner but as one who reminds. May God protect your flowers,[57] O my lord and [ . . . ], our master and teacher Jacob the wise, the discerning, the benefactor and g[enerous one, "the Diadem] of the Speakers," him and his brothers; may their Rock protect them and save them from all bad [de]crees, and may He pass on to them your merit and good deeds, [and p]eace. Also, I ask my lord to arrange for me the *geṭ* (divorce document). May I be able to merit to see your countenance. Peace. I wish for it to be done dis[creetly] and not in public.

## 28. "I remain like a man locked up in prison, [and] I am causing a burden for the people of the house"

The suppliant, Isaac by name, writes to Ephraim b. Shemarya, head of the Palestinian congregation in Fustat, who exercised extended authority over the entire community and at times even beyond it to other local communities in Egypt (1007 to his death in 1055). As the letter is in Hebrew, Isaac was probably a newcomer trying to eke out a living in a profession like teaching. In alluding to his learning he appeals, very typically, for special consideration. Like many other needy Jews at poll-tax season, he was unable to pay and so was hiding out where he lived and had become a burden on his hosts or landlord. He asks Ephraim to speak to the poll-tax collector, perhaps to secure a reduction (the poll tax was graduated according to economic status: see below) or some other relief.[58] Goitein surmises that Isaac was a local communal leader.[59]

The first few lines contain some rhymed prose.

TS 8 J 21.6[60] (Hebrew)

"And peace with you and peace with Him who support you," etc.
(1 Chronicles 12:19).
To brother and friend, / great in knowledge, / beloved and cherished, soul bound up with soul, engraved on my heart, the great, my right eye, my powerful arm, his honor, gre(atness and) hol(iness), (our) mas(ter) and tea(cher) Ephraim the ḥaver of the great Sanhed(rin),[61] / glory of the ḥavers, who is exalted / among those invited to assemble, / may God be your succor / and place over you His

[57] Hebrew: *peraḥim*, referring possibly to disciples or children.
[58] *Med. Soc.*, 2:387–89.
[59] *Med. Soc.*, 1:54.
[60] Ed. Mann, *Jews*, 2:109–10 (omits a few phrases); cf. 1:102; *Med. Soc.*, 1:54; 2:190; 2:527n32; 2:389 and 612n36; Hassanein Rabie, *The Financial System of Egypt A.H. 564–741 A.D. 1169–1341* (London, 1972), 110; Elinoar Bareket, *Fustat on the Nile: The Jewish Elite in Medieval Egypt* (Leiden, 1999), 92, 97, 139.
[61] Title awarded by the Jerusalem yeshiva, also called the Sanhedrin, after the name of the Palestinian yeshiva in late antiquity.

cover, / son of his honor, gr(eatness and) ho(liness, our) ma(ster) and teacher Shemarya the teacher, who rests in Eden, the garden of God.

From the day we parted until this day I have heard no news of what you have done for me. No one has told me what has been done lately on my behalf. I remain like a man locked up in prison, [and] I am causing a burden for the people of the house. Now, you have always done great kindnesses for me; perpetuate your kindness this time when we meet, and do not be neglectful, for my heart and eye are counting on the kindness of the Rock, first, may His name be blessed, and on your kindness. Many scholars have come here from the Land of Edom (Europe) and from the Land of Israel. Let me be like one of them among my people. Earn merit for what you do for me. As you know, Moses our teacher, of b(lessed) m(emory), achieved merit and bestowed merit on others, and the merit of others depends upon h[im], as it is s(aid): "He executed the Lord's judgments [margin] and His de(cisions) for Is(rael)" (Deuteronomy 33:21). Time is pressing. If you can speak on my behalf with the collector of the poll tax,[62] that would be good. If, God forbid, that is difficult for you, let me know and I shall turn elsewhere, be it right or left. I fear I will come out of this without a solution and be put in prison.

(Above:) May your welfare increase like the multitude of the locusts. Isaac, your admirer, asks that your welfare increase.

## 29. "He was of the givers and not of the takers"

The following letter is rather famous, as it has been claimed as evidence of Jewish Khazars living in Kiev-Rus in the high Middle Ages. The Khazars were a Turkic tribe that settled in the Caucasus region, whose royal family converted to Judaism around the eighth century. A Turkic postscript is found at the bottom of the page. The letter emanates from the community of Kiev (so the name of the city has been deciphered) and recommends a certain Jacob ben Ḥanukkah for charity. Jacob had been seized by non-Jewish creditors of his brother's, who had been killed by brigands and plundered of his money. Jacob had stood surety for his brother's loan, so he was left with responsibility for the unpaid debt. The community had redeemed him from captivity in the hands of the creditors by paying part of what he owed. Then, apparently, they sent him to collect as much as possible of what remained of the loan from Jewish communities elsewhere. Signatures at the bottom, as in other letters of recommendation for foreigners, give the letter the weight of a legal document,

[62] Hebrew: *baʿal ha-mas*, translating Arabic *ṣāḥib al-jāliya*, "collector of the poll tax"; *Med. Soc.*, 2:612n36.

authenticating the suppliant's story and verifying his need.[63] Two of the signatories are parnasim, which in Europe signified leaders of a community, not lower-ranking social-welfare officials, as in Egypt. Encouraging readers of the letter to be generous, the missive explains that Jacob is not a lowly beggar, but from a "good family," and usually "of the givers and not of the takers."[64] Voicing the unexpectedness of his poverty (a conjuncture, in our terms), the community writes that "cruel Fate was decreed against him." These and other typical notions show that ideas of poverty and charity were shared by Jews from the Muslim domain with Jews from Europe, and that at least the ideas of poverty and charity in the Geniza documents, if not all the practices, can be taken as more universally applicable to medieval Jewry outside of the Arab world.

Jacob evidently ended up in Fustat or at least passed through.

TS 12.122[65] (Hebrew)

[ . . . ] the first among the foremost, He who is adorned with the crown, "Final and First," who hears the whispered voice and listens to utterance and tongue, may He guard them "as the pupil (of one's eye)" (cf. Deuteronomy 32:10), and make them to dwell with Naḥshon[66] on high as at first, men of truth, despisers of gain, doers of lovingkindness and pursuers of charity, guardians of salvation whose bread is available to every wayfarer and passerby, holy communities scattered to all (the world's) corners: may it be the will of the Master of peace to make them dwell as a crown of peace.

Now, our dignitaries[67] and masters, we, the community of Kiev, inform you of the troublesome affair of this Mar Jacob b. Ḥanukkah, who is from a [good] family. He was of the givers and not of the takers,[68] until a cruel Fate was decreed against him, in that his brother went and took mone[y] from gentiles; this Jacob stood surety. His brother went on the road, and there came [bri]gands who slew him and took his money. Then came the creditors [and t]ook this (man) Jacob captive, they put chains of iron on his neck and fetters about his legs. He stayed there an entire year [ . . . and after]ward we took him in surety; we paid out sixty [coins] and there ye[t . . . ] remained forty coins; so we have sent him among the holy communities that they might take pity on him. So now, O our masters, raise up your eyes to heaven and do as is your goodly custom, for you

[63] For other examples see Cohen, *Poverty and Charity*, chapter 2, note 28.

[64] On this phrase and its midrashic antecedent, see chapter 1, note 11.

[65] Ed. Norman Golb and Omeljan Pritsak, *Khazarian Hebrew Documents of the Tenth Century* (Ithaca and London, 1982), 1–71. The translation is Golb's with slight modifications.

[66] Praised in rabbinic lore for being the first to enter the Red Sea after Moses parted its waters. Babylonian Talmud Soṭa 37a.

[67] Hebrew: *aluf*, a high military rank in the Bible which was used as a title in the Babylonian yeshiva in the Middle Ages.

[68] See above, note 64.

know how great is the virtue of charity. For "charity saves from death" (Proverbs 11:4). Nor are we as warners but rather as those who remind. "It will be to your merit as an act of charity before the Lord your God" (Deuteronomy 24:13). You shall eat (the) fruits (thereof) in this world, and the capital fund (of merit) shall be yours perpetually in the world to come. Only be strong and of good courage, and do not put our words behind your back; and may the Omnipresent bless you and build Jerusalem in your days and redeem you and also u[s] with you.
A(men?) A(men?) A(men?) BQZ[69]
Abraham the parnas [ . . . ]el bar MNS   Reuben bar
GWSTT' bar KhYBR (Khaybar?) Kohen   Simson
Judah, called SWRTH   Ḥanukkah bar Moses
QWFYN bar Joseph   MNR bar Samuel Kohen
Judah bar Isaac Levi   Sinai bar Samuel
Isaac the parnas   (in Turkic runes) HWQWRWM, "I have read (it)."

## 30. "Act on our behalf in keeping with your habit with scholars and members of the Sanhedrin"

The author of this letter of appeal on behalf of his family had just made the laborious journey with them from Jerusalem. The most interesting thing about the letter is that the name of the addressee is in a different hand and inserted into the formulaic greeting in two blank spaces left for that purpose. This means the writer had no idea to whom he would appeal for charity at his destination until he got there. Perhaps he came armed with more than one such letter-form to fill in and disseminate as needed. Associated with the yeshiva in Jerusalem, he relies upon the general willingness to support needy scholars. He also uses common religious rhetoric to appeal to his would-be benefactor, motifs we have seen above, such as equating charity with an offering in the Temple (see also below).

The beginning is in rhymed prose.

TS 6 J 3.1[70] (Hebrew)

May abundant greetings / and scented blessing / and double consolation / and fulfillment of every request / be bestowed upon our precious master and teacher Abraham ha-Kohen the precious, may your Rock protect you and be your succor, son of our teacher Joseph, (who) r(ests) in (the Garden of) E(den). We request from your honor, our precious one, to act on our behalf in keeping with your habit with scholars and members of the Sanhedrin (the yeshiva), for we have

[69] A. Brandt suggested to the editors to read *b(arukh) q(ore) z(eh)*, "b(lessed be he who) r(eads) t(his)" (Golb and Pritzak).

[70] Published in S. Assaf and L. A. Mayer, eds., *Sefer ha-yishuv*, volume 2 (Jerusalem 1944), 31 (wrongly marked 6 J 31); rev. ed. Gil, *Ereṣ yisrael*, 2:621.

the burden of a wife [and] children. We have just made the extremely laborious journey from Jerusalem to Fustat. May our Rock consider what you do for us as if it were a complete offering and a basket of first fruits, and may he double your reward. May He in His mercy so do and fulfill, and may the outcome be (your) welfare.

(signature:) descendant of Yeshuʿa the ḥaver son of Ṣedaqa, (who) r(ests) in E(den).[71]

## 31. "The benefactions of my lord the elder are w[ell known] to all who t[urn] to you"

Samuel b. Jacob ha-rav b. Samuel ha-rav writes to Abraham b. Ḥaggai supplicating his help and appealing to his reputation as a generous benefactor and as one "who loves Torah scholars." The writer is a recent arrival, whose use of Hebrew suggests that he hailed from a European country. As in so many other letters, he emphasizes that, up to now, he has not turned to anyone for charity, and, as in other missives, he plays on the theme that charity functions like a sacrificial offering to God.

TS 10 J 10.4 (Hebrew)

In the name of the Merciful

"The righteous man holds his way, he whose hands are clean, etc." (Job 17:9).[72]

I send peace, peace / to the man of peace / from the Lord of peace, / "peace, peace" / [ . . . ] his face in his cloak and reveal them. / Behold I dreamt a dream, / (his) ho(nor), gr(eatness and) ho(liness our) ma(ster) and t(eacher) Abraham the precious elder, the wise and the discerning, who fears heaven and loves Torah and those who study it, whose gift to all is great whether in secret [or in p]ublic, may he be blessed by Him abundantly, son of (his) ho(nor), gr(eatness and) ho(liness our) ma(ster) and t(eacher) Ḥaggai (who) r(ests) in the G(arden of Eden).

I inform my lord the precious elder that I am among those who remember your deeds and I yearn for your benefactions. Since I arrived here I have d[e]sired to see my lord the elder and I always pray for you. I came here out of great [need]. The benefactions of my lord the elder are w[ell known] to all who t[urn] to you, in keeping with your congenial habit. Since I arr[ived here I have not asked] a thing from anyone. If you now would d[o me a kindness . . . ] grant me something with which to sustain myself [ . . . ] even a small coin [ . . . ] may the Omnipresen(t), b(lessed be) H(e) [ . . . ] (margin:) give you the good tidings of absolution and forgiveness [and consider] whatever you do on my behalf as if

[71] There are tiny letters above and below the signature, probably abbreviating a biblical verse (which cannot be determined) and functioning as authentication of the signature.

[72] The verse concludes: "grow stronger." There is a blank space of a couple of lines after this.

it were a complete offering upo[n] the altar. May you merit "to see the goodness of God and to visit his sanctuary" (Psalm 27:4). If I did not know about your habit and kindnes[s and] goodness I would not be bothering you. I have nothing of the sereneness of our forefather[s], and I have no means of sustenance. May the h(oly one) b(lessed be) H(e) grant that you be favored by all those who see you, [and] the outcome be your welfare. Your student Samuel b. Jacob the Rav b. Samuel the Rav (who) r(ests in) E(den).

## Chapter Four

# INDIGENT CAPTIVES AND REFUGEES[1]

AS IN ISLAM, where captives constitute one of the eight classes of people to whom payments are due from the alms tax (*zakāt*; Sura 9:60); and as in Christianity, where, in the Gospel parable of the Last Judgment (Matthew 25:31–46), aid to captives constitutes one of the six charitable acts ensuring salvation;[2] so too in Judaism, ransom of captives is considered a paramount charitable miṣva. Captives were especially in need of charity because their fate if not ransomed was slavery, if not worse. Their suffering is already cited in the Talmud as reason for deeming their ransom a preeminent religious duty. In the Middle Ages, seizing human beings and later selling them was an everyday occurrence. In the Geniza period, Muslim and European corsairs exploited the Jewish commitment to redeem captives by routinely capturing Jewish travelers for redemption by a Jewish community. The letters and other documents describe numerous instances of ransoming of captives in Alexandria and of contributions from other Egyptian Jewish communities toward the cost. A single person fetched the hefty sum of 33⅓ dinars according to Geniza evidence, corroborating what is known from Muslim sources about Muslim captives. Through the Geniza correspondence we obtain glimpses, not only of how the community dealt with the problem, but also of the actual experience of the captives themselves—and hear their voices.

### 32. "I am a woman *who was taken captive*"

We begin with the voice of a female captive who had been ransomed from Crusaders. She had just arrived (in Fustat) from one of the small Jewish communities in the Egyptian Delta. She invokes a topos—help for the wayfarer—that we saw frequently in connection with the "foreign poor." Captives were by definition foreigners, but their dire situation largely canceled out the low prioritization that foreigners had according to the halakha of "the poor of another town." She addresses "the holy congregation," rather than an individual.

[1] See Cohen, *Poverty and Charity*, chapter 3.

[2] It was considered an aspect of charity in the Byzantine Empire. See John J. Boojamara, "Christian *Philanthropia*: A Study of Justinian's Welfare Policy and the Church," *Byzantina* 7 (1975), 365–66.

This is typical, as we shall see below in the letters on women and poverty. While men showed no reluctance to appeal to individuals (other men, of course), women, it seems, were more accustomed to turn to Jewish officialdom or to the community. Turning to a man outside her family meant unwanted exposure, unless the man had some official function in the community. This preference for appealing to the community or its representatives was strengthened, especially for the widows, most of whom had children in tow (like the woman here), because of the rabbinic concept, mentioned in several Geniza letters, that the court is "father of orphans and judge of widows." Notice, too, the use of exhortative biblical verses at the beginning.

The time of this missive must be after 1099, the year the Crusaders captured Jerusalem, though it is difficult to pinpoint the date. During the intermittent warfare between the Muslims and the Latin Kingdom of Jerusalem in the twelfth century, Crusaders had many opportunities to take Jews (and of course Muslims) prisoner.

ENA 4020.62 (formerly Uncatalogued 98)[3] (Judaeo-Arabic)

*"Thus says the Lord: Do justice and deeds of charity, for my salvation is near to come and my charity to be revealed"* (Isaiah 56:1). *"Blessed are those who do justice and deeds of charity at all times"* (Psalm 106:3).

I inform the holy congregation—may God enhance its splendor—that I am a woman *who was taken captive in the land of Israel.* I arrived here this week from Sunbāṭ "naked," with no blanket and no sleeping carpet. With me is a little boy and *I have no means of sustenance.* I beseech now God the exalted and beseech the congregation—*may you be blessed*—to do with me what is proper to be done *with any wayfarer. May the Holy one, blessed be He, repay you many times and be your help so that you shall never be driven from your homes.*[4] *And may He bring the redeemer in your days. Amen.*

## 33. "You do not need anyone to goad you to perform *religious duties*"

This letter is famous because it comes from Maimonides (d. 1204). It is a circular appealing for money to ransom Jewish captives—one of three or possibly four, if not five, circular letters from Maimonides about ransoming of captives

[3] Ed. S. D. Goitein, "New Sources on Palestine in Crusader Days" (in Hebrew), *Eretz-Israel* 4 (1956), 149–50; idem, *Ha-yishuv be-ereṣ yisrael be-reshit ha-islam uvi-tequfat ha-ṣalbanim* (Palestinian Jewry in Early Islamic and Crusader Times), ed. Joseph Hacker (Jerusalem, 1980), 288–89; translated into English by Goitein in *Med. Soc.*, 2:170 (slightly revised here). Cf. also Cohen, "The Voice of the Jewish Poor," 253.

[4] The last phrase, in Aramaic, occurs elsewhere, CUL Or 1080 J 8, line 16, *Med. Soc.*, 2:500, App. C 92. Cf. also *Med. Soc.*, 2:555n59.

from his early years in Egypt. While the Talmud declares ransoming Jewish captives a "great religious duty" (*miṣva rabba*), Maimonides goes further and gives extra prominence to this duty in his Code, the Mishneh Torah (Hilkot mattenot ʿaniyyim 8:10). He uses language that reflects the stark realities of Egyptian daily life: "The ransoming of captives has precedence over the feeding and clothing of the poor. Indeed there is *no religious duty more meritorious than the ransoming of captives*, for not only is the captive included in the generality of the hungry, the thirsty, and the naked, but his very life is in jeopardy."

Maimonides sends an emissary and a parnas, who together carried the letter to read publicly to communities and collect money to bring back to Fustat. As part of the exhortation, Maimonides mentions the contributions he personally and others have already made to the cause and urges strong and immediate participation. He asks to be informed of the total donated and instructs the addressees to turn monies collected over to his emissary. The letter was written by the scribe Mevorakh b. Nathan and bears Maimonides' signature. The other circulars fill out a picture of intense activity in this endeavor.[5]

Goitein read (from a facsimile published elsewhere)[6] the date as Tammuz (1)480 (of the Era of Documents), that is, the summer of 1169, and connected the appeal with the Crusader sack of Bilbays near Fustat (Old Cairo) the previous year. In Goitein's view, this act of leadership on Maimonides' part shortly after settling in Egypt established his reputation and led to his appointment as head of the Jews by the Fatimid caliph shortly thereafter. Shailat prefers to read (1)481, hence the summer of 1170, and connects the episode with a collection of money on behalf of captives that, according to yet another document, was sent to Maimonides from the city of al-Maḥalla in the Egyptian Delta. His hypothesis about the date of the letter does not negate the significance of Goitein's interpretation for Maimonides' rise to prominence.

JTS MS 8254.7[7] (Judaeo-Arabic)

(begins in mid-sentence . . . ) *may He cover them with the cover of His wings*, what all the comm[uniti]es of Israel have contributed, *may God bless them* and what they have done concerning the *captives*, *may God release them from imprisonment*.

[5] Cohen, *Poverty and Charity*, chapter 3.

[6] By Marguiles (see next note) and in Norman Bentwich's *Solomon Schechter: A Biography* (Philadelphia, 1940), opp. p. 143. Goitein assumed the manuscript was in Cambridge but could not find it there. It was (and is) actually in New York.

[7] Formerly ENA 2896. Ed. Y. Shailat, *Iggerot ha-Rambam* (Epistles of Maimonides), 1:64–65. Earlier publications by S. H. Margulies, "Zwei autographische Urkunden von Moses und Abraham Maimuni," *Monatsschrift für Geschichte und Wissenschaft des Judenthums* 44 (1900), 8–13, and by Goitein, *Ha-yishuv*, 312–14, and idem, "Maimonides, Man of Action: A Revision of the Master's Biography in Light of the Geniza Documents," in *Hommage à Georges Vajda*, ed. G. Nahon and Ch. Touati (Louvain, 1980). The translation below incorporates some improved readings by Mordechai A. Friedman, "New Sources from the Geniza for the Crusader Period and for Maimonides and His Descendants" (Hebrew), *Cathedra* 40 (1986), 75n39. After seeing a photograph of the document

We are [sending] you a letter with the honorable, *his h(onor), g(reatness), (and) h(oliness), our master and teacher* Aaron ha-Levi, *the hon(orable), the excellent scribe, (may his) R(ock) p(rotect him)*. He will read it to the community. He is accompanied by a parnas sent from our midst. When he reads it to *you, my brothers,* take heed of it as is to be expected from the likes of you, and you will gain thereby the great reward. Act upon it in the same way as we, all the *judges* and the *elders and the student(s)*, have all acted, going around, night and day, urging people in the synagogues, the markets, and at the doors of dwellings, in order to collect something toward this great goal. Having contributed as much as we ourselves are able, you, too, should do for them as befits your generosity and your [renown] as seekers of *merit* [through] kindness and love. Write to tell us the total amount you obtain on their behalf, through God the ex(alted's) favor and your own. Exert yourselves to collect it quickly and send it to us with *our above-mentioned dignitary*, R. Aaron ha-Levi. You do not need anyone to goad you to perform *religious duties*. May God the exa(lted) not let you experience adversity *and may he protect you and enfold you with his abundant mercy. May your welfare increase forever. Tamm[uz] (1)480 (of the Era of Documents).*

Moses the son of Maimon, *(may the) m(emory of the) r(ighteous) be (blessed)*.

## 34. *"Why has my lord left me out of his gifts?"*

"Ephraim the poor, poor foreigner," the author of this missive and of one other letter of appeal written earlier,[8] was a refugee from the west. Named Ephraim b. Isaac of Ceuta, Morocco, he had fled thirty-five years earlier from the threat of the Almohads, who conquered that part of Morocco and then Spain in 1147. The addressee (named in the first letter) is Moses, also an immigrant to Egypt. Ephraim lived about fifteen years in Sicily after leaving North Africa, but left there as a refugee after being plundered and losing everything. In Egypt he worked as a silversmith, "needing nobody's support," until, three years before writing to Moses, he contracted ophthalmia and lost half his eyesight. That meant the end of gainful employment in his profession. To get by he took on some students as a tutor, teaching them Bible, for wages of four dirhems per week. Strapped, he turned to his Maghrebi countrymen in Egypt, ten of whom assumed the charitable obligation of paying his poll tax. Still struggling, he had

sent him by the Seminary librarian, Friedman ventured the opinion that Margulies, who thought the date was (1)484 = 1173, might be correct and suggested further that Maimonides may already have been head of the Jews when he led the campaign to ransom the captives. I examined the letter at the Jewish Theological Seminary under bright light and also ultraviolet light and did not see any letter after the *tp*, which stands for 480, hence I agree with Goitein's reading of the date.

[8] TS 12.3, trans. by Goitein, *Med. Soc.*, 5:77 (the main part of the letter).

turned to Moses for assistance, asking him to write to his own brothers to help him out and also requesting a personal gift of "a little wheat."[9]

The present letter, a sequel, expresses Ephraim's disappointment with his would-be benefactor. He repeats his request for wheat (here itemizing the amount, perhaps somewhat more than the "little wheat" he asked for in his first letter). In a postscript he adds a request for cash.

The unusual confluence of two letters dealing with the same thing provides us with a more nuanced view of the vicissitudes of private charity and the plight of the foreign poor than single letters of appeal normally can. Another example of this is the pair of letters from the widow of the cantor Ben Naḥman translated in chapter 6.

TS 8 J 20.24 (Judaeo-Arabic)

I wrote to your excellen[cy . . . ]. I entreat[ed] you to kindly send your slave 4 irdabbs of wheat // above the line: their price is about 15 dirhems per irdabb, // 2½ of them at their price, and 1½ irdabb to be at the disposal of your slave, your poor foreigner. *I come not as a warner but as one who reminds*. Your slave is living off the charity of some of my countrymen and friends and masters // above the line: who pay on my behalf the poll tax. // May God grant you life and remember them with kindness *as well as all those who act kindly toward me. Why has my lord left me out of his gifts? Does scripture not say: "You shall rejoice in all the goodness that the Lord God has given to you and your house, you and the Levite and the stranger who is in your midst*," (Deuteronomy 26:11) "*for I am a stranger along with you*" (Psalm 39:13). Who, moreover, among *the poor of Egypt (Fustat)* is more deserving than I, who am *incapacitated? Our teacher* Moses sold me for little or nothing. I present this petition to your excellency, *and "let not the downtrodden turn away disappointed*" (Psalm 74:21). One does not have to wish you well over and over again. Your sla[ve] will serve *at your feet* as long as he remains in Fustat, thanking you before God and man. *May the Omnipresent, blessed be He, double your reward and welfare and the welfare of my lord "the Diadem" your brother. And peace to my lord your son, may the Holy one blessed be He grant him life and protect him. Amen.*

Written by me
Ephraim the poor, poor foreigner

In the name of love, I seek refuge in your kindness [ . . . ] your excellency, I informed you in letters. I ask from your excellency 60 dirhems, one dinar on your [a]cco[u]nt, leaving one half. As for me, I [ . . . ] silver and not gol[d] and [ . . . ] ir[dabb . . . ] dirhems each per irdabb. *And p[eace].*

[9] Arabic: *qamḥ*. Goitein translated "flour," but that is usually distinguished from wheat by being called *qamḥ daqīq*, e.g., TS Arabic Box 18(1).33, lines 14–15 (*qamḥ*, *qamḥ daqiq*, and *raghīf khubz* ["loaf of bread"] in that order and in the same breath). That letter is translated above, no. 9.

## Chapter Five

# DEBT AND THE POLL TAX[1]

DEBT WAS A CHRONIC affliction of the poor in the European Middle Ages, "the poisonous remedy for poverty," as Michel Mollat calls it.[2] Like captives, debtors constitute one of the eight categories in Islam to whom the poor-due is to be paid (Sura 9:60), and the Muslim is enjoined to be patient with hard-pressed debtors, even to the extent of remitting what they owe as a charitable act (Sura 2:280).

The documents from the Geniza exhibit the same nexus between debt and poverty among the Jews. We have already seen in several previous letters of the poor how debt and the poll tax—which became a debt for the poor who could not afford to pay it on time—lay at the root of their predicament. For both the marginally self-sufficient (the "working poor") and those who were normally comfortable, once a conjuncture interfered with their livelihood and they were confronted with their inability to purchase basic daily needs, they might have to borrow. Or, already in debt, they would be unable to repay their obligations and so risked the wrath of their creditors. In either case, charity might be their only resort. The annual poll tax incumbent upon non-Muslims was a harsh burden for the poor or nearly poor. Nonpayment could result in physical mistreatment by the authorities or even imprisonment. For that reason, private appeals for money to help discharge the poll-tax debt abound, as do lists of donations to subsidize the poll tax of the indigent.

Islamic lawyers were divided on the question whether the poor should be exempt from the poll tax and on what defined the poverty line. The Geniza documents illustrate vividly that the poor (and the invalid and the old, who also usually were poor) were not released from this annual obligation, either in the Fatimid or in the Ayyubid period.[3] Even the young were liable. The poll tax was felt all the more directly and harshly because in Egypt, at least, Jews paid as individuals and the tax collector and his agents hounded delinquents.

In general, however, the poll tax was the only discriminatory obligation imposed on the non-Muslims that was rigorously enforced, even when most

[1] See Cohen, *Poverty and Charity*, chapter 4.

[2] Mollat, *The Poor in the Middle Ages*, 6.

[3] *Med. Soc.*, 2:381, and in a thorough article on the subject, Eli Alshech, "Islamic Law, Practice, and Legal Doctrine: Exempting the Poor from the Jizya under the Ayyubids (1171–1250)," *Islamic Law and Society* 10 (2003), 1–28.

others, especially in the Fatimid-Ayyubid period, were not. Moreover, Jews (as well as Christians) knew that payment of the tax was the key to the protective guarantees of the *dhimma* system. So it was stated—echoing an opinion in Islamic law—in a tenth-century anecdote about Jewish life in Baghdad, that "the poll tax is in defense of a person's life, and by force of it the Jew observes his religion, his Sabbath, festivals, and Day of Atonement, and all else he chooses to do in his religion, and no one disturbs him." This statement is also echoed in a Geniza letter from the first half of the fourteenth century.[4] What follows from this, of course, is that the poor lived in apprehension and fear of the consequences when they could not afford to pay or when individuals or the community were slow to take up the slack.

## 35. "Bring contentment to my soul"

The writer of this letter, Joseph, a scholar without great assets, is in dire straits because of debts and dependents and sureties on his behalf. He requests a donation. The gifts will be like the first fruits brought to the holy Temple in Jerusalem, an allusion (which we have seen before) to the notion in rabbinic Judaism that charity took the place of sacrifices to God after the destruction of the Second Temple. Praying for his would-be benefactor, "May you never be ashamed in your life," he expresses the common motif of the Jewish "shamefaced poor." He adds a Messianic hope from the book of Isaiah that God will "fulfill through you the verse referring to the 'Seven weeks,' 'I will bring them to My sacred mount and let them rejoice in My house of prayer.'"

TS 8 J 18.25 (Hebrew)

(Begins in midsentence) gave a hand to find relief from the hardship that found us. Now, therefore, my masters, bring contentment to my soul, assign me [ . . . ] the Creator to find favor in your eyes to call upon the people to help us and bestow aid upon us like one of the needy. For we are in dire straits on account of debts we have, child care, and sureties on our behalf. I, Joseph, come to bow down and entreat my masters: If you do kindness to people from all places, do so,

[4] Tenth-century anecdote: Cohen, *Under Crescent and Cross*, 71; Fourteenth-century letter: ENA NS 21.12, lines 1–4, trans. Goitein, *Tarbiz* 54 (1984–85), 89–90. Goitein notes that the same letter quotes Isaiah (60:17), *ve-nogsayikh ṣedaqa*, which is understood as "those who oppress you [by taxing you] treat you charitably [by not harming you]." Opinion found in Islamic law: "God ordained to impose one dīnār on every adult and did not draw a distinction [between people]. Since the jizya is paid so the payer's life is spared (*li-ḥaqn al-dam*—the same language used in the tenth-century Jewish anecdote), and in return for living in Dār a-Islām, the rich and poor are equal with regard to sparing life and the interest to live [in Dār al-Islām]." Quoted in Eli Alschech, "Islamic Law, Practice, and Legal Doctrine," 24n75.

too, to your slave. I know that you are aware of the difficulty scholars encounter finding food and supporting themselves. So, I come to remind your honors, and may you be considered as those who bring first fruits. May the Rock of Israel be your succor and save you from all trouble and distress and grant you favor in the eyes of all who see [you], and may you never experience shame or disgrace in your lifetime. May there be fulfilled through you the verse referring to the "Seven weeks," "I will bring them to My sacred mount and let them rejoice in My house of prayer," etc. (Isaiah 56:7), with all Israel included in all the blessings. A(men), a(men), a(men), s(ela).

## 36. "Your slave knows that he has nothing and that he is poor"

Writing to a nagid (head of the Jews), our author explains that he is owed sixty dirhems by Abu'l-ʿIzz b. ʿImrān, a poor person (*faqīr*). He proposes, as a charitable act, to let him work off his obligation. A copyist had been copying quires of the Torah for the letter-writer, but had left for Palestine. Knowing that Abu'l-ʿIzz has a good handwriting, the writer now wants to have him discharge his debt by taking over the project. He asks the nagid to order him to do so, at a rate of at least two quires per week. The offer conforms with the midrashic recommendation, codified by Maimonides, that the highest form of charity is to give the poor a loan or gift or remunerable work (Hilkhot mattenot ʿaniyyim 10:7). It illustrates, therefore—as do Geniza documents elsewhere—a correlation between the ideal realm of normative law and the concrete realm of practice.[5]

TS 6 J 1.8 (Judaeo-Arabic)

The slave kisses the ground, paying obedience to God the ex(alted), before the seat of our lord the *nagid, may your glory be exal[t]ed and your honor be increased, and may (God) grant your sons long life, bless them, protect them, and see that they acquire great prestige. Amen.* I inform you that the elder Abu'l-ʿIzz b. ʿImrān, *(may his) R(ock) p(rotect him)*, owes me money. Your slave knows that he has nothing and that he is poor. The truth is that your slave was having quires of the *Torah* copied for him, but the person who was copying them left for Palestine (Shām). Your slave heard that the most illustrious elder Abu'l-ʿIzz, (*may his) R(ock) p(rotect him*), has a good manuscript hand, so your slave asks our lord, *may your glory be exalted,* to order him to [c]opy at least two quires per week (he doesn't stipulate how many weeks), that is, if he confirms that he owes me. If he can only give a little, I shall drop the claim, though I shall not drop my hope for the mercy of God the ex(alted). It amounts to about sixty dirhems. Let him copy for me until he discharges what he owes. When he discharges it, I will forgive the advanced

[5] See elsewhere in this anthology, and passim in Cohen, *Poverty and Charity*.

payment for his copying before he copied anything.[6] This favor I ask from God the ex(alted) and from our lord, *may your glory be exalted.* May Go[d] bring redemption during the lifetime of our lord. Everything in our lives comes from God and from our lord. May God ma[k]e you ever the refuge for those seeking [r]efuge [ . . . ] in His mercy and make you [ . . . ] in His presence with all. *And peace.*

## 37. "Help would free me from complaining"

Adhering to the literary form of the Arabic petition, this letter asks a nagid for assistance. The petitioner, Yaʿqūb b. Abuʾl-Yumn, is poor and explains why he has been unable to earn money. It is holiday time—a popular occasion for asking for charity, as already noted—and he wants to be able to celebrate properly. He cannot leave his house, however, on account of the poll tax. His letter is almost a carbon copy of scores of pauper letters from early industrial England in which illness and unemployment underlie an urgent request for welfare payments.

ENA 2738.37 (Judaeo-Arabic)

Your slave Yaʿqūb
b. Abuʾl-Yumn

*In (your name, O Mercifu)l*

"*Happy is he who is thoughtful of the wretched; in bad times may the Lord keep him (from harm)*" (Psalm 41:2).
God the ex(alted) knows the state the slave of *your excellency the nagid, may your rule be established forever*, is in. I inform your highness about my situation, my poverty and indigence, my desolation and illness. I ask you kindly, may God perpetuate your strength, to help me during this noble *holiday* with something with which I may celebrate. Your slave, were he no[t] confined to the house, unable to go out on account of the poll tax,[7] and had he not been sick for eight months, would have been able to earn a living. Help would free me from complaining. You are suited to do this. *May the holy one, blessed be He, double your reward and be your succor and grant you a (good) e[nd] and hope. And may your excellency's welfare increase and not diminish. And so may it be His will.*

[6] A difficult phrase. The writer seems to be saying that he had earlier advanced Abuʾl-ʿIzz some money for the job he was proposing and now, as a further charitable act, will reduce the debt by that amount.

[7] Either he was under house arrest for nonpayment, or did not want to be caught by the tax collector in the street or the marketplace.

## 38. "I ask you, by God, not to disappoint the request of your slave from you"

The writer of this letter, a foreigner from Jerba (the island off the coast of Tunisia), claims that he has been unjustly placed under house detention by the Muslim authorities. House arrest was imposed for unpaid debts in general, not just for the poll tax. Unable to acquit himself of his entire obligation, he had been paying interest for nine months as well as the fee for house arrest (payment for the guardsman, called *tarsīm*), the normal procedure in such cases, a form of "debtor's prison." He solicits assistance from a notable, a Jewish courtier with connections to the Muslim government. Like so many other suppliants in this society and their English pauper counterparts in the age of the Industrial Revolution, he cites burden of family among his woes. There are several spelling errors in the text, e.g. *tarsīm* and *muslim* spelled with a *sin* rather than a *samekh.*

Verso has some Arabic writing, seemingly unrelated.

TS 10 J 6.17 (Judaeo-Arabic)

[ . . . *h]onor, gre(atness and) hol(iness), our mas(ter) and tea(cher) the great Dignitary*[8] *[ . . . ] his welfare,*[9] *[ . . . ho]nored and precious, and whose reputation is wise, above and not below, the wise and discerning, who does many [good deeds] and much beneficence to all wayfarers, with the poor, and also with scholars;*[10] *who stands ready to help the people of the Lord with all his ability and might; may [G]o[d] be your succor and grant you favor, kindness and mercy in the eyes of* God *and man.*[11]

Your slave informs your excellency about his terrible situation of dearth and family burden, of which God the exalted is aware—*may* God *from His holy habitation strengthen you and from His throne support you, make your ways succeed and bless all you do, make you "a head rather than a tail" [and remove] your enemies from before you.* Your slave is from Jerba. *He (God) knows the mysteries* of the adversity that your slave has experienced, the house arrest[12] by the Muslim religious authorities,[13] which is unjust and not inconsiderable. For nine months your slave has been paying interest of three dirhems per month on two dinars, as well as monthly dues for house arrest. Your slave appeals to your gate only out of deep

[8] See chapter 1, note 49.

[9] This word, Hebrew *shelomo*, is written above the line and I am not certain where it was meant to be inserted.

[10] Our suppliant seems to be claiming all three reasons for being counted by his would-be benefactor among the deserving poor.

[11] The standard wish for those who depend upon the favor of rulers, based on Proverbs 3:4.

[12] Arabic: *tarsīm*, literally "the fees paid to the guardsman who was stationed outside the house."

[13] Arabic: *al-sharīʿa min muslim.*

faith in my heart *in heaven's mercy* and your noble nature. I ask you, by God, not to disappoint the request of your slave from you. *And may your welfare increase and not d[iminish]. Amen sela.*

## 39. "I am hiding out in the house like the women"

A man in debt and unable to meet his commitments petitions for help collecting charity promised by the nagid but not received, namely, the pledges (usually made in the synagogue) for a particular week. He has been hiding out from a creditor, confined to the house ("like the women"), and has therefore not been able to earn anything through work. The refrain about suffering children (here described as "dying" from hunger) represents a common motif to gain sympathy, a rhetorical strategy of the poor that we have seen before, but it is credible. It is a cross-cultural motif, echoed also in the letters of English paupers, who also suffered from seeing their children go hungry.

The pledges meant to be earmarked for the petitioner had been transferred to a cantor. This could have been for charity or, what's more likely, for the cantor's salary. What we seem to have here is a case of transferring monies collected for one charity to another communal purpose. The Talmud, quoting a tannatic source not found in the Mishna (a *baraita*), permits the transfer of funds from the *quppa* to the *tamḥui* and vice versa and changing their use "for whatever they wish."[14] The two terms, *quppa* and *tamḥui*, refer in the Talmud, respectively, to alms (mainly food) for the local poor and alms for "the poor of the whole world," particularly foreign Jews. The Hebrew words, however, do not appear in the hundreds of Geniza documents for Fustat, leading to the conclusion that the two institutions were unified there into one fund serving all the poor, both local and newcomers. (See discussion of this in Cohen, *Poverty and Charity*, chapter 8.) Monies could also be used for salaries of communal officials (a cantor, for instance). Indeed, many accounts of charitable donations and expenditures include both disbursements for direct charity (purchase of bread for the communal dole, for instance) and salaries for communal servants (cantors, beadles, etc.) The term embracing both direct charity and communal needs was *mezonot*. See nos. 70, 72, and 73 below.

Maimonides' codification of the law on changing the use of charity funds (Mishneh Torah, Hilkhot mattenot ʿaniyyim 9:7) seems to reflect this broadened application. His language is slightly altered from the talmudic law by the addition of two significant words at the end, to read "for any need of the community (*mi-ṣorkhei ṣibbur*) they wish." Maimonides' Spanish predecessor Rabbi Joseph ibn Megas (d. 1141), whose teachings he greatly admired, argued vociferously against using quppa or tamḥui receipts for anything other than the

[14] Bava Batra 8b.

needs of the poor.[15] I believe that Maimonides' language, a clear departure from the language of the Talmud and from the ruling of his respected forerunner, reflects the practice of his own time and place, on which he put his imprimatur. The sixteenth-century commentator on Maimonides, RaDBaZ (Rabbi David Ibn Abi Zimra, chief rabbi of Cairo in the first half of the sixteenth century) noted the departure and added, "this is the custom."[16] This seems, therefore, to be an instance—one of several in the Mishneh Torah—where Maimonides' formulation of a law bears the imprint of everyday life as reflected in the Geniza documents.[17] Obviously, the disgruntled writer of our letter didn't approve of the custom.

TS 8 J 17.27[18] (Judaeo-Arabic)

"*While you shall be (called) Priests of the Lord," etc.* (Isaiah 61:6) [ . . . Your slave . . . ][19] kisses the ground before *(our) m(aster) and t(eacher) Joseph ha-Kohen the beloved Dignitary, Crown of the Priests, Diadem of the Dignitaries*, and informs you that I am [going through] adversity that none but the Creator of all existence knows. I am hiding out in the house like the women.[20] I cannot go out except [in the] evening. I am fleeing from a debt that I owe. I am unable to do any gainful work unless I go out. My little ones are dying of hunger because I have been hiding out. Our lord the Head promised me the pledges of a week (jumʿa). When the week I was to have claimed the pledge that he promised arrived, I was told that it had gone to the elder Bū Saʿd the *cantor, (may his) R(ock) p(rotect him)*. I therefore ask my master please to intercede on my behalf so that I am paid that w(eek's pledges), for I have heard that nothing is accomplished without the decision of my master, may God grant you success. I am all the more dependent upon you.[21] *And peace.*

## 40. "They threw him into prison"

House arrest was preferable to outright imprisonment in a Muslim jail. This legal document, a verification of bankruptcy, was drawn up in 1175 in Minyat Ziftā, a town in the Delta. It was evidently shown to the Jewish authorities in Fustat, where it eventually ended up in the Geniza. Five persons testify to the

[15] *Ḥiddushei Ha-RI Megas le-masekhet Bava Batra*, ed. Moshe Shemuel Shapira, 2nd ed. (Benei Berak, 1979), 7b.

[16] See RaDBaZ, ad loc.

[17] I discuss this example in *Poverty and Charity*, chapter 8, and other examples elsewhere in that book.

[18] Cf. *Med. Soc.*, 2:37, 544n13, and Cohen, "The Voice of the Jewish Poor," 244.

[19] The tarjama, containing the petitioner's name, would have appeared in the upper left-hand corner of the page, but that has been torn away.

[20] Normally, only the men went out in public, to work, to synagogue, and elsewhere, while the women, like their Muslim counterparts, stayed at home.

[21] Arabic: *kayfa mā kuntu kuntu lāẓim lakum*. Alternative translation: "However I am, I adhere to you."

poverty of Sulaymān b. Ḥasan, who was imprisoned for insolvency when his Jewish creditor brought him before a Muslim court. The man did not have money to pay a police guard, who would have held him under house arrest, a preferable fate. The document is in the hand of Shabbetay b. Abraham, the well-known judge and communal leader of Minyat Ziftā for over forty years, who succeeded his father, Abraham b. Shabbetay.

CUL Add. 3423[22] (Judaeo-Arabic)

We the undersigned witnesses on this wr[it] state that we know the situation of Sulaymān b. Ḥasan, and that he is poor, with few possessions. We do not know if he possesses any real estate or cash. He owes Baqā ha-Levi b. Ṣāliḥ three and a half dinars, which the latter has claimed from him in *a Muslim court*. He is not able to pay the fee[23] for the police guard.[24] So they threw him into prison. He has asked us, *the undersigned*, to report what we know about his situation. This was on the same Monday the eighteenth of *Sivan* 1486 (June 9, 1175) in the city of Minyat Ziftā, so that it be *a conveyance of right and a proof*. She'erith ha-Kohen b. Yakhin ha-Kohen *(who) r(ests in) E(den)*

Ṣedaqa b. Hillel ha-Kohen *(who) r(ests in) E(den)* — Berakhot b. Yakhin *(who) r(ests in) E(den)*

Josiah b. David *(who) r(ests in) E(den)* — Nadiv b. David *(who) r(ests in) E(den)*

## 41. "Your servant is in a desperate situation in all his affairs"

A letter and a responsum, on either side of the same sheet of paper, tell the story of a man in distress, especially because of debt. Some parts of the letter are confusing because it is difficult to determine the antecedents of the pronouns, which are invariably in the third person. I have tried to clear things up by using the second person where I think the reference is to the addressee of the letter and first person when the referent is the writer. The letter likely concerns an earlier stage of the case, discussed in yet another responsum edited in the publication.

TS 13 J 9.11[25] (Judaeo-Arabic)

Recto:
Your s[la]ve kisses t[h]e ground [*be*]*fore the excellent [seat of our lord], may it be uplifted and increase and may you live forever*, and informs you that I had presented

[22] Cf. *Med. Soc.*, 1:204, 2:48, 4:461n196.
[23] Arabic: *juʿl*.
[24] Arabic: *raqqāṣ*.
[25] Ed. and trans. M. Friedman, in *Genizah Research after Ninety Years: The Case of Judaeo-Arabic*, eds. Joshua Blau and Stefan C. Reif (Cambridge, 1992), 88–90. I have consulted Friedman's translation.

*before your excellent seat, may it be uplifted,* a petition containing a partial explanation of my situation. One of the students of our lord came forth (from the capital, apparently) and told your servant (i.e., the writer) on behalf of our master that you would not be ready to execute the matter until after the *holiday*. You had earlier generously promised to execute the matter as it was known to you. Your servant is in a desperate situation in all his affairs and I ask you in your munificence not to neglect me but to pay full attention to my weak state (meaning, poverty) and desolation.[26] The knife has reached the bone.[27] My greatest adversity is the matter of this creditor and the fact that he is one of the better people,[28] so that he is justified and I am the one who wrongs him and myself. I do not blame him, for I have fallen in with him *because of my many sins*. The purpose of this (petition) is that when my master meets with the illustrious head,[29] *our master and teacher* R. Abraham *the great Rav, may his glory be exalted and his honor increased,* you, my master, should tell him what you know to be the truth about your servant's situation and ask him to procure 60 dirhems in any way possible and send for the creditor and ask him to divide the sum into installments of 10 dirhems per month. That is what he requested, since he knows (my) situation. He is well aware of my extreme predicament.[30] The *writ* in his hand divides it into 20 dirhems per month. Let it be promised to him that the 60 dirhems be paid in six monthly installments. If that is done, it will be help from God *by the merit of our lord*. The matter is easy. The matter can be paid off by the end of *Passover*, God willing, with the help of our lord and *by the merit* of his father, *(may) the m(emory of) the r(ighteous be) b(lessed)*.[31] Your servant has informed you of this after having kissed your feet. *May the welfare of his excellency our holy lord, increase forever and never diminish. Forever, sela amen.*

Verso (the responsum):[32]

Concerning Reuben against whom there is a bi[ll of debt . . . ,] and he lacks the means to pay and does not have that with which to support himself or his family, to the extent that, were he able, he would swear to his fellow litigant with *a solemn oath* that he has nothing and is without means. And some of the food and furnishings are not designated for him but for others. And his opposing party is oppressing him and summons him *to a gentile (i.e., Muslim) court*.[33] If he admits

[26] Arabic: *li-qiṭʿatihi*, literally, being "cut off," in this case, from assistance or from employment.

[27] Arabic: *qad waṣalat al-sakīn al-ʿaẓm*, a very common expression for despair in the Geniza letters.

[28] Arabic: *min aṭrāf al-nās*; translation follows Friedman (see above, note 25), 89n28.

[29] Meaning head of the Jews.

[30] Friedman (see above, note 25), 88n23, suggests reading the phrase squeezed in above the line: *mā anā fīhi min al-ʿasra.*

[31] Referring to Moses Maimonides.

[32] Friedman's translation.

[33] A common strategy when one litigant thought he could get a better deal from the Muslim court, or use its enforcement powers against the other person.

it, he (the creditor) may become violent and have him arrested. And he does not heed the ruling of *Jewish* law.[34] If he denies it, the qāḍī may require of him *an oath*, and he is afraid of the (heavenly) *punishment*. *May you instruct us*: if the violating opposing party transgresses and summons him *to a gentile court*, is he allowed to swear that he does not owe him anything in this case and be virtuous or not?[35] And, being well aware of the situation of the debtor and knowing the truth of his destitution, may the judge send after the violent opposing party and tell him, "if you summon him *to a gentile court*, you will no longer have any claim on him and you will be obligated such and such by *Jewish* law"? *May our lord instruct us and may he be granted a double reward by heaven.*

## 42. "To be paid for the poll tax of the *cantor*"

Two "elders" are requested to convey one dinar to al-Makīn Abuʾl-ʿIzz al-Levi, which they had pledged for the first installment of the poll tax of a cantor. Though respectable members of the Jewish "clergy," cantors, like many other communal "servants," received relatively low salaries and so their names often appear on alms lists as recipients of funds collected for public charity.

Mosseri L 129.1 (II 127.1)[36] (Judaeo-Arabic)

The shaykh Mukarram and the shaykh Abū Manṣūr, *(may their) R(ock) p(rotect them)*, shall kindly deliver to the most illustrious shaykh al-Makīn Abuʾl-ʿIzz the Levite *(may his) R(ock) p(rotect him)* a gold dinar, which they pledged[37] during a collection for the first installment of the poll tax, to be paid for the poll tax of the *cantor*. *And peace.*

[34] Arabic: *li-ḥukmi sharīʿat yisrael*, using the Islamic term for religious law, as common among the Jews of the Arab world.
[35] According to the halakha, a Jew was permitted to lie under oath to gentile authorities in order to save himself or other Jews from dire consequences. Babylonian Talmud Bava Qama 113a; Maimonides, Mishneh Torah, Hilkhot shevuʿot 3:1.
[36] *Med. Soc.*, 5:511n80.
[37] Arabic: *asmawhu*, literally, "put the names down."

# Chapter Six

## WOMEN AND POVERTY

TO WHAT EXTENT did Jewish women in medieval Egypt, by virtue of their gender, become victims of poverty, and what strategies did they employ to deal with their plight? The Geniza provides ample opportunity to investigate these questions, particularly because through the letters preserved in this treasure trove we are able to hear the voices of women themselves. These kinds of data are almost entirely absent from Islamic historical sources, where we hear—if we hear at all—about upper-class Muslim women, but virtually nothing about women from the underclass of society. The Geniza, of course, gives us only a partial picture of women and poverty. The needy women who appear in the Geniza records are mainly those who were not able to find succor in the bosom of their families. Those who did, did not leave a documentary trail.

The poor women who appear in the Geniza letters fall into predictable categories. There are the widows, the classic group of female poor in most societies, well known from the Bible and from early Christian literature. They show up in abundance, too, often with children in tow, in pauper letters from early industrial England.[1]

In their susceptibility to indigence, divorcées were not much better off than widows. Both had claim to the "delayed" marriage payment promised by their husband in the marriage contract as well as to the principal amount of the dowry they had brought with them into the marriage and recorded in the contract. But then, as now in modern society, women could not always easily collect, or collect everything. Even when the money was there, widows and divorcées, alike, had to hope that their husbands or their husbands' heirs would pay up. Jewish law did not automatically award widows any additional part of their husbands' financial estate. They were, however, eligible under certain conditions for maintenance for themselves as well as for their children after their husbands' death (not divorcées, who could only collect maintenance for their children). Sometimes they took possession of other property of their husbands if their husbands had specifically stipulated this in their wills or made a gift to their wives prior to their death (often with the condition they

[1] Sokoll, *Essex Pauper Letters*, Index, s.v. widows.

not remarry).[2] Depending upon the amount of their husbands' contractual obligations and their own success collecting, widows and divorcées might suffer greatly from the loss of their marriage.

Wives of absentee husbands also appear among the needy. Some husbands were absent for business reasons, others had deserted their wives and children. The women's letters often disclose stories of pitiful deprivation; we have seen some of this already in previous chapters. The alms lists below (chapter 8) also show a huge representation of their gender in receipt of public charity.

## 43. "I and my children never, ever uncover our faces"

In this appeal, typically addressed to the community ("your excellencies, my masters, the illustrious lordly judges, and . . . the elders of Israel"), a widow and mother of four, weighed down by debt, asks for "something to conceal myself (*astur bihi nafsī*) and the fo[ur] who are with me." She thus voices the common plaint of the mastūr(a), the "concealed," who strives to maintain him- or herself economically without having to "uncover his/her face," especially by resorting to the public dole. Turning to an individual for private charity, or to the community through its leaders for ad hoc assistance (as here), helped minimize the shame that these people, ranging from the working poor to the well-off, felt when poverty temporarily struck.

Mostly, the women called or calling themselves "wife" were actually widows.[3] In this case, however, the word "widow" itself is squeezed in above the line in the heading next to the word "wife," suggesting that the word "wife" alone was felt to be insufficient to alert the addressees as to how destitute she was (even with her mentioning her orphans). Widows were in a more needy category than married woman. She plays hard on the sympathies of her would-be benefactors when she writes that without their (quick) help, she and her little ones will die.

The letter is written in the same hand as that of the man who wrote the next one (no. 44), which is also couched in the first person. Together, they nicely illustrate the point that letters from women were normally "scribed" by a man but preserved the woman's voice, often in the first person.[4] The juxtaposition of two letters of women penned by one and the same copyist affords an opportunity to address the general issue raised in the Introduction about writers and those who had letters written for them. What repeats itself is the form—the form of the Arabic petition. Only the scribe would have been familiar with this aspect of the narrative from experience writing other letters of appeal or mis-

[2] *Med. Soc.*, 3:251.

[3] See Cohen, *Poverty and Charity*, chapter 5.

[4] On the blurred boundary between writing one's own letter and having one's own letter written by someone else, see above, p. 8 and the Introduction to my *Poverty and Charity*.

sives asking for redress of a grievance. But even here there is variety, also presumably the work of the scribe, since the actual "writers," two women, probably did not know the different and proper ways of addressing a correspondent in Arabic etiquette (though this possibility cannot be excluded).

The repeating features in these two letters are formulaic, or rather, rhetorical. One is the motif of being "naked and starving." A second is the offer of prayers on behalf of the benefactors. Praying for the living was common, though prayer for the soul of the benefactor after his death, as in the "pro anima" prayers of the poor for their deceased benefactors in Christianity, is not found in the Middle Eastern Jewish context. It crops up occasionally in Christian Europe, however, in Jewish communities in medieval Spain.[5] Thirdly, we find the reminder that charity is rewarded by God. The factual matter, however, varies greatly, and that is the contribution of the respective widows, in their own voice—despite their illiteracy. Our scribe did not standardize (hence fictionalize) the facts. He heard the women's stories and incorporated them faithfully into the texts, in the first person, as if they were being written by them. The pair of letters illustrates, therefore, the general reliability of the historical data in these letters. Moreover, the style—the work of the scribe—in and of itself forms a historical datum of significance, for it reflects social expectations and the mentality of both takers and givers in the calculus of poverty and charity.

The biblical quotation from Isaiah, found elsewhere, too, in the letters of the poor (see no. 45), alludes to a midrashic metaphor comparing "sowing" to giving charity.[6]

TS 13 J 18.10[7] (Judaeo-Arabic)

Your slave woman, the wife // widow //,[8]
destitute and debt-ridden[9]
with four orphans

*In the name of "Him who looks after the poor and broken-spirited"* (Isaiah 66:2).
I have made God the ex(alted) my intercessor with your excellencies,[10] my masters, the illustrious lordly judges, and with *the elders of Israel,*[11] *may their Rock [bless*

[5] See Judah Galinsky, "'I am Donating to Heaven for the Benefit of my Soul': Jewish Charitable Bequests and the *Hekdesh* Trust in Thirteenth-Century Spain," *The Journal of Interdisciplinary History* 35:3 (Winter, 2005), 423–40.

[6] The midrashic interpretation says *ein zeriʿa ella ṣedaqa,* "sowing means giving charity," e.g., Bava Qama 17a, Avoda Zara 5b. Cf. also Cohen, "The Voice of the Jewish Poor," 250.

[7] *Med. Soc.,* 3:305.

[8] The word *armala* is written above the line. See commentary above.

[9] Arabic: *miskīna madyūna.*

[10] An unusual twist on the usual theme of asking for human intercession with God or another person.

[11] The elders form an additional category of communal notables, who often assisted the judges or other religious or administrative officials in carrying out communal business. See *Med. Soc.,* 2:58–60.

*them] with the best of blessings*, so that [you kindly bestow] upon me something to conceal myself and the fo[ur] who are with me, and with which I can satisfy my hunger and theirs. We are five souls, desolate,[12] naked, and starving, having no one to turn to except God the ex(alted) and my masters the illustrious elders, "*who sow by all waters*" (Isaiah 32:20), who act with kindness toward all. I and my children never, ever uncover our faces, not to a group of people or to individuals.[13] However, necessity has now forced us to do this. May you look upon us with a merciful eye and obtain reward because of us. May you not neglect us. After this petition[14] the only thing left is life through your kindness or death as a result of your neglect, far be it from you. May God the ex(alted) accept from us our pious prayers for you. *May your welfare increase for ever.*

## 44. "Appoint someone to take up a collection for me"

In this petition, scribed by the same man as the previous one, a different woman appeals to a different addressee, the nagid, to arrange a collection so she may buy a new veil for the upcoming holidays. She implores him: "To whom shall I apply if not to you, and to whom shall I turn?" This kind of direct appeal to the head of the Jews by a seemingly insignificant person was entirely characteristic of that society. We also have petitions in the Geniza, or better, drafts of petitions, written in Arabic characters and addressed by "average" Jews to a vizier or a sultan, seeking assistance.[15] The phrase at the end of this document, "to you belongs the lofty decision," is a conventional feature of Arabic petitions that is found in some but not all Judaeo-Arabic examples. This same scribe left it out of the previous letter.

There is some other writing at the top of the letter and on the verso, both in Hebrew and in Arabic characters. The letter was either reused or never sent (a draft?).

TS 13 J 18.3[16] (Judaeo-Arabic)

Your slave woman who is alone[17]
desolate, and destitute
the daughter of Rāfiʿ the silk worker
(or: silk merchant)

[12] Arabic: *munqaṭiʿīn*, lit., "cut off" from family help or from employment.

[13] Arabic: *mimman lam nakshuf yawman qaṭṭu wujūhanā li-jamāʿa wa-lā li-furād.*

[14] Arabic: *ruqʿa.*

[15] Khan, *Arabic Legal and Administrative Documents*, 354–58 (no. 85), a petition to a vizier from a poor man concerning a debt; 369–71 (no. 89), a petition to the Ayyubid sultan al-ʿĀdil (probably al-ʿĀdil I, 1200–18) from a poor man requesting a reduction of his poll-tax rate.

[16] Cf. *Med. Soc.*, 2:36–37; Cohen, "The Voice of the Jewish Poor," 251. This is in the same handwriting as the previous letter (TS 13 J 18.10).

[17] Arabic: *al-waḥīda.*

*In (your) name, O Mer(ciful)*

I am writing this petition[18] with my blood and tears, seeking aid from God // be pra(ised) // and your excellency my master, the most illustrious head, the great Nagid, the noble lord, may God perpetuate your leadership over *Israel*,[19] make constant (Divine) favor and your happiness, protect you and take care of you, and destroy your enemies and those who envy you.[20] I am distressed, impoverished, alone, enduring va[riou]s kinds of suffering and especially "nakedness."[21] I have no outergarment to conceal me,[22] nor anything to cover my head. I sent you a petition before this one about the same thing, but you did not favor me with anything. You know, may God perpetuate your greatness, that I and people like me have nothing but the mercy of God the ex(alted) and your mercy. To whom shall I apply if not to you and to whom shall I turn. I ask you (margin:) not to turn me away disappointed by your lack of favor. If you will be so kind, appoint someone to take up a collection for me so that I can buy a veil[23] to cove[r] my head during the upcoming holiday, may God bless you and allow you to celebrate it for many years to come. Accept from me my pious prayers and earn abundant recompense. To you belongs the lofty decision. And peace and praise be to illustrious God.[24]

## 45. "My husband . . . left me a 'widow during (his) lifetime.'"

A docket on the margin of this letter, recorded by officials upon receipt, says it all: "The wife of Maʿānī who fled." The poor woman, whose husband had fled to Alexandria, leaving her "a widow during his lifetime," applies to the "courts" (meaning, the judges) and the community. The colorful expression, in Arabic *armalat al-ḥayāt*, is found in Hebrew in the Bible (*almenut ḥayyut*, 2 Samuel 20:3). It stands in, here and in other letters, for the normal rabbinic expression, *ʿaguna*, literally, "anchored," that is, to the missing husband because his death cannot be attested—like the English "grass widow." Our distressed lady is almost blind and has to care for a three-year-old daughter. Times were hard, she says, for the rich as well as for the poor. This must have been a

[18] Arabic: *ruqʿa*.

[19] Meaning the Jewish community.

[20] Typical language in letters to the head of the Jews or to a Jew holding a position in Muslim government (some heads were also active at court), who sometimes experienced enmity or opposition, either from other Jews or as part of Muslim court intrigue. Some examples of this, particularly of internal Jewish political conflict, can be found in Cohen, *Jewish Self-Government*.

[21] Meaning lack of adequate clothing. See Cohen, *Poverty and Charity*, chapter 6.

[22] Arabic: *yasturunī*. Here meant in the physical sense, but also loaded with the metaphorical overtone of mastūr, "concealed from the embarrassment of poverty."

[23] Arabic: *miqnaʿa*.

[24] The words "praise be to illustrious God" are written in Arabic characters.

time of crisis in Egypt accompanied by general dearth. As we have seen before, she (or, more probably, the man who scribed her letter) quotes Isaiah 32:20, in which the word "sow" is interpreted midrashically to mean giving charity. Here, too, appears the popular verse in the epigraph, "Happy is he who is thoughtful of the wretched; in bad times may (the Lord) keep him from harm" (Psalm 41:2). She asks for something "that I can 'cover myself' with," by which she means, conceal her indigence by restoring her economic self-sufficiency, the ubiquitous sentiment of the mastūr and the mastūra.

TS 13 J 18.18[25] (Judaeo-Arabic)

"*Happy shall you be who sow by [a]ll waters, Who let loose the feet of (cattle) and (asses)*" (Isaiah 32:20).[26]
"*Happy are those who act justly, who do right*[27] *at all times*" (Psalm 106:3).
"*Happy is he who is thoughtful of the wretched; in bad times may (the Lord) keep him from harm*" (Psalm 41:2).
"*May the Lord guard him and preserve him; and may he be thought happy in the land. Do not s(ubject him) t(o the will of his) e(nemies)*" (Psalm 41:3).

My masters the "*courts,*" *(may their) R(ock) p(rotect them)*, and the community, *may they be blessed*, are aware of the current situation and how difficult it has been for those with means, all the more so the weak and poor. I am a woman with poor sight. I cannot [dis]tinguish night from day and cannot find my way since my husband le[ft me and f]led to Alexandria and left me a "widow during (his) lifetime." In my charge is an infant girl three years old. We are starving, naked, *and lacking strength*. Were it not for God the exalted and the elder Abū ʿAlī, *(may his) R(ock) p(rotect him)*, who remembers us occasionally, we would not be in any shape. I call out concernng my situation to God and the community, *may they b[e] blessed*, to look into my situation before I die of starvation and hopefully put together something that I can "cover myself" [with, *and] may your reward from heaven be doubled. May [your] welfare [increase for ev]er.*

Margin (docket): The wife of Maʿānī who has fled.

[25] *Med. Soc.*, 2:314.
[26] See above note 4.
[27] The Hebrew is *ṣedaqa*, which in the Bible usually denotes "righteousness" and, according to most scholars, took on the meaning of "charity" only later, in rabbinic Hebrew. Moshe Weinfeld believes *ṣedaqa* has the sense of "charity," that is, "social justice" for the needy, in many parts of the Bible, beyond the one verse in Aramaic in the late Book of Daniel (4:24) recognized by other scholars. See Weinfeld, *Social Justice in Ancient Israel and in the Ancient Near East* (Jerusalem and Minneapolis, 1995).

## 46. "The house in which I and the orphan girl were sheltered fell down"

A widow in distress, with one orphaned daughter, petitions a high-ranking notable in the community for assistance. Her house had collapsed. Officials in the community had a halakhic responsibility to care for orphans, many of whom lived with their widowed mothers.[28] Knowing that, this woman employs here a common strategy of appealing especially for her fatherless daughter. The widow was herself an orphan, as we learn from the heading, hence deserving of special attention on those grounds (she was probably a young mother). Through a slip-up, she is called "the orphan girl, *son* of (*bn* = *ben* instead of *bnt*) al-ʿĀbid." We would have known more about her plight had the letter not been torn off. Little must have been lost, though, as most such appeals are anyway short.

TS 8 J 18.19 (Judaeo-Arabic)

Your slave who prays for you
The orphan girl, son [*sic*] of al-ʿĀbid, *(who) r(ests in) E(den)*

*In your name, O Lord*

I inform my master the most illustrious head,[29] may God make permanent His support (for you), that the house in which I and the orphan girl were sheltered fell down and we were left bewildered, not knowing what to do. You, may God make your high place permanent, look after the condition of orphans. You know that I am a desolate woman about to die. You earn my prayers and those of the orphan girl day and night, because she does not have [ . . . ].

## 47. "Your slave has been banished, she and her son, from her house for three months"

The next two documents tell a fascinating story of hardship and poverty. They are a pair of petitions from the widow of the cantor Ben Naḥman, describing her plight to "your excellency the Gaon," whom I take to be the gaon and head of the Jews, Maṣliaḥ ha-Kohen b. Solomon (in office 1127–39). Her poverty resulted, in part, from being ill treated by the family of her late husband, so her petition is in the nature of a request for a redress of grievance.

[28] On the lot of orphans see. *Med. Soc.*, 3:302ff, and Cohen, *Poverty and Charity*, chapter 5.

[29] Arabic: *rayyis*. Not the head of the Jews, who would have been addressed as "our lord" (*sayyidunā*), not "my master" (*mawlāya*).

Goitein summarized the first letter in the context of the family,[30] but not the second, which was drafted by the same scribe two months after the first petition and which furnishes additional details about her case, further fleshing out the circumstances surrounding her predicament.

Her predicament resembles that of many wives in the Geniza documents. Married at a young age, the couple typically moved to the husband's parents' home. Especially if the groom was young, he would live with his bride among his own extended family in the clan house or compound. Thus, the young woman entered strange surroundings, dominated by the senior women in the residence, including her husband's mother, older sisters and sisters-in-law, and other blood relatives. Under the best circumstances, the young girl received loving treatment from her new family. For the wife of a traveling husband, this compensated for leaving the bosom of her own family. But complaints about difficult relations between a wife and her in-laws are common.[31] Often, the only recourse the woman had was her own brothers, especially if her father was old or sick, or even dead, not unusual given the ubiquity of illness in that society and short life expectancy. Brothers, therefore, assumed some responsibility for protecting their sisters, even married sisters, when they could.[32]

Our young wife had lost her husband and had one child, an orphan by Jewish law. She, herself, was ineligible to inherit her husband's estate—only to receive her dowry back, insofar as it was still intact, as well as the "late" installment of the money promised by her husband in the marriage contract in the event of divorce or his death. The latter was considered a debt against his estate and against the claims of any creditors. Sometimes, to protect their wives from painful litigation, husbands would appoint them executrix over their estates, or make provision before they died for their wives to continue living in their house after they were gone.

Our widow claimed just this—that her husband had gifted her a share of his part of the family compound before his death. That was the beginning of the problem, which reached severe proportions, including physical violence, desolateness, and poverty. We have, of course, only her story. While reading the two versions of her petition, the early one and the later one, we wonder why, two months after the first, she appealed to the head of the Jews again. It seems that the widow submitted the second petition because her brothers had failed to help her, and because she wanted to add details to strengthen her case. New elements in the second petition include: (1) her brothers, to whom she had turned after submitting the first petition, had not been able to come to her assistance, tied up as they were trying to evade the poll-tax collector (they too were not people of means); (2) she had once held the deed to the apartment,

[30] *Med. Soc.*, 3:259.
[31] *Med. Soc.*, 3:173.
[32] Ibid., 20–24.

but it was now in the hands of her mean-spirited and physically abusive stepson; (3) her husband's sister owed her five months' rent, evidently from another apartment her husband had bequeathed to his wife, intending that the rent from that would help her sustain their son with food and other needs, apart from the shelter (unless the rent was for staying in the apartment from which the widow and her son had been evicted five months earlier). Perhaps, too, she had not heard from the gaon and wanted to exhort him to respond. Perhaps after receiving her first petition the gaon had heard from the other parties with counterclaims, making her second petition all the more necessary.

We have, here, then, the facinating story of a woman thrust into indigence by social circumstances typical of that society. The saga is all too realistic to have been invented, even though the actual "scribing" of the petitions was almost certainly done by a man (the same man). For the reasons stated above, this does not vitiate the authenticity of her own voice or distort her personal strategies.

We now let the widow of the cantor Ben Naḥman speak in her own voice—twice—as transcribed by another person, who employed the form of the Arabic petition, appropriate in an appeal to the ruler of the Jewish community.

TS 10 J 16.4[33] (Judaeo-Arabic)

Your slave, the wife (= widow) of
[the] cantor Ben Naḥman

*[I(n the name of the)] M(erciful)*

Your slave informs *your excellency the Gaon, may your r[ul]e be established forever,* [about the situati]on of your slave and her son, their hunger and nakedness. That is because your slave has been banished, she and her son, from her house for three months without being able to enter it. For whenever I enter the house, Bayān, the son of my husband, pounces upon your slave and inflicts pain on me in my most vital organs and vulnerable places, intending thereby to harm me. The last // [t]ime // your slave left the house, had not a Turk happened to be passing by, he would have killed me. I st[r]etched out my hand and had just begun to cry out for help when he happened by. Also, he (her stepson) and his aunt have banded together against me and concocted improper things about me. The reason for your slave's forbearance all this time until today has been the fear lest, God forbid, the bo[y] go astray[34] and it be blamed on me. Otherwise your slave would have s[o]ught the help of God the ex(alted) and of your noble gate.

[33] Ed. Cohen, "Four Judaeo-Arabic Petitions of the Poor," 459–64; cf. *Med. Soc.*, 3:259.

[34] Arabic: *yakhruj al-ṣabī ʿan al-ṭarīqa*, which means "convert to Islam."

[But] now the knif[e] has reached the bone and your slave app[eals] for help to [God] the ex(alted) and your noble gate, to be shown favor [and] have her case considered and have pity shown on her. I have *a right* in that house, *praised be God*. If your slave does not trust in God the ex(alted), I shall go my way.

*May t(he) h(oly one) b(lessed be) H(e) double your reward and be [your] succor.*

## 48. "A long time has passed and I wish that you would kindly look upon me with a merciful eye"

Second of the two petitions from the widow of the cantor Ben Naḥman, written two months after the first (no. 47). Apart from the content (described in the commentary to no. 47), we have here another example (like nos. 43–44) of two letters from the pen of the same scribe, but this time dealing with more or less the same matter. We see even more clearly the relationship between formulaic rhetoric (saying what is required and expected from a formalistic viewpoint) and actual information (the details of the case).

TS 13 J 13.6[35] (Judaeo-Arabic)

Your slave, the wife (= widow)
of the cantor Ben Naḥman

*[I(n the name of the)]* M*(erciful)*

Your slave informs *your excellency the Gaon, may your rule be established foreve[r]*, about her situation and that of her son, their hunger and nakedness. To date, [because of] these people, I have been banished for five months. We are perishing from the su[ffering] we have experienced. I am de[solat]e with no one to speak about [m]y case. A long time has passed and I wish that you would kindly look upon me with a merciful eye. Your slave's brothers are not able to show themselves in public on account of the poll tax.[36] My husband did not pass away[37] and forsake me without having me dwell in the house, sustaining myself and my son with whatever else comes from rental income. However, my husband's children and their aunt threw me out and forcibly took control of the place. The documents regarding the house were in my possession, and when the wall fell into disrepair and they needed to repair it, the deed to the house was taken from me. They have had it until the present. Since they took the documents from me they have been saying: "We owe you nothing. The house is ours, and you have no share in it." Your slave's belongings have been in the apartment

[35] Ed. Cohen, "Four Judaeo-Arabic Petitions of the Poor," 459–64.

[36] That is, they were hiding out from the tax collector.

[37] Arabic: *mā marra rajulī min hunā* (she refers to his death with a euphemism similar to one used in contemporary English-speaking societies: he "passed away").

since the day I left the house. My husband's sister owes your slave five months' rent that I have not collected from her.

It is very proper that you show favor to your slave and her son. *May t(he) h(oly one) b(lessed be) H(e) double your reward and be your succor.* May he grant you noble holidays like these. To you belongs the lofty decision in this matter. *May your welfare and the welfare of your sons increase and not diminish. And so may it be his will.*

## 49. "This is *child support* for her daughter for two full months"

A parnas is instructed to pay a divorcée child-support (mezonot)[38] for her daughter, 60 dirhems for two months, out of money held by a certain merchant. In return, she must henceforth cease saying bad things about her ex-husband, especially since she was going to receive more than what was allowed by Jewish law. The parnas is enjoined to collect the amount each month from a merchant (known from elsewhere) and pay her.

Goitein dates the letter to circa 1115.

ENA 4011.17[39] (Judaeo-Arabic)

*In your name, O Merciful*

My lord the *parnas*, may God support you, shall [r]eceive from the elder Abu'l-Riḍā Solomon b. Mevorakh,[40] may God watch over him forever, 60 waraq

[38] Goitein consistently translates "alimony," which, notwithstanding the similarity between the rabbinic Hebrew *mezonot* (food, sustenance) and Latin *alimonia,* is not always precise. In American law, alimony is the allowance made for the wife (or, today in many states, a spouse of either gender) for support upon divorce or legal separation, and differs from child support. In Jewish law, a husband had no automatic ongoing obligation toward his divorced or widowed wife, only toward his children, although in practice the wife often adminstered the disbursements from his assets or estate, as in the present instance. Occasionally mezonot appears to be distinguished from child care, and could be rendered "alimony." An example seems to be found in Mosseri A 7 [VII 7], a legal document regarding money still owed on a settlement between a husband and his divorcée, which called for "*mezonot* and what is required from him for his child when he dies or during his lifetime" (line 4). The term is used in both ways in one and the same legal document, TS NS J 51, ed. Elinoar Bareket, *Shafrir miṣrayim: ha-hanhaga ha-yehudit be-Fustat ba-maḥaṣit ha-rishona shel ha-me'a ha-aḥat-ʿesreh* (Jewish Leadership in Fustat) (Tel Aviv, 1995), 220–23: "The court obligated him to bestow upon her 'alimony' (*mezonot*)" (line 14); "he obligated himself to pay his divorcée Rayyisa bat Moses as 'child support' (*mezonot*) a half dirhem each day" (verso, lines 10–11). Moving in another direction, mezonot in the Geniza could designate a wide range of distributions, from food for the poor and child support for orphans, to contributions toward the salaries of the generally poorly paid communal officials, such as cantors, teachers of poor children, and kosher meat inspectors. See Cohen, *Poverty and Charity,* 218–20.

[39] *Med. Soc.,* 2:539n65; 3:271.

[40] Mentioned in a letter relating to the India trade; cf. *Med. Soc.,* 2:539n65.

dirhems[41] and pay them to the divorcée of Abu'l-Baqā' Samuel, telling her that this is *child support*[42] for her daughter for two full months. He should direct her to desist from saying improper things about him and to have all her close and distant relatives[43] stop interfering. She should be informed that the amount he is allocating her each month is more than what she should be given by law. She should be informed what that amount is and henceforth no one should protest. It is firmly established that each month my lord the *parnas* shall receive the prescribed amount and deliver it to her, if God wills. *Salvation*

[41] The waraq dirhem was a low-value silver dirhem, but in the Fatimid period (969–1171) the word was used interchangeably with the word for the standard dirhem; *Med. Soc.*, 1:388. In the present instance it sounds like the two are being distinguished, in which case the coin would have been less than the standard 1:40 per dinar.

[42] In the Hebrew singular *mezona.*

[43] Arabic: *kull min ahlihā wa-min ʿashīratihā*; cf. *Med. Soc.*, 3:425n2.

## Chapter Seven

# LETTERS REGARDING PUBLIC CHARITY

THOUGH BEST documented in the alms lists and donor registers, which appear in the next two chapters, the Geniza letters also reveal much about the public charity of the community. At the outset it must be noted that public charity in the Geniza world was not nearly so well-differentiated from private philanthropy as was public poor relief in early modern European countries, where population growth, hard economic times, expanding numbers of the urban poor—accompanied by an intensified fear of public begging and vagabondage—as well as new proposals by both Protestants and Catholics to improve social welfare, gave birth to state-run, "secular" philanthropy, in some places (notably England) supported by public taxation.

In the Geniza world, public charity was preeminently a religious act—a *miṣva*, in Hebrew—as it had been in Judaism for centuries. Furthermore, the structures of communal charity had been established already in postbiblical times, when Jews everywhere became increasingly urban, and the older, agriculturally based means of relieving the needy documented in the Bible no longer sufficed.[1] Also, in the "mixed economy" of Jewish charity in the Geniza world, the neat dichotomy often assumed in modern poor relief between voluntary, private (personal) charity, and obligatory, public (and impersonal) philanthropy, was absent. People answered the call of private appeals from the poor, left money to the poor in their wills, established pious foundations for purposes including relief of poverty, and at the same time contributed directly to the public dole. Moreover, in the Geniza society, "public" giving was, in theory at least, voluntaristic, even if it was felt to be obligatory—a manifestation of the religious mind seeking to satisfy God's commandments. Public Jewish charity in our period nicely illustrates Marcel Mauss's principle, based on the study of a very different society, that the gift is "in theory . . . voluntary but in fact . . . given and repaid under obligation."[2] Furthermore, in that

[1] This development has been traced recently by Frank M. Loewenberg, *From Charity to Social Justice: The Emergence of Communal Institutions for the Support of the Poor in Ancient Judaism* (New Brunswick and London, 2001).

[2] Marcel Mauss, *The Gift: Forms and Functions of Exchange in Archaic Societies*, trans. Ian Cunnison (London, 1954), 1.

closely knit, residentially compact society of ethnoreligious Jewish solidarity, the social distance between givers and takers was drastically reduced. Much familiarity marked the relationship between social welfare officials and the local poor. Lastly, in the Geniza community of the high Middle Ages, we do not find any evidence of formal taxation (as opposed to solicitation for contributions) to support poor relief. If the example of the mandatory Islamic alms tax (zakāt) ever tempted Jews to imitate its example, we find no evidence of this in the Geniza (even the evidence for government collection of zakāt for the poor from Muslims in Egypt during the classical Geniza period is scant).[3] In its lack of organized taxation for charity, the Jewish community of the Geniza differed from many medieval Jewish communities in Christian lands that taxed their members to generate revenues for charity long before the rise of the European poor laws.

## 50. "Kindly . . . assist the bearer of this letter, Isaac al-Darʿī, for he is an acquaintance of mine"

Collections toward the poll tax, a heavy annual burden for the poor, as we have seen, formed part of public charity. We will see this in some of the charity lists below. Here, Moses Maimonides, head of the Jews 1171–77 and 1195–1204, asks the provincial community of Minyat Ziftā in the Delta to arrange a collection toward the payment of the poll tax for Isaac al-Darʿī (from Draʿ in Morocco), a newcomer to Egypt and an acquaintance of Maimonides'. Isaac owed the tax for himself and his son. This, then, is an appeal for public assistance on behalf of the needy.

TS 12.192[4] (Judaeo-Arabic)

May God grant long life to your excellency, my prop and support, the elder "the Trusted" (al-Thiqa) "the Trustworthy" (al-Amīn),[5] and perpetuate your honor. The one who esteems you, your slave Moses, greets you and expresses distress that you are so far away and asks you kindly to assist the bearer of this letter, Isaac al-Darʿī (of Draʿ, a town in Morocco), for he is an acquaintance of mine. Ask the *ḥaver (may his) R(ock) p(rotect him)* to charge the community with his care, so that he gets the money for his poll tax in your town. He has to pay two

[3] Sabra, *Poverty and Charity in Medieval Islam*, 39.

[4] Ed. Richard Gottheil, *Gaster Anniversary Volume*, eds. Bruno Schindler and A. Marmorstein (London, 1936), 173–80; rev. ed. with facsimile Simha Assaf, *Meqorot u-meḥqarim be-toledot yisrael* (Texts and Studies in Jewish History) (Jerusalem, 1946) 163–65; cf. *Med. Soc.*, 2:498–99, App. C 82b; 2:46; 2:382 (partial translation). The letter is also translated in full, with discussion, by Joel L. Kraemer, "Two Letters of Maimonides from the Cairo Genizah," *Maimonidean Studies*, ed. Arthur Hyman, vol. 1 (New York, 1990), 87–92. My translation adheres mostly to that of Goitein.

[5] Assaf speculates he might be Mishael al-Thiqa, the father-in-law of Maimonides.

poll taxes, one for himself and one for his son. If possible, your excellency, let him pay it in your town, Minyat Zifta. So do it, because he is a newcomer[6] and thus far has not paid anything. He is on his way to Damietta on a matter important for me. On his way back, action should be taken for him according to your means. *May your welfare increase, as well as the welfare of the ḥaver and his son and the welfare of her*[7] *son, (may his) R(ock) p(rotect him).*

Moses b. Maimon, *(may) the m(emory of) the r(ighteous be) b(lessed)*

Verso:

To his excellency the most illustrious and most noble elder "the Trusted" "the Trustworthy," may his honor be perpetuated.

(Below, in Arabic letters): By means of Ibrāhīm al-Darʿī.[8]

## 51. "I won't ask for anything else from you again until the end of next month"

Wages of teachers of poor or orphaned children whose families could not afford private, home instruction constituted part of the public charity budget. When wages weren't paid on time, teachers themselves wound up among the poor. Below we shall see teachers both on accounts of communal expenditures and on alms lists. This short letter from Solomon ha-melammed ("the teacher") to Abuʾl-ʿIzz, also a teacher, complains about arrears in payments for his professional services, called jumʿa, "week," meaning payment for a week. He is in dire need. The sender seems to be the same person who wrote the next letter (no. 52), and the addressee appears to be the same addressee. The handwriting is different.

TS 6 J 4.16 (Judaeo-Arabic)

The slave Solomon *the teacher*

informs the master, the *teacher*, the elder Abuʾl-ʿIzz, *(may your) Ro(ck) pr(otect you)*, that it has been a long time since I received anything. *By Jewish law*,[9] I need to receive the pledges of that week (*jumʿa*) in cash or as a credit toward my account with your brother "the Illustrious *Schola*r" Abuʾl-Muna, *(may) his Ro(ck)*

[6] Arabic: *ṭāriʾ*.

[7] This could refer to a son of the ḥaver's wife by a previous marriage.

[8] In Arabic, apparently in Maimonides' own hand. This must have been a relative or friend of Isaac's from Morocco, to whom Maimonides sent the letter so Ibrāhīm could, in turn, hand it to Isaac for delivery to al-Thiqa in Minyat Zifta. As a newcomer, the indigent Isaac would not have had a proper address; Kraemer, op. cit., 90.

[9] Hebrew expression: *ve-din yisraʾel*, an oath, similar to saying "by God." See chapter 3, note 53.

> *pr(otect him)*, against what I owe him. I won't ask for anything else from you again until the end of next month, *Shevat*. I am owed the same amount by Ibn al-Dihqān.[10] I have no more patience over this delay, *etc*. I am in straits, warding off my worst instincts,[11] knowing as I do about my situation. Please be beneficent with that which God has given to you or accredit my account with your brother for what I owe him. *May your welfare increase and not diminish. N(eṣaḥ) s(ela)*.

## 52. "Do not impede the messenger, but send him the dirhem quickly"

Copied on the reverse side of a legal document dating from the time of the nagid Abraham Maimonides (d. 1237), this letter, like the previous one, addresses Abu'l-ʿIzz and requests that arrears be paid to the letter-bearer for the writer, named Solomon, a needy person. Here, as there, Solomon is a teacher, and presumably the arrears mentioned here, as there, are for his teacher's wages.

TS 6 J 3.10v (Judaeo-Arabic)

> May the elder A[bu]'l-ʿIzz pay the bearer [on]e dirhem because my need for it is urgent. God knows the situation I am in, so do not impede the messenger, but send him the dirhem quickly. May He open to you his treasure and relieve you from (having to resort to) *human beings. May your welfare increase, as willed by him who lov[e]s you. Solomon (may) h(eaven) w(atch over him) and i(ncrease his good fortune)*.[12]

## 53. "My wife and sons are coming up from Alexandria and they wrote to me that they do not have the fee for the boat"

This letter illustrates an important part of the public charity system. Addressed to the Fustat parnas Eli b. Yaḥyā by a blind person, it requests a pesiqa, a pledge drive. Such ad hoc collections formed one of the most common methods for providing charity to the needy. They were distinct from the regular distributions of bread, wheat, clothing, and cash, even though money for those purposes was also often raised through pledges and collections. The act of making a pesiqa was called, in Arabic, "putting one's name" (on a list).[13] It

[10] Alternative translation: I should get the same amount in my account with Ibn al-Dihqān.

[11] Translation uncertain.

[12] The abbreviation is *n-m-sh-w-l*, for *naṭreh min shemaya ve-gavreh le-mazleh*, which is Aramaic. See elsewhere in the Geniza, Gil, *Be-malkhut yishmael*, 4:955, index, s.v.

[13] E.g., TS 13 J 20.24, line 8: *(a)smu lahu 40 dirham*, "pledge for him 40 dirhems" (a needy French Rabbi in the Egyptian town of Bilbays); cf. *Med. Soc.*, 2:122. And the following note.

was a kind of vow, with all the religious obligations entailed in vows in Judaism,[14] and we may imagine that Maimonides, who himself organized many of these pesiqot in Egypt, had it in mind at the beginning of chapter 8 of his laws of charity in the Mishneh Torah when he wrote as his topic sentence: "Almsgiving is included in the category of vows." By virtue of its ad hoc nature, the pesiqa was serviceable for private as well as public charity, and indeed the pesiqa system illustrates how the boundaries between public and private charity could often be blurred.[15]

The writer needed money to bring his family from Alexandria—he writes "coming up" (Hebrew: *ʿolim*) because from Alexandria one sailed up the Nile. Being blind, he would have been eligible for the weekly bread dole; here he asks for an allotment above and beyond the normal food ration—in the form of a pesiqa for his family. The parnas Eli b. Yaḥyā, one of the two most prominent social welfare officials during the second half of the eleventh century, had helped him before. The petitioner invokes biblical verses that others requesting pesiqot also use in their letters.

Verso contains a different letter, by a man from Raḥba (in Iraq). He complains that the Jews of Fustat had not given him needed assistance and appeals to the addressee to help him out.

TS 8 J 16.29r[16] (Hebrew)

To your honor, greatness, and holiness, excellent diadem and crown.

To our master and teacher Eli the parnas, the trusted, the wise and discerning, the righteous, the perfect and straight, who has done me many favors since I came. I, your slave, the blind, fast every Monday and Thursday. For a year I have not eaten meat. I pray for you and your son R. Ephraim day and night that God grant that you see sons from him and rejoice in the[m], amen. Your slave entreats God and you to do for me a kindness by arranging [on my behalf] a pesiqa, because my wife and sons are coming up from Alexandria, and they wrote to me that they do not have the fee for the boat. So do for me a kindness this time, also, and your latter kindness toward me will be better than the first. "You will decree and it will be fulfilled, and light will shine upon your affairs" (Job 22:28). "Do not fail your servants" (Joshua 10:6). "Let not the downtrodden turn away disappointed" (Psalm 74:21). May the God of Israel grant you good old age and a good end and that you spend your days well. Amen.

[14] See *Med. Soc.*, 2:544n9, apropos TS 8 J 16.13, "On the Day of Atonement they made pledges for a collection (*asmaw pesiqa*) which became a vow (*neder*) incumbent upon them." See also Cohen, *Poverty and Charity*, chapter 8.

[15] For more on the pesiqa system, see Cohen, *Poverty and Charity*, 220–24.

[16] Ed. Scheiber, *Geniza Studies*, 78–79 (Hebrew section); cf. *Med. Soc.*, 5:90.

## 54. "Collect for me a *pesiqa of charity,* from you and from the congrega[tion] that prays at your house"

The writer of this letter asks a prominent physician to arrange for him a *pesiqat ṣedaqa*, a charity pesiqa, in his private synagogue—and first to give himself. The suppliant cannot go to work because of illness, a common complaint. The form of the letter mimics that of the Arabic petition, with one slip-up.

TS NS J 389[17] (Judaeo-Arabic)

*Truth*[18]

I kiss the ground before and inform[19] my master [ . . . ] *the honored Dignitary, the wise and discerning, physicia[n], C[rown] of the Sages and Physicians, may God bless you and protect you and give you long life and lengthen your days with goodness and your [y]ears with pleasantness, and give you a son living and strong.* I inform you that your slave is experiencing adversity on account of sickness and dearth and lack of income,[20] as well as nakedness.[21] Your slave req[uests] that you give charity to your slave [and that] you collect for me a *pesiqa of charity*, from you and from the congrega[tion] that prays at your house.[22] *May God open up for us and you His good treasury and His full and wide hand.* Do not turn your slave away disappointed. May you be charitable toward your slave [at a]ll times. *And peace.*

*Truth*

[17] *Med. Soc.*, 2:500, App. C 90. To the right of the letter, one sees the ends of four lines, apparently in the same hand, beginning opposite the space between the second and third lines. One word is *ḥazzān*, "cantor." Possibly the letter itself was part of a scribe's notebook and the writing to the right is part of another letter.

[18] Hebrew: *Emet*. This superscripture (repeated at the end) is sometimes found on money orders (similar to the modern check), where it abbreviates the verse *Emet Me-ereṣ Tiṣmaḥ*, "truth springs out of the earth" (Psalm 85:12), and warns that any misuse of the payment order will eventually be discovered; *Med. Soc.*, 1:241. Here, Goitein notes, its seems out of place. He takes it as a "refined allusion to the second half of verse 12 of Psalm 85: 'Truth springs out of the earth and justice looks down from heaven,'" the Hebrew word for justice [*ṣedeq*, the same word as *ṣedaqa*] at that time denoting charity." Ibid., 2:500, App. C 90. In letters such as this one (see also no. 56) the superscripture may vouch for the deservedness of the subject.

[19] The word "and inform" (*wa-yunhī*) is in the wrong place here. It should follow the name of the petitioned and his titles, as correctly below, where the word is repeated in the right place. Omit the word mentally and the sentence reads smoothly.

[20] Arabic: *maksab*.

[21] Arabic: *ʿury*, meaning lack of adequate clothing, the cross-cultural metaphor for this kind of deprivation in different societies. See Cohen, *Poverty and Charity*, chapter 6.

[22] Goitein speculates that he "kept a private synagogue, probably because his patients were mostly government officials and other high-standing persons, whom he usually had to visit early in the morning. It would have been impossible for him to do so had he attended the public service which naturally was of longer duration." *Med. Soc.*, 2:166.

## 55. "The only thing that is delaying me is the balance of the pesiqa"

This man was about to settle in Palestine. He requests to be sent the balance of a pledge drive (pesiqa) that had been arranged on his behalf and also asks that another pledge drive be arranged for his son by the *gabbai*, the collector of donations for charity. The writer had sent a similar appeal to the judge Ḥananel, an in-law of Moses Maimonides. It was considered a privilege to give money to the needy to travel to the Holy Land and the writer plays on that sentiment, promising (as usually in these letters) to pray for the welfare of his would-be benefactor.

Mosseri L 291 (Ia, 21)[23] (Hebrew)

What shall I say to my beloved Kohen, the righteous and pure R. Phineas. I send you this day a letter of entreaty and supplication, for the sake of the Creator, who[se] word you revere and fear, that you not delay me anymore. We are on the road to the Land of Isra(el), and the only thing that is delaying me is the balance of the pesiqa that is in your honor's hands. From here on there should be no giving up. Rather, have it collected today and tomorrow I shall depart for there, in honor of you. Similarly, I sent a letter to his honor my lord the Rav and Judge R. Ḥananel. For the sake of the Creator, please do not keep me waiting another minute beyond today, because we are about to leave. Also speak to the collector about a small pesiqa for my son today. Don't make me delay till tomorrow to depart for there. Know that your reward will be very great in this world and in the next. I pray for your honor at all times, and may the O(mnipotent) save you from every trouble and injustice and reward your actions in th(is) wo(rld) and in the w(orld) to come and reward you with sons who study Torah, as I, your beloved and admirer, who prays for your honor, wish. David b. Benjamin, m(ay his) s(oul be) b(ound) in the (bundle of life).

Verso: To his honor the pious Kohen R. Phineas

## 56. "Kindly arrange a collection for the bearer for two chickens and bread"

A cantor is asked to arrange a collection in the synagogue on a Thursday morning for a poor, old, sick man. Such ad hoc collections (the word *pesiqa* is not used here) benefited those whose indigence required somewhat more (or

[23] Ed. Mann, *Texts*, 1:463–64. Cf. Goitein, *Tarbiz* 50 (1980–81), 383.

more immediately) than the semiweekly bread dole or the less regular distributions of wheat, cash, or clothing. This person needed chicken and bread, the chicken being above and beyond the ration provided for the poor in the public dole. The sick craved (or their doctors prescribed) meat to help them recover from their illness.

Since cantors performed multiple functions and were regularly on duty, so-to-speak, in the synagogue, they were called upon to help administer charity. Thursday, like Monday, was a day when more men attended synagogue services than usual, in order to hear the recitation of the weekly Torah portion, so these days (as well as Sabbath and holidays) were convenient for collecting pledges of gifts for the poor. Giving charity in the synagogue was, and continues to be to this day, a particularly meritorious religious act.

The superscripture, "Truth," is found here as on no. 54.[24]

TS 6 J 8.4[25] (Judaeo-Arabic)

*Truth*

May the *cantor* Abu'l-Riḍā, *(may your) R(ock) p(rotect you)*, kindly arrange a collection for the bearer for two chickens and bread on Thursday morning in *the synagogue*, when *the holy Torah* is taken out. He is *poor, old, and sick, and lacks strength. And peace.*

## 57. "He is one of the blind and receives his share with them"

We shall find many handicapped persons receiving bread and other alms from public charity, on the alms lists (below). The blind seem to have sometimes come to the pick-up point (probably the synagogue) in groups, led by a seeing person, to collect their due. This note to the cantor Aaron requests that he look after a needy man, named Shabbat, who is "one of the blind and receives his share with them, but claims that they cheat him, for they take from (New) Cairo." It is not clear what the second part means. Goitein writes: "It would be odd to assume that 'the blind' of Fustat had to walk twice a week the two miles to Cairo to get their shares. The complainant must therefore have been a Cairene who came to a dignitary in Fustat to lodge a claim with him."

The writer is called "Rosh ha-Seder," a title granted by the Babylonian yeshiva. Goitein originally thought this person was Elḥanan b. Shemarya, head of the Jewish community at the beginning of the eleventh century until about 1025, who held that title. On the basis of handwriting and other considerations, Elinoar Bareket thinks the writer was Sahlān b. Abraham, head of

[24] See note 19.

[25] *Med. Soc.*, 2:463, App. B 91 (1200–40). Verso has some writing in a different hand, apparently lines from a eulogy for someone who had died.

the Babylonian congregation ca. 1030–50, who was the nephew of Aaron the cantor, the recipient of this note. Sahlān was also designated "Rosh ha-Seder."

CUL Or 1080 J 48[26] (Hebrew)

Rosh ha-Seder[27]

Our beloved and eminent ma(ster) and t(eacher) Aaron the cantor the precious one, may our Rock protect you and increase your welfare and blessings forever. Our hearts are unto [you and] our yearning for you is great. Our entreaties (to God) are on your behalf, may the Omni(present) fulfill them and apportion to you good things and save you from all snares, through His kindness.

The bearer of this note[28] is Shabbat. He is one of the blind and receives his share with them. He told us that they cheat him by taking from (New) Cairo. He [reque]sts that I write to you to look into his matter with them. May you, blessed be God, do in this (matter) as you are granted abundance from heaven.[29] May your welfare and blessings inc[rease] forever.

Perfect covenant.[30]

[26] Ed. Goitein, *Joshua Finkel Jubilee Volume*, eds. Sidney B. Hoenig and Leon D. Stitskin (New York, 1974), Hebrew section, 125–26, cf. *Med. Soc.*, 2:454, App. B 57a (1040–80); Bareket, *Fustat on the Nile*, 190, 249.

[27] "Head of the Row," a title in the Babylonian yeshiva, held by both Elḥanan b. Shemarya and Sahlān b. Abraham (as well as by others).

[28] Hebrew: *movil peṭeq zeh*, a translation of the Arabic *mūṣil hādhihī al-ruqʿa*, one of many such direct translations from Arabic epistolographical terminology found in Hebrew letters. This aspect of Jewish acculturation in the Arab world has been little studied.

[29] Hebrew and Arabic: *ka-asher tuwaffaq min ha-shamayim*. A standard Hebrew blessing, here seamlessly interwoven with a standard Arabic blessing.

[30] Hebrew: *berit tam*, the *ʿalāma*, or signature motto, of the writer, who, according to Bareket, is Sahlān b. Abraham.

# PART TWO

## CHARITY LISTS

# Chapter Eight

## ALMS LISTS

THE ALMS LISTS and donor lists in the Geniza complement the letters and form, like them, a unique source for social history. Very little of this type of material has survived for other societies in a comparable period.[1] The voices of the poor and of those who helped relieve their poverty resound here as they do in the letters, though they are silent voices that can be made audible with a little historical imagination and thick description. Inert though they appear, the lists divulge much about the dynamics of the Jewish public welfare system.

The documents fall into two categories, beneficiary lists and donor lists, corresponding to two appendixes in Goitein's *Mediterranean Society*, volume 2. In the research for my book, *Poverty and Charity in the Jewish Community of Medieval Egypt*, I identified more than sixty additional lists not noted by Goitein. At the end I bring a legal document and a will that pertain to our subject.

Among other things, the beneficiary and donor lists permit us to make a rough socioeconomic taxonomy of the poor and nonpoor, relying on the fact

[1] Food distributions in the ancient, pre-Christian world, did not, strictly speaking, constitute charity; they were for citizens, some of whom might incidentally have been needy. A list for the corn dole in ancient Egypt (Oxyrynchus, second half of the third century C.E.), preserved in a papyrus, is taken to be representative of the corn dole in Rome itself, for which no such lists exist. J. R. Rea, *The Oxyrynchus Papyri, Volume XL* (London, 1972). Also from the Greek papyri is a list of recipients of wheat of unknown provenance from the early third century C.E. Anna Świderek and Mariangela Vandoni, *Papyrus Grecs du Musée Gréco-Romain d'Alexandrie* (Warsaw, 1964), 65. Several lists were discovered among the Jewish Aramaic papyri from the island of Elephantine in Upper Egypt (fifth century B.C.E.), including contributors to the local temple and even a list of people receiving rations of wheat as members of the Persian military garrison (that was the function of the Jewish community there) (Cowley, ed. *Aramaic Papyri*, 65–76, 78–83), but no poor lists. Lists ("poor rolls") are mentioned in early Christian sources, but I do not know of any that have survived in their actual form. See Peter Brown, *Poverty and Leadership*, 11, 60 (Brown writes: "would that they had survived!"), 65, 78; and, regarding the so-called matricula, a list of names of the poor receiving assistance from the church (none of which have survived, Peter Brown tells me), see Michel Rouche, "La matricule des pauvres: Evolution d'une institution de charité du Bas Empire jusqu'à la fin du Haut Moyen Age," in *Etudes sur l'histoire de la pauvreté* (Paris, 1974), 83–110. Recently Princeton University acquired an Arabic document on papyrus from the seventh century that may contain a record of distributions to the poor or orphans. Princeton University Papyrus Acc. No. 2002-143. I thank Petra Sijpesteijn for her help with this papyrus.

that people are often recorded with their occupation (X the grave digger, Y the physician, for instance).[2] Three categories can be discerned: professions that appear only on beneficiary lists, constituting the true underclass of the chronic poor; occupations that are found only on donor lists, representing the non-poor; and a middle group of people who appear on both. These floated back and forth between subsistence (greater or lesser), when they were working, which kept them out of "deep" poverty, to borrow Paul Slack's term in his study of poverty in early modern England,[3] and total impoverishment, which led them to the dole.

In the underclass of *chronic poor* are to be numbered, for instance, gardeners, water carriers, doorkeepers, porters, flour dealers, messengers, shoemakers, blacksmiths, grave diggers, supervisors of kashrut, and treaters of wounds—most of these menial occupations or jobs that paid very poorly. Among the *nonpoor* we find, not unexpectedly, merchants, brokers, bankers, government clerks, tax-farmers, and physicians. Occupations from essential food and textile trades also appear. The *middle group* contains people who held regular, if poorly paying jobs, like synagogue beadles and cantors. They appear more often as beneficiaries than as donors, but as synagogue functionaries they could hardly avoid giving to public charity, and thus we find some of them on donor lists. Others in this middle group who oscillated between being "takers" and "givers" include carpenters, tailors, masons, cooks, elementary school teachers, butchers, cheese makers (and others in the food industry)—people, in other words, whose income depended very much on the availability of work or on the flow of customers. At the upper end of the middle group we find people in the silk trade, a staple commodity in the economy of Egypt, and dyers, who served the almost insatiable appetite of the Geniza people and their Muslim neighbors for colored garments. We are not surprised to find bankers and money assayers and people in the medical profession as donors. But even these people could end up on the dole. In those days bankers were mostly money changers who may also have held deposits for merchants, and pharmacists were mainly purveyors of medicinal herbs. Jewish physicians, while overwhelmingly found among the nonpoor, could also experience economic hardship—there was a lot of competition![4]

Remarkably, this taxonomy roughly correlates with the picture of non-Muslim class differentiation portrayed in the famous early book on taxation, *Kitāb al-kharāj*, by Abū Yūsuf (d. 798). Discussing the graduated poll tax of 12-24-48 dirhems, which he recommends to his patron Caliph Hārūn al-Rashīd (786–809) for Iraq, Abū Yūsuf states that the lowest rate was to be paid by "those who work with their hands, such as the tailor, the dyer, the shoemakers

[2] See Cohen, *Poverty and Charity*, chapter 1.

[3] Slack, *Poverty and Policy in Tudor and Stuart England*, 39, and passim.

[4] More on this, including a fuller list of examples, in Cohen, *Poverty and Charity*, chapter 1.

(*al-iskāf wa'l-kharrāz*),[5] and the like." From the wealthiest, "such as the banker, the clothier, the estate owner (*ṣāḥib al-ḍayʿa*), the merchant, and the healer and the physician (*al-muʿālij wa'l-ṭabīb*), and all who practice a professional craft (*ṣināʿa*) or commercial trade (*tijāra*)," forty-eight dirhems should be collected. Finally, in the middle category Abū Yūsuf numbers those who pursue the same occupations as those in the "wealthy" category, but should pay only twenty-eight dirhems if their income was not sufficient to afford the higher rate.[6] This would roughly correspond to those in our own middle group who appear mostly as givers and in the minority of instances as takers.

(In the lists I have indicated in some cases that I am uncertain about the spelling or vocalization of a name.)

## Alms Lists

### Notes on the documents

Square brackets [ ] enclose a lacuna in the manuscript; three dots enclosed in brackets indicate letters or words difficult to decipher.

Double square brackets [[ ]] indicate something crossed out.

Slashes // // indicate something added above (sometimes below) the line; single slashes (/ /) are used when only a single letter is so added.

A question mark indicates an uncertain reading or translation.

Words set in italics are in Hebrew or Aramaic in the text.

One Egyptian raṭl (pound) = ca. 450 grams.

One qinṭār = 100 raṭl.

One wayba = ca. 15 liters or about 4 gallons.

Six waybas = 1 irdabb.

One dinar (gold coin) = normally about 40 dirhems (silver coins) in the Fatimid and Ayyubid periods (969–1250), but this exchange rate fluctuated with the silver content of the dirhem.

Waraq = a dirhem of low quality silver.

One loaf of bread weighed about 1 pound and cost, on average, 1/5 dirhem when not subject to price fluctuations.

Nine waybas of new wheat or 11 waybas of old wheat cost 1 dinar in a document from ca. 1005–1035.

An artisan or middle-class (not wealthy) family could live on 2 dinars per month.

Fast of Av—Jewish fast day commemorating the destruction of the Holy Temple in Jerusalem, usually celebrated in August.

[5] In a Geniza document, these two words for shoemaker are found, along with a third, *ḥadhdhā*; *Med. Soc.*, 1:422n81. See also Cohen, *Poverty and Charity*, 57.

[6] Abū Yūsuf, *Kitāb al-kharāj* (Cairo, 1392/1972), 123–24.

"b." stands for ben, "son of," but since this is often a family name (Arabic *ibn*), it cannot always be assumed that the person is actually the son of the person named.

Occupational names like "son of the tailor" may be family names and may not necessarily identify the occupation of the father.

*Umm* is the Arabic word for "mother," *abū* for "father," usually forming part of honorific names.

*Rayyis* = "head" and may mean the head of the community, a physician, a functionary in government service, or other positions of authority.

*Ḥaver* = "member," namely, of the yeshiva in Palestine, hence a scholarly graduate of that institution, qualified to serve as head of a congregation.

"Wife" translates, usually, Arabic *imraʾa/marʾa*, and Goitein thinks this is a euphemism for "widow," which it probably is most of the time.

"House" (Hebrew: *bayit, beit*) can mean "household/family," or "wife," following a midrashic saying: "his house means his wife" (who conducts the affairs of the household).

R. stands for "rabbi" and means a person of learning, but not the synagogue rabbi as we know it today.

"Elder" translates Arabic *shaykh* (occasionally Hebrew *zaqen*) and connotes an honored position in the community, but not necessarily a person of old age.

"Supervisor" translates Hebrew *shomer* (occasionally Arabic *ḥāris*) and connotes a person who supervises the ritually correct (kosher) production of a food item.

Maghreb = North Africa.

Andalusia = Muslim Spain.

Ḥijāz = the part of Arabia including Mecca and Medina where non-Muslims are officially forbidden to reside.

Rūm = Christian lands, sometimes specifically the Byzantine Empire.

Bodl. = the Bodleian Library Geniza Collection, Oxford.

TS = Taylor-Schechter Geniza Collection in Cambridge University Library.

ENA = Elkan Nathan Adler Geniza Collection, Jewish Theological Seminary of America, New York.

Westminster College = another collection in Cambridge.

Hebrew words and expressions are not italicized. Original spellings are retained (e.g., Iṣḥāq, Iṣḥaq). The layout of the lists and the positioning of the lines, especially in facing columns, reproduce as closely as possible the layout on the manuscript pages (as can be seen in the accompanying illustrations).

58. TS NS J 41[7]

Goitein describes this list as follows: "Distribution of about 430 loaves of bread, weighing 450 pounds, to 104 households on the Friday before the Fast

[7] Cf. *Med. Soc.*, 2:442, App. B 17, ca. 1107.

[8] Arabic: *unfiqa fī al-ʿaniyyim*, which Goitein translates "spent on the poor," by which I think he means, money was spent to buy 430 loaves.

of Av (which fell on Sunday)." The heading states: "Dispensed to the Poor,[8] may God, in his mercy, make them rich." I count 408+ loaves (one figure is effaced). It appears that the scribe originally wrote "six" (*sitta*) qinṭār, then changed the word "six" to the numeral (Hebrew letter) 4. The page is folded down the center, with holes for the binding string in the center, indicating that this page was originally bound with others in a scribe's notebook. Column I is on the right but there is no necessary continuity between it and column II, on the left. There may have been at least one intervening page. This would account for the discrepancy between the stated number of pounds (loaves—one loaf weighed one Egyptian pound [*raṭl*]) baked and the computed total number of loaves dispensed. Columns II and III could form the end of a subsequent list in that same quire, written by the same scribe.

Typical and predictable entries include widows (most of those called "wife" are probably widows); lots of women in general (ca. 25); orphans listed alone; an orphan girl and her brothers (she was probably an older sibling and collected on behalf of all of them). Widows and orphans form the classic "weak" persons in Judaism and Christianity. Since orphans are fatherless children, they often lived with their widowed mothers or with other family. Interestingly here, as elsewhere generally in the alms lists, orphans are not recorded along with their guardians, even their own mothers. This apparently accords with the rabbinic dictum that "the court is the father of orphans." Since orphans were entitled in their own right to support (food, clothing, and school fees) from the Jewish court and, by extension, from the community, they appear in the alms lists alone, without the names of their guardians, even though, generally, the latter received and took charge of the allotments to which the orphans were entitled.[9] The orphans of the Karaite on this and other lists were obviously not discriminated against, another sign of the well-known cooperation between the two denominations, Rabbanite and Karaite, in Fustat. A Karaite appears as a donor to charity in no. 75.

The list contains a fair share of foreigners, identifiable by their toponymic or by some other marker (e.g., Eliakim and his traveling companion, *rafīq* in Arabic; Greek forms of names like Symeon, Dānīl; the word "newcomer," Arabic ṭāri', meaning someone freshly arrived [and perhaps not yet paying the poll tax locally]); a person from Qalhā, a village in the Egyptian Fayyūm, a region that was racked by famine and civil war during the years 1069–72 (called *nahb al-Fayyūm* in the Geniza documents),[10] perhaps explaining the multitude of Qalhāwīs on the poor rolls in the capital; people designated acquaintance (Arabic: maʿrifa), namely, those known to someone locally who vouched for their deservedness (they occur all over the lists; see below);[11] proselytes,

[9] See my article "Halakha and Reality in Matters of Charity during the Geniza Period," 329–32, and Cohen, *Poverty and Charity*, chapter 5.

[10] *Med. Soc.*, 3:208.

[11] See also Cohen, *Poverty and Charity*, chapter 8.

usually former Christians from Europe who fled with little resources to the lands of Islam to escape harrassment at home and to gain protection as poll-tax-paying dhimmīs; parents living with their children (sometimes married children); people in low-paying and economically marginal professions (e.g., grave digger, washer of the dead, supervisor of milk, cantor [many more of them in subsequent lists], tailor). The supervisor (Hebrew: *shomer*) was the eastern counterpart of the *mashgiaḥ* of Ashkenazic lands. He watched to see that food was prepared in accordance with the kosher dietary laws, and he was paid a low wage for this service. The ill or disabled (e.g., blind people, a man with tremors) occur here as elsewhere ubiquitously in the alms lists. As in other cultures, illness looms large as a cause, or a symptom, of poverty in the Geniza. Notice that two blind men are listed next to each other at the end of Column III, which I take to mean that they were led together to the pick-up point (probably in the synagogue compound) by a seeing person (on the blind see many letters above). Three entries clustered together call for comment: the mother-in-law of Elia and the orphan boy; Elia; and Elia "the short." These people appear elsewhere (see below) in a group of alms recipients from Rūm. They were needy foreigners, recently arrived. Goitein dates this list around the time of those dated lists from 1107 (see below), which he connects with the flow of refugees from persecution in Europe at the time of the First Crusade (1096). Many if not most of these Jews of Rūm probably hailed from Byzantine Asia Minor and had fled to Egypt, either in the wake of the Seljuk Turks' victory at the battle of Manzikert in 1071 or, more likely, from the Crusaders passing through Asia Minor in 1098.[12] The Greek names in these lists (Symeon here, for instance) strengthen this conclusion. Those with Arabic names would have been descendants of Jews who migrated to Byzantine Asia Minor following the Byzantine conquests in Muslim Syria in the 960s and 970s.[13] Elijah was a popular Hebrew name among Greek Jews.[14] Clearly, Elia "the short" had that nickname to distinguish him from his namesake and fellow countryman in the same Rūm cohort of immigrants. The mother-in-law of Elia collected in her own right. She probably did not live with Elia. But who was the orphan? Not the son of Elia, obviously—he was still living. Perhaps the youngster was her grandson from another son's marriage, or an unrelated orphan whom she had taken into her house, a kind of foster-child arrangement;[15] or perhaps this was a third Elia. The isolated notation "received" is found here and on other lists, possibly indicating that the person collected his ration from someplace else (directly from the bakery?).

[12] See Cohen, *Poverty and Charity*, 84–85.

[13] See David Jacoby, "What Do We Learn about Byzantine Asia Minor from the Documents of the Cairo Genizah?" in his *Byzantium, Latin Romania and the Mediterranean* (Aldershot, 2001), 87.

[14] See Joshua Starr, *The Jews in the Byzantine Empire 641–1204* (Athens, 1939), index s.v. Elijah.

[15] See Cohen, *Poverty and Charity*, 236–37.

Goitein analyzed the rations in dozens of bread lists and came up with the figure of four loaves per adult per week, dispensed twice, on Tuesday and Friday (two loaves on average each time). The nutritional value of this ration was low.[16] When a person collected more than two loaves, he or she was fetching rations for other family members, normally children, who usually got one loaf since they needed less. A figure of 3 would mean two loaves for the adult and one for a child.

**Col. I**

1. In the name (of God)
2. Friday the 8th of the month of
3. Av, may its mourning be turned into joy.
4. Dispensed to the poor, may God in his mercy
5. make them rich, [[six]] 4 and a half qinṭārs (450 pounds)
6. of bread
7. the orphans of the astrologer 8 the man from Acre 6
8. Abū Kathīr 6 Noah 3 Sittān 2
9. Abū Hilāl 4 ʿAyyāsh 3
10. Ibrahīm of Tyre 4 the neighbor (f.) 2
11. the Ṣūrānī 6 the acquaintance of Abū Surūr 4
12. Samīḥ 4 Umm ʿUbayd 3

**Col. II**

1. Maʿlaʾ 5 an orphan girl and her brothers 43. the wife of the deceased man 4
2. the sons of Raḥamim 3 Symeon 4 Nathan 3
3. the wife of the deceased man Eliakim 2 his traveling companion 2
4. the female proselyte 4 Malīḥa 3
5. Yaʿqūb 1 Zaʿfarān 8
6. Sibāʿ 4 the children of Abū Saʿīd 6
7. Umm Furayj 2 Wahīb 3 Shalom 3
8. Umm al-Khayyāṭ (mother of the tailor) 2 Kināna 1
9. the Mumḥe b. al-Ḥallāʾ (maker of ornaments/jewelry) 8 Umm Sabīʿ 3
10. Dānīl and his son 2 Shilḥiyā ("the Berber woman") 3
11. her sister 3 [[Umm]] Zuhayr and his father-in-law 6
12. Yāfūnī 2 the newcomer from Rūm 6
13. the "runner" Kohen 6 his mother and maternal aunt 4
14. the brothers of the deceased man 3 Umm ʿAynayn Ḥamd 4

[16] Cohen, *Poverty and Charity*, chapters 6 and 8.

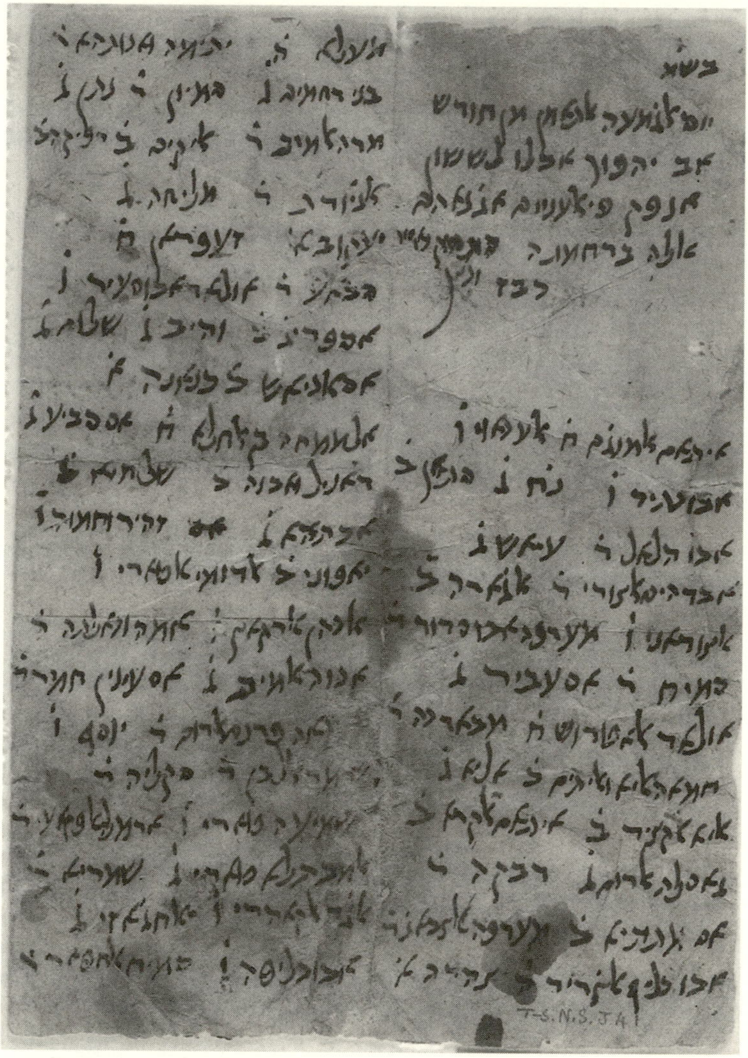

Fig. 2. Page from an alms list, distribution of bread to the poor, ca. 1107; (no. 58) TS NS J 41

13. the children of the deaf man 8
Mubāraka 4

14. the mother-in-law of Elia and the
orphan boy 2 Elia 3

15. Elia "the short" 2 the orphans of
the Karaite 2

16. the female washer of the dead of
the Rūm 3 Rebecca 4

17. Umm Matatya 2 the acquaintance of the dyer 4

18. Abū Khalīf the blind man 5 his
in-law

15. [the mother-in-]law of the parnas
of the Rūm 4 Joseph 6

16. the su[p]ervisor of milk 4 the
woman from Sicily 4

17. Shamī'a the newcomer 6 the
widow of the seller of fuqqā' (honey
sherbet) 4

18. the afflicted newcomer 3 Shemarya 4

19. the proselyte from Cairo 6 the
man from Hijāz 3

20. Ab[ū] Khalīfa 6 Samīh the grave
digger 4

Verso

**Col. III**
1. two acquaintances of Azhar 16 b.
Yahyā 4

2. the acquaintance of the man from
Damietta 6

3. the daughter of al-Thulayth[17] 2 the
daughter of al-Jady[18] 2

4. the sister of Ishaq 2 b. Sa'āda 2

5. the son of the writer/singer of
liturgical poetry 6 Sa'āda 4

6. Umm Miryam 2 Abū Shaykha 2

7. Barakāt the fortune teller? (al-
munādalī)[19] 4

8. Salāma 4 the man from Qalahā 3

9. Umm Zarīfa 4 the wife of 'Awād 4

---

[17] I am uncertain about the spelling of this name.
[18] Perhaps born under the zodiac sign Capricorn ("the goat") and so named.
[19] In another context, Goitein cites a word, *yimandilū*, which he tentatively connects with the modern Egyptian *mandal* meaning magic divination. *Med. Soc.*, 2:536n133.

10. Umm Hilāla 2 the man with tremors 3

11. the worker and/or dealer in lead 5 the wife of the furrier[20] 5

12. b. Dānīl 8 a newcomer 2

13. the Rayyis b. Joseph (may his) m(emory be) b(lessed) [. . .] the glassmaker 4

14. // the son // of the mother-in-law of al-Muṭālibī 2 (a *mim* above the line = *fa-sallam*, received)

15. a newcomer elder of Baghdad 6

16. the cantor b. al-Quḍāʿī (son of the healer of stomach ailments) 6 the mother-in-law of b. al[-. . .]. 4

17. the acquaintance of Abuʾl-Munā 8

18. the daughter of Ḥashīka 5 Abū Mukhtār 4

19. his sister 3 the wife of the tanner 3

20. Yaʿqūb the blind man 3 Makhlūf the [b]lind man 2

59. TS Misc. Box 8.9[21]

Goitein describes this as a "[l]ist in the same hand as B 17 [= no. 58], headed 'Fourth Friday, 550 Pounds,' specifying about 140 households receiving approximately 600 loaves of bread. Most of the names in the preceding section [no. 58] recur in this one, as well as in B 19–24 (= nos. 60–65), but from which group it is separated by many different names."

Again, we have here a leaf from a notebook. Column I is parallel to and to the left of column IV, and column IV ends two-thirds of the way down the page, a sign that it contains the final column in a section recording a single

[20] There was a trade in furs coming from Tunisia and Sicily (see *Med. Soc.*, 1:154), so this furrier, whose widow and orphaned children appear on many alms lists, was evidently an immigrant to Egypt.
[21] Cf. *Med. Soc.*, 2:442, App. B 18, ca. 1107.

distribution. Whether these four columns are indeed consecutive needs to be investigated as well as the possibility that no. 58 and no. 59 come from the same notebook. The dimensions are similar.

Many names are repeated from the previous list, which makes it datable around the same time. Many foreigners are present. Not seen in the previous list: other low-paying and economically marginal professions (a night watchman,[22] a female teacher, glassmakers, synagogue beadles, a dyer, a scribe); ill and disabled (a semiparalyzed woman). This list (like most of the alms lists) also includes a large number of women (ca. 35). The entry Judah and an orphan must represent a man taking care of an orphan in his household, perhaps the child of a deceased relative. The female washer of the dead for the Rūm, evidently one of the Rūm herself who spoke their language (Greek probably), had perhaps arrived with them from Byzantium. She is distinguished in the list from the local female washer of the dead from Fustat. There was also a special parnas of the Rūm (whose mother-in-law appears on several lists), and he, too, had a special function. As a fellow countryman of the others, and knowing their language, he could help the charity administrators determine their need and hence their allocations.[23]

**Col. IV**

1. Joseph the night watchman 5 the wife of the tanner 5
2. Yaʿqūb 3 Makhlūf 2 b. al-ʿAmmānī 4
3. Barakāt the supervisor 4 ʿAyyāsh 4
4. the mother-in-law of the Rūm [. . .]
5. Maʿlā' 10 a blin[d woman] 5 a woman from Ma[lī] 2
6. a female teacher 3 KL[. . .] 3 Abū a[l-. . .]
7. Naʿīm 4 a cantor from Ascalon 6
8. a newcomer from Baghdad 6
9. the orphans of the furrier 5 Shilḥiyā 4

**Col. I**

1. Friday the 4th
2. five and 1/2 qinṭārs (550 pounds)
3. Abū Kathīr 6 the woman from Sicily 2
4. R. Menaḥem 5 the o[rph]ans of Ibrahīm 3
5. Abū Mukhtār and his sister and his son 9
6. Zaʿfarān 8 a man from Andalus and his son 5
7. the wife of ʿAwāḍ 5 Hārūn of Jerusalem 4

[22] One of the police and security officials; cf. *Med. Soc.*, 2:86. He was a Jew.

[23] *Med. Soc.*, 2:79.

10. a semiparalyzed woman 2 Shalom the scribe 3

11. the female washer of the dead for Fustat 2

12. Sulaymān the supervisor 4

13. Umm I[b]rahim 4 Hilāl 2

8. the woman from Barqa 4 Afūnī[24] 2

9. the female proselyte 4 the sons of Raḥamim 4

10. a female guide (of the blind) 1 Nathan 2 b. Shekhanya 6

11. the acquaintance of the dyer 3 al-Ṣūrānī the Kohen

12. the mother-in-law of Elia and the orphan boy 2 the acquaintance of Umm Surūr 4

13. Elia "the short" 2 the wife of the deceased elder 4

14. Abū Khalīf and his [. . .] 5 Ṣāliḥ 4

15. Mubāraka 4 Umm Furayj 2

16. a newcomer from Rūm 4 the two acquaintances of Azhar16

17. Sittān [. . .] the acquaintance of the man from Damietta 7

18. b. Yiḥye 3 the daughter of al-Thulayth 2

Verso

**Col. II**

1. the daughter of al-Jady 2 the sister of Isḥaq 2

2. b. Saʿāda 4 the son of the writer/singer of liturgical poetry 8

3. Sibāʿ 4 Simḥa 4

4. Wahīb 3 the orphans of the astro[lo]ger 8

**Col. III**

1. Yaʿqūb the dyer 3 Simon 4

2. b. Nissim 4 Abū Shaykha 2

3. the man from the Ḥijāz 3 Umm Yūsuf 3

4. Umm Mi[r]yam 2 the fortune teller? (al-munādalī)[25] 4

[24] I am uncertain about this name.

[25] See above, note 18.

5. Abū Khalīfa 6 the man with tremors 3

6. Ibrahīm of Tyre 4 the female proselyte 2

7. b. al-Ḥallāʾ (maker of ornaments/jeweler) 6 Elia 3 Umm Sabīʿ 3

8. the divorcée of Abu Saʿīd 6 Judah and an orphan 8

9. the orphans of the Karaite 2 a man from Baghdad 3

10. Kināna 1 Umm Hilāla 2

11. Eliakim and his traveling companion 4 Malīḥa 3

12. an orphan girl 4 the in-law of R. Joseph 8

13. Umm Khalīf 3 Umm al-Khayyāṭ 2

14. the Kohen from Rūm 4 his mother 4 the brothers // of the deceased man // 3

15. Samīḥ the Kohen 4 Umm ʿUbayd 3

16. the son of the aflicted man 1 [. . .]m 4

17. Umm ʿAynayn Ḥamd 4 the children of the deaf man 8

18. b. Nafīʿ 10 the glassmaker 3

5. Symeon 4 the female washer of the dead for the Rūm 4

6. [R]ebecca 4 Umm Matatya 2

7. [an o]rphan from Rūm 2 b. Yūsuf 10 the glassmaker 4

8. the daughter of Ḥashīka[26] 5 the acquaintance of

9. Abuʾl-Munā 8 Shemarya 4

10. Salāma 4 Umm Ẓarīfa 4

11. the man from Qalahā 3 Maʿlāʾ 5

12. the worker and/or dealer in lead 5 the wife of the seller of fuqqāʿ (honey sherbet) 4 [[3]]

13. Zuhayr and his mother-in-law 6 the man from Baʿalbek 6

14. b. al-Quḍāʿī (the son of the healer of stomach ailments) 6 the teacher from Acre 6

15. Ṣadaqa the beadle 10 the son of the woman from Palestine 3

16. Furayj the beadle 14 b. al-Jāzifīnī 8

17. b. Abuʾl-Ḥayy [. . .] the preparer of vinegar sauce or other appetizers (al-kāmukhī) and his father-in-law 11

18. the orphans of U[mm Ka]thīr[27] 4 Sulaymān 4

[26] Sometimes spelled Ḥasīka, though I am uncertain about the vocalization of this name.

[27] The missing letters could as easily be completed "A[bū Ka]thīr," but an Abū Kathīr appears alive (though poor) elsewhere collecting alms on these lists from the same time (including on this very document), which makes "Umm Kathīr" a better guess.

19. the acquaintance of Ab [*sic*] Sḥaq 4 the supervisor 3

20. the producer/seller of fine things and his mother-in-law 6 Makḥūl 4

19. the wife of Ḥūrāra 3 Umm Ibrahīm 3

20. Umm Kaḥlā' 5 the supervisor from Tiberias 6

21. the Maghrebi woman 2 Sabī' 5

60–63. TS Box K 15.5, 15, 39, 50

Pages from a booklet recording distributions of bread, one section beginning, as befits a title page, "List of the Poor of Old Cairo—may God in his mercy make them rich and help them in his grace and kindness." When the folded pages are placed one on top of the other, it becomes evident that there is no necessary continuity from column to column and that some bifolios are missing. The date November 1107 is found on one heading (no. 62). The handwriting is that of the scribe Abraham, son of the well-known scribe and cantor Aaron ha-Mumḥe b. Ephraim, who also wrote nos. 64 and 65.

60. TS Box K 15.5[28]

Col. IV lists separately the Rūm, Jews who came from Byzantium (probably) as a group at the end of the eleventh or the beginning of the twelfth century. Many of their names appear on the previous two lists, though not all together, as here. The two women Mubāraka are probably freed slave girls, as that was a common name they took (see no. 66). As elsewhere, this register includes many ill or disabled, many women (ca. 40), including, typically, widows, wives of men who could not work because of illness or disability, women with children (either widows or perhaps deserted mothers), older women, men with humble occupations, and foreigners. Entries (here and in other lists) styled "house of (*beit*) X" seem, on the face of it, to refer to "households," though, as Goitein believes, very often the word "house" means "wife," following the Jewish adage, "*beito—zo ishto*" ("his house means his wife").[29] The wife of the deceased man (in one list he is called "the deceased elder") was probably called such because, being a foreigner, the scribe did not know her husband's name and the man might anyway have died in his place of origin. There is also an entry on these lists for the brothers of the deceased man, doubtless that widow's brothers-in-law.

[28] Cf. *Med. Soc.*, 2:445, App. B 19.

[29] Based on a midrashic explanation of the biblical account of the high priest Aaron, of whom it is said "Aaron is to offer his own bull of sin offering, to make expiation for himself and for his household" (*beito*) (Leviticus 16:6 and elsewhere). See Mishna Yoma 1:1.

The bread was purchased with a single gift from the head of the Jews Mevorakh b. Saadya—three dinars, a substantial sum, which bought six hundred pounds (loaves). Thus, here one loaf of bread cost ⅕ of a dirhem, a typical price when circumstances did not push the price up or down.

**Col. I**

1. List of the Poor of Old Cairo,

2. may God in his mercy make them rich

3. and help them in his grace and kindness.

**Col. IV**

1. Sh[. . .]

2. b. Abū [. . .]

3. the acquaintance of Abū Zik[ri . . .]

4. Four hundred [. . .]

5. which is one hundred sevent[y . . .]

6. Remaining, eighty loaves.

7. From twenty-e[ig]ht loaves

8. dispensed on this day

9. eight[tee]n loaves.

10. The Rūm

11. Mubāraka 4 Mubāraka [. . .] the Kohen from Rūm 4

12. his mother and grandmother 4 Elijah al[- . . .] 3 his mother-in-law 3

13. the wife of the blind man 3 Khalīf t[he b]lind man 3 his in-law 2

14. Umm al-Khayyāṭ 2 Ḥasan the elder [. . .]

15. Shemarya 4 b. al-Kharazī (maker of beads) 2 [. . .] 2

16. [. . .] 2 the orphans of the Karaite 2 David 4

17. Kināna 2 a semiparalyzed woman 2 the mother-in-law of the pa[r]nas 2

18. Eliakim 2 Elijah 3 Judah 3

19. an orphan 2 the Kohen 3 the wife of the deceased man [. . .]

20. the wife of the man afflicted with an intestinal ailment 3 Judah 4

21. Isaac 2 the female washer of the dead and her mother 3

22. Umm Matatya 2 Solomon the scribe 2

23. the woman from Rūm and an orphan 4 a man from Rūm 2

24. a blind man from Rūm and his guide 5 the in-law of Joseph 2

25. a woman from Rūm 3 an errand boy from Rūm 3

124

Verso

**Col. II**

1.

2. On the [. . .] day

3. of Marhesh[van] (November)

4. Available six hundred [loaves]

5. weighing six qinṭārs (600 pounds).

6. Their price three dinars,

7. which I have received from the Chief of the Dignitaries (sar ha-sarim; i.e., the nagid Mevorakh)—may he live forever.

8. b. Daniel 8 Joseph b. al-Munajjim (the son of the astrologer) and his mother 8

**Col. III**

1. [. . .]q 2

2. [the house of] b. Saʿāda 4

3. the house of b. Y[iḥye] [. . .] b. al-Murahhiṭ (the son of the writer/singer of liturgical poetry) 6

4. the stricken man 2 ʿAyyāsh 4

5. the Mumḥe b. Shekhanya 6 b. al-Ḥilāl 8

6. Umm Khalīf 4 the glassmaker 3

7. b. Nafīʿ 6 the sister of b. Nafīʿ 2

8. the producer/seller of fine things 4 his mother-in-law 2

9. Sibāʿ 4 the cantor b. al-Kāmukhī (the son of the preparer of vinegar sauce and other appetizers) 3

10. Samīḥ 4 Wahīb the glassmaker 3

11. al-Sūrāniyya 5 Joseph the night watchman 4

12. Hārūn of Jerusalem 2 the wife of Abraham 4

13. Sittān 3 [[2]] Umm Furayj [. . .]

14. the wife of the furrier 5 the wife of Abū Saʿīd 4

15. Jacob the blind man 3 Umm Ẓarīfa 3

16. Salāma 5 the woman from Qalahā 3

17. Umm Ibrāhīm and her son 3

18. the cantor Saʿīd 3 Abu Mukhtār, his son and daughter 9

19. Umm Hilāla 2 Sulaymā[n] the supervisor of milk 4

20. Zuhayr the lame 4 Abū Khalīfa 4

21. Samīḥ the grave digger 4 the son of the deaf man 8

22. Maʿlāʾ 5 the man from Andalusia [. . .]

23. Abū Kathīr the silk worker 4 Hilāl 2

9. the man from the Ḥijāz 3 the man from Acre 6

10. al-Makḥūl 4 the mother-in-law of the woman from Palestine 3

11. the wife of Maʿlāʾ 8 and his in-law 4

12. Wahīb 4 and Abū Wahīb 4

13. the female teacher 3 the wife of Ḥadāda [. . .]

14. the blind woman 5 the wife of b. al-ʿA[mm]ānī 4

15. Umm Lubuwwa 3 the man from Ma[l]īj 8

16. the wife of the tanner 6 her neighbor (f.) 4

17. Abū Saʿīd // the silk worker // the blind man 4 the woman from Malīj 2

18. Sabīʿ the blind man 6 Saʿāda 2

19. Makhlūf the blind man 3 [[the in-law of Joseph 6]]

20. Umm Ibrahim 2 the in-law of Ghālib 5

21. [Ṣ]āliḥ 4 the cantor from Baʿalbek 6

22. the wife of Jacob 4 b. al-Quḍāʿī (the son of the healer of stomach ailments) 8

23. the son of al-ʿAmmānī 8 Umm ʿUbayd 4

| | |
|---|---|
| 24. the female washer of the dead from Fusṭāṭ 2 Barakāt 4 | 24. the coo[k] [. . .] Simon 4 |
| 25. the wife of ʿAwāḍ 4 [Ḥasan the gl]ass maker 4 | Abū Shay[kha. . .] the [ac]quaintance of b. Isḥaq 4 |

61. TS Box K 15.15[30]

On this bifolio from the same scribe's notebook, in col. IV, line 4, the number 23 was written, representing the subtotal of the allocations from the top of that column; then it was crossed out when additions were postscripted ("added to . . ."), amounting to eight more loaves. Hence the new total of thirty-one in line 8. The postscript seems to be a revision to allocations registered above in the same list. The new names are not found in the Rūm clusters but the five named persons (the sixth is the daughter of one of them) occur together on other pages, e.g., no. 64 below, facing columns II and I.

After the revised subtotal come the Rūm as a group. Another revision at the bottom of col. IV takes into account the addition of 13 loaves to the allocation for the Rūm: 89, which permits us to algebraically provide the number 3 for the effaced first entry in the column. The total that follows (500+, the last two digits are effaced) represents the grand total of distributions of bread for the day. The smaller sums (usually 110+; 89 in this case) at the end of many columns represent subtotals. The entries "3 orphans 3" in col. IV, line 10 and "an orphan 1" in col. I, line 10 reflect the fact that children needed and received less than adults.

These tiny details illustrate a general feature of the public charity system. Revisions were constantly made in the light of individual and family needs and in the light of resources (money available in the community budget and amount of bread that could be baked). For example, in this list, col. IV shows an entry for Zaʿfarān—six loaves—and in the opposite column, from another day's distribution, Zaʿfarān—eight loaves. The lists were prepared in advance, and adjustments could be made each time, as in col. IV, lines 4–7, or when people arrived at the pick-up point. In many places on the lists we actually see that numbers of individual allocations have been crossed out on the spot and another number, smaller or larger, substituted (an example in col. IV, line 10 here). Maʿālī in the first line of col. IV was one of the bakers. He received some loaves as part of his compensation, or perhaps the cash equivalent. The item "transport" (*ḥumūla*) in the following line represents the allocation for the porter who delivered the bread to the pick-up point (the load would have been heavy).

[30] Cf. *Med. Soc.*, 2:443, App. B 20.

Two entries seem odd, but they appear to reflect a reality of family life: separated from each other are (1) the producer/seller of fine things and his mother-in-law, and (2) the divorcée of the producer/seller of fine things. The divorcée collected two loaves, hence for herself only, and he collected six, four for himself and presumably his children, and two for his mother-in-law (sometimes the allocation is broken down in separate entries: four for him [and his children] and two for her). We may speculate that the ex-wife was incapable of taking care of any dependents, even her own children.

The foreigners from Malīj and Qalhā represent many such immigrants from provincial towns in Egypt seeking assistance in the capital. The man from the Egyptian port city of Damietta was well enough established to vouch for other newcomers entering the Fustat poor roll.

| **Col. IV** | **Col. I** |
|---|---|
| 1. Solomon the scribe [3] Maʿālī 3 | |
| 2. the neighbor (f.) of the tanner 2 transport 3 | |
| 3. the ac(quaintance) of Abū Kathīr 4 Umm Ibrahim 2 | |
| 4. Aaron 4 the blind man Abū Saʿīd 2 [[23]] | |
| 5. Added to Shamīʿa 1 and to his daughter 1 | |
| 6. and to Maʿlā' 1 loaf and to Umm Hilāla 1 | |
| 7. and to Sabīʿ the blind man 1 and to b. al-Murahhiṭ (the son of the writer/singer of liturgical poetry) 3 | 1. Dispensed for them also |
| 8. The Rūm 31 | 2. on Friday the 21st of that (month) |
| 9. Umm Yūsuf 2 the mother-in-law of Elijah 2 | 3. five qinṭārs, numbering |
| 10. Mordechai [[2]] 3 three orphans 3 | 4. five hundred sixty-seven (loaves) |
| 11. Zaʿfarān 6 Umm ʿAynayn 3 | 5. the cantor al-Quḍāʿī (healer of stomach ailments) 6 the man from Baʿalbek 5 |
| 12. the orphans of the furrier 4 Shemarya 3 | 6. Abū Mukhtār 9 b. al-Kharazī (son of the maker of beads) 2 |

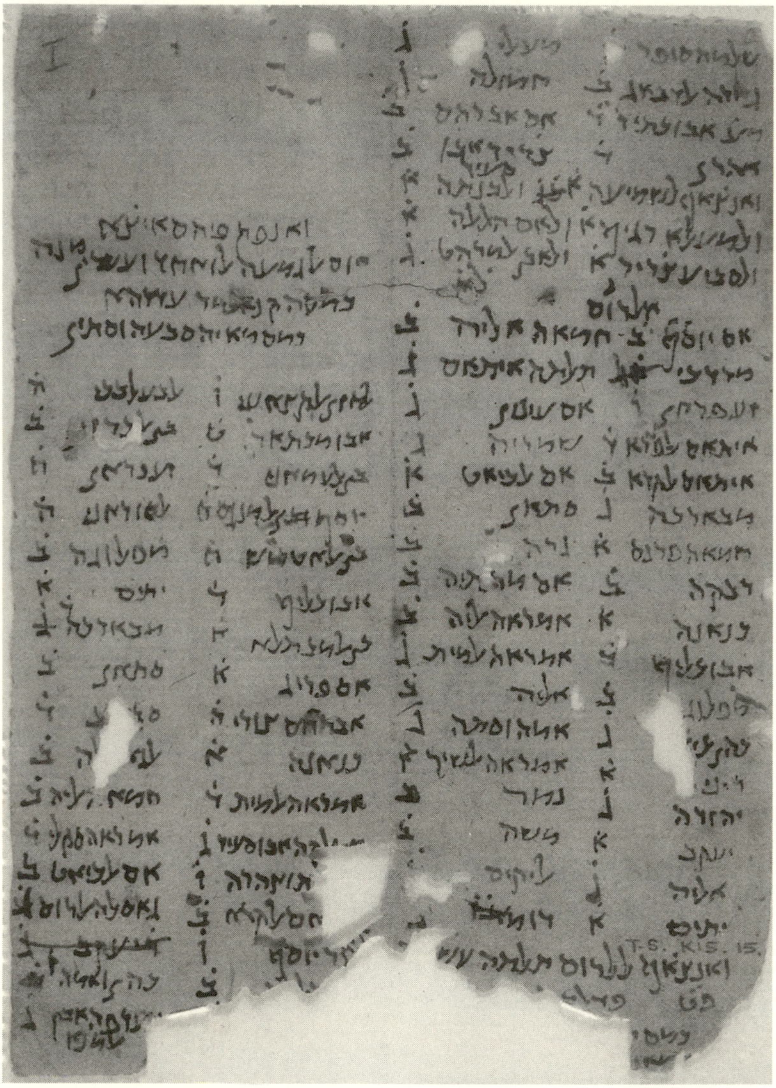


Fig. 3. Page from an alms list, distribution of bread, 1107; (no. 61) TS Box K 15.15

13. the orphans of the Karaite 2 Umm al-Khayyāṭ (mother of the tailor) 1

14. Mubāraka 3 Sittān 2

15. the mother-in-law of the parnas 1 his grandfather 2

16. Rebecca 2 Umm Matatya 2

17. Kināna 1 the wife of Elijah 2

18. Abū Khalīf 4 the wife of the deceased man 3

19. a semiparalyzed man 2 Elijah 2

20. the Kohen the tai[lor] 3 his mother and his grandmother 3

21. Dīnī[31] 1 the wife of the elder 1

22. Judah 3 Namer[32] 2

23. Jacob 1 Moses 2

24. Elijah 3 Eliakim 2

25. an orphan 1 a man from Rūm 2 [[76]]

26. added to the Rūm thirte[en]

27. 89 Thi[s being . . .]

28. five [qinṭārs . . . numbering five]

29. hundre[d] . . . [loaves]

7. the son of al-ʿAmmānī 4 Zaʿfarān 8

8. Joseph [[and]] b. al-Munajjim (the son of the astrologer) 8 al-Sūrānī 5

9. the son of the deaf man 8 the semiparalyzed woman 2

10. Abū Khalīf 4 an orphan 1

11. the son of the afflicted man 1 Mubāraka //4// [[3]]

12. Umm Furayj 1 Sittān 2

13. Abraham of Tyre 5 Sib[ā]gh 4

14. Kināna 1 the female was[h]er of the dead 2

15. the wife of the deceased man 4 the mother-in-law of Elijah 2

16. the [div]orcée of Abū Saʿīd 3 the wife of the man from Sicily 4

17. [. . .]t and his in-law 6 Umm al-Khayyāṭ 2

18. [the or]phans of the Karaite 2 the female washer of the dead for the Rūm 3

19. [. . .] Joseph 6 [[R. Jacob 3]]

20. [. . .]l[. . .] 2 the Kohen and his mother //7// [[. . .]]

21. [. . .] the acquaintance of Abu'l-Munā

[31] I am uncertain about the vocalization of this name.

[32] *Namer* (a biblical animal, probably a leopard) seems to be the Hebrew equivalent of the Greek *pardoleon*. See Jacoby, "What Do We Learn about Byzantine Asia Minor," 86.

Verso

**Col. II**

1. Umm Ibrahim 3 Umm Ẓarīf[a] 3

2. the wife of the man from Qalahā 3 Salāmūn 4

3. Aaron of Jerusalem 2 an orphan 1

4. Nathan 2 Raḥamim 3

5. Ṣāliḥ 4 Ṣadaqa 10

6. the woman from Malīj 2 the wife of the silk worker 4

7. the mother-in-law of Muṭālibī 2 the wife of Elijah 2

8. the wife of Judah 3 the Kohen [. . .] 2

9. the acquaintance of Mu[ṭ]ālibī 2 Umm ʿAynayn 4

10. an orphan 1 Umm Yūsuf 3

11. Eliakim 2 b. Abū Saʿīd 2

12. Samīḥ 4 Wahīb the glassmaker 3

13. Umm Khalīf 3 Judah and his in-law 3

14. Sulaymān [[and his mother-in-law]] 3 Sham[ī]ʿa 6

15. the wife of the tanner 3 her [mother-in]-law 2

**Col. III**

1. 4

2. [[D]] the ac[qu]aintance of Azhar 8 the ac(quaintance) of the man from Damietta 3

3. the daughter of al-Thulayth 2 the sister of Isaac 2

4. the daughter of al-Jady 2 b. Saʿāda 4

5. Joseph the night watchman 4 b. al-Murahhiṭ (the son of the writer/singer of liturgical poetry) and a stricken man 8

6. the house of b. Yiḥye 3 Barakāt the glassmaker 3

7. Samīḥ the Kohen 4 the wife of ʿAwāḍ 4

8. Wahīb 3 the woman from Qalahā 3

9. Umm Ẓarīfa 3 the w(ife of) the seller of fuqqāʿ (honey sherbet) 3

10. Simḥa 3 the son of the afflicted man 1

11. Hilāl 2 the ḥaver son of R. Joseph [. . .]

12. the son of the man from Andalusia 2 the orphans of Joseph 5

13. Salmān 8 the daughter of Ḥasīka 4

14. the house of al-Jāzifīnī 8 Ṣadaqa the beadle 10

15. b. Nafīʿ and his sister 8 the acquaintance of b. Ṭībān 4

| | |
|---|---|
| 16. Solomon the scribe 3 b. Daniel 8 | 16. the producer/seller of fine things and his mother-in-law 6 Isaac and his in-law 4 |
| 17. Elijah 3 Joseph the night watchman 5 | 17. the [. . .] 4 Naʿīm 4 |
| 18. the divorcée of the producer/seller of fine things 2 the man from Malīj 6 | 18. Simon 4 Jacob the dyer 3 |
| 19. Makhlūf the blind man 2 the orphans of Joseph 8 | 19. Abū Khalīfa 6 [N]aḥum 2 |
| 20. the acquaintance of [Az]har 8 the acquaintance of the man from Damietta 6 | 20. b. al-ʿAnānī 4 Umm Kaḥlāʾ 5 |
| 21. the orphans of b. [Yiḥ]ye 3 the dau[gh]ter of al-Thulayth 2 | 21. b. al-Ḥilāl [. . .] |
| 22. the daughter of al-Jady [. . .] the house of b. Saʿāda [. . .] | 22. the wi(fe of) Maʿlāʾ and his in-law 10 and H[. . .]kallām (physician treating wounds) 3 |
| 23. Abū Khalīfa 6 b. al-Murahhiṭ (the son of the writer/singer of liturgical poetry) 8 [. . .] | 23. the female teacher 3 the wi(fe of) Ḥu[rā]ra 3 |
| 24. the errand boy from Andalusia 2 Simḥa [. . .] | 24. the blind woman 5 the son of the orphan woman 4 |
| 25. b. al-Murahhiṭ (the son of the writer/singer of liturgical poetry) 4 the Mu[mḥ]e [. . .] | 25. [. . .] 3 the in-law of Joseph 8[33] |
| 26. Furayj 4 [[3]] and R[. . .] | 26. Makhlūf 2 the supervisor from Tiberias 5 |
| 27. Hilāl 2 Shemarya [. . .] | 27. [U]mm ʿUbayd 3 the wife of the tanner 3 |
| 28. the acquaintance of b. Ṭībā[n] 4 [. . .] | 28. [. . .] 10 Jacob 10 |
| 29. the wife of F[. . .] | 29. [. . .] Abū Hilāl [. . .] |
| | 30. [. . .] |

[33] The number 8 (letter *ḥet*) is not totally clear (one letter seems to have been overwritten by another), but elsewhere in these lists this same Joseph receives two loaves (once), six loaves (twice), and eight loaves (four times).

62. TS Box K 15.39[34]

This page contains the all-important date, which Goitein originally read as Tuesday, 18 Marheshvan (Nov. 5), 1107 (*Med. Soc.*, 2:443) but which I read in Cambridge as 11th of Marheshvan, October 30, 1107. Goitein dates it correctly in *Med. Soc.*, 1:56.

Originally, the baker Maʿālī baked 490 pounds of bread, amounting to 539 loaves, less than on the other days. It was not enough. So ten more pounds (loaves) were added from "old bread," left over from the previous distribution, bread that would have been stale (the hungry will eat even stale bread).

In several places the names of the baker Maʿālī and of another baker, Ṣadaqa, appear, interrupting the list of names of beneficiaries. I take this to mean that the names that follow in the column were assigned to them, respectively. When people came to the pick-up point they collected their rations from one or the other of these bakers. Possibly the list was known to the bakers in advance so they could determine how many loaves they should bake each time.

In the separate section listing the Rūm, the entry for the wife of the deceased man whom we encountered above includes here (only) her late husband's son and her own daughter (from another marriage), four loaves, but most of the time she got three or four loaves, so she was probably always collecting for herself and the two children. Once she got only two, a single adult's semiweekly ration; once (two weeks later than this list, no. 63) the scribe wrote one, a mistake, which he corrected to three.

| **Col. IV** | **Col. I** |
|---|---|
| 1. alef The Rūm | 1. bet |
| 2. Judah 4 Mordechai the blind man 4 | 2. In (your) name, O Merci(ful) |
| 3. the orphans of the Karaite 2 b. Nathan 2 | 3. D[i]s[pensed] for the poor, may God make them rich |
| 4. the mother-in-law of Elijah 4 Zaʿfarān 8 | 4. Tuesday, the 11th of |
| 5. the acquaintance of the dyer 4 the wife of the deceased man 2 | 5. Marheshvan (1)419 (October 30, 1107) |
| 6. Abraham and his brothers 5 Eliakim 2 | 6. four hundred ninety pounds, numbering |
| 7. Khalīf the blind man 5 an orphan 2 | 7. five hundred thirty-nine (loaves) |
| 8. the wife of Elijah 2 the tailor Kohen 4 | 8. from Maʿālī the baker, to which were added ten, |

[34]Cf. *Med. Soc.*, 2:443, App. B 21.

9. and his grandmother and mother 4 the wife of the deceased man and his son and her daughter 4

10. Umm Ḥamd al-ʿAynayn 4 Dīnī 2

11. the wife of the elder 2 Rebecca 4

12. Umm Yūsuf 4 Kināna 2

13. Elijah 4 the female washer of the dead 2

14. an orphan 2 an orphan 2

15. a se[m]iparalyzed woman 2 Sarah 1

16. Shemarya 4 Umm Matatya 2

17. the mother-in-law of the parnas of the Rūm 2 Umm al-Khayyāṭ 2

18. an errand boy 1 a man from Rūm 1

19. Michael 2 Moses 2

20. a woman from Rūm and an orphan 4 the in-law of Joseph 8

21. [[Simḥa the grave digger 4]] [[the son of]] a man from Rūm 1

22. [. . .] 1 a man from Rūm and an orphan 5

23. [[149]]

24. 124

9. making five hundred pounds (loaves), ten being old loa[ves] (margin: ten [[old loaves]] in old loaves, from [. . .])

10. b. Daniel 8 Abū Mukhtār and his son and his sister 9

11. the Kohen of ʿUkbara 6 Mubāraka 5

12. Sittān 3 Umm Furayj 2

13. Ḥasan the glassmaker 4 the mother of the blind man 2

14. Abū Shaykha 2 the Maghrebi woman 2

15. the man from Acre 6 the orphans of the furrier 5

16. Abraham of Tyre 4 the wife of his son 2

17. Shamīʿa 6 [U]mm Ibrahim 4

18. the slave girl of Mukhtār 3 the supervisor of the milk 4

19. Yaʿqūb the night watchman 5 the cantor al-Quḍāʿī (healer of stomach ailments) 6

20. Abū Khalīfa 6 Samīḥ the Kohen 4

21. Wahīb the glassmaker 3 Jacob the blind man 2

22. Sibāʿ 4 Hilāl 2

23. the wife of Abū Saʿīd the blind man 4 Umm Hilāla 2

24. Joseph b. al-Munajjim (the son of the astrologer) 8 Zuhayr 4

25. Hārūn of Jerusalem and his wife 4 Salāma 4

26. the wife of the man from Qalahā 4

27. Umm Ẓarīfa 3 Ṣadaqa the beadle 8

28. b. al-Kharazī (son of the bead maker) 2 Maʿlāʾ 5

29. the man from Malīj 6 163

Verso

**Col. II**

1. the wife of the silk worker 4 the son of the man from Andalusia 2

2. Barakāt the supervisor and his father-in-law 7 Ṣāliḥ 4

3. the orphans of Joseph 8 Umm Ibrahim 2

4. supplied by Ṣadaqa

5. the acquaintance of Azhar 8 the acquaintance of the man from Damietta 8

6. the daughter of al-Thulayth 2 the sister of Isḥaq 2

7. the daughter of al-Jady 2 the orphans of b. Yiḥye 4

8. the wife of b. Saʿāda 4 b. al-Murahhiṭ (the son of the writer/singer of liturgical poetry) 8

9. the man from the Ḥijāz 3 b. Shekhanya 6

10. Maʿālī

11. the wife of ʿAwāḍ 5 the lame man 3

**Col. III**

1. Abū Kathīr Umm Ibrahim

2. Ṣadaqa Ṣadaqa

3. Maʿālī and his porter 5 the supervisor from Tiberias 6

4. the wife of the man from Sicily 4

5. [[amounting to 282]] [[something on it]]
(written on the left side) I put aside the ten old loaves for the Rūm so that the total is two hundred seventy-two

12. the ḥaver R. Solomon 8 the acquaintance of Abu'l-Munā 8

13. the daughter of Ḥasīka 4 the wife of the tanner

14. b. al-Ḥilāl 8 ʿAyyāsh 4

15. Sabīʿ and an orphan and his mother 6 the mother-in-law of al-Muṭālibī 2

16. Ṣadaqa

17. Abū Saʿīd the blind man 4

18. b. Nafīʿ 6 his sister 2

19. Isḥāq and his in-law 6 the glass-maker 3

20. the producer/seller of fine things 4 the acquaintance of b. Ṭībān 4

21. the house of the woman from Palestine (al-Shāmiyya) 3 Yaʿqūb the dyer 4

22. Maʿālī

23. the wife of Maʿla' and her in-law 10 al-Kalāsiyya 3

24. Abū Hilāl 4 the wife of Ḥurāra 3

25. the female teacher 3 the blind woman 6

26. the cantor from Baʿalbek 6 al-Makḥūl 4

27. Naʿīm 4 the wife of the deaf man 8

28. Simon 4 Makhlūf the blind man 2

29. Simḥa the grave digger 4 the son of al-ʿAmmānī 4

30. Ṣadaqa Ṣadaqa

31. the wife of the seller of fuqqāʿ (honey sherbet) 4 Umm Lubuwwa 4?

32. Maʿālī Maʿālī

33. Umm Nasāba 2 the female washer of the dead for Fustat

34. Ṣadaqa Ṣadaqa

63. TS Box K 15.50[35]

Distributions for the following Tuesday, November 12, 1107 (one week after no. 62), comprising 547 loaves weighing five hundred pounds, with about seventy women's names, several repeated, since more than one distribution is accounted for in these bifolios. The list records, separately, both the orphans and the widow (written: wife) of a furrier. This again accords with the halakhic rule that "the court is the father of orphans." They were eligible for alms in their own right, as wards of the court or by extension the community, even if their mothers were still living. Hence they are listed separately.[36] Many foreigners are identifiable by toponymics. Several ill or disabled, several other orphans, several siblings (perhaps also orphans), several entries of people who are vouched for by a local resident ("acquaintance of X"), the female proselyte found on other pages from these lists from 1107, and persons working in various low paid occupations appear. The ḥaver R. Joseph, a scholar, collects rations. Elsewhere in these contemporaty lists we find two other ḥaverim, a sign that scholars also sometimes found themselves on the bread dole; or the bread was a salary supplement.

**Col. II**

1. Also dispensed for them
2. Tuesday the 25th of that (month)
3. five qinṭārs (500 pounds), numbering five hundred
4. forty-seven (loaves)
5. Sabīʿ and an orphan 5 Mukhtār 3
6. Barakāt 3 Saʿadya 3

**Col. III**

1. the Maghrebi woman 2 Elijah 3
2. Abū Khalīf 4 the semiparalyzed woman 2
3. Elijah of Rūm 3 Judah of Rūm 3
4. the son of our master Joseph 8 Furayj the man with tremors 3
5. Hilāl 2 Umm Hilāla 2
6. Umm Rebecca 4 Umm Matatya 2

[35] Cf. *Med. Soc.*, 2:443, App. B 22.

[36] See above no. 58.

7. Shemarya 4 Joseph the night watchman 5

8. Joseph and his brothers 8 the orphans of the furrier 5

9. Samīḥ the Kohen 4 Wahīb 3

10. Dīnī 1 the female washer of the dead for the Rūm 2

11. the wife of the deceased man [[1]] 3 the wife of the elder from Rūm 1

12. Abū Mukhtār 3 and his sister 3

13. Sulaymān the supervisor 3 Shamīʿa 6

14. Umm al-Khayyāṭ 3 the orphans of the Karaite 2

15. the man from Sicily 4 Umm Ibrahim 4

16. Umm Khalaf 3 the acquaintance of the dyer 4

17. Eliakim 2 Ḥasan the glassmaker 4

18. Abraham of Tyre 4 the wife of his son 2

19. Umm ʿAynayn 4 the man from Damsī[s] 3

20. Umm Yūsuf 3 the wife of Bū Saʿīd 5

7. the errand boy from Andalusia 2 the wife of ʿAwāḍ 5

8. [the] man from the Ḥijāz 4 Umm Ẓarīfa 3

9. Salāma 4 [t]he woman from Qalahā 3

10. a woman from Rūm 1 the orphans of Joseph 8

11. b. Shekhanya 6 b. al-Quḍāʿī (the son of the healer of stomach ailments) 6

12. the mother-in-law of Muṭālibī 2 transport of one qinṭār 5

13. Kināna 1 [. . .] 10

14. three orphans from Rūm 4 Abraham and his sister 3

15. b. al-ʿAmmanī 4 b. al-Kharazī (son of the maker of beads) 2

16. the man from Acre 6 the female proselyte (al-gera)[37] [. . .]

17. the mother-in-law of Elijah and an orphan 2 the mother-in-law of the woman from Palestine (al-shāmiyya)

18. the in-law of Namer 2 the acquaintance of Azhar 5

19. the female washer of the dead for Fustat 2 the acquaintance of the man from Damietta 6

20. the sister of Isaac 2 the daughter of al-Thulayth 2

[37] The Hebrew *gera* is not the standard form for female proselyte, which is *giyyoret*, appearing only in postbiblical Hebrew. Gera in the Bible is the cud of an animal (which chews it) or a coin (the twentieth part of a shekel). In a rare instance in a midrash, Ruth the proselyte is called gera (Bereshit Rabba, Vilna ed. 88:7; the passage is not attested in any but one late manuscript of Bereshit Rabba or in any of the later midrashic anthologies that draw material from Bereshit Rabba; see the critical edition *Bereschit Rabba* by J. Theodor and Ch. Albeck, 2nd printing [Jerusalem 1965], 3:1086 in the notes). Possibly there were two different lady converts to Judaism drawing from the poor dole in Fustat at the same time and the scribes employed the odd form to distinguish one from the other.

21. Mubāraka 4 Rayyisa 2

22. Sittān 2 Umm Furayj 2

23. Umm Sālim 3 b. Nathan 2

24. Sibāʿ 4 the Kohen from Rūm 4

25. his mother and grandmother 4 Jacob 1

26. the Kohen 2 Zaʿfarān 8

27. Maʿlāʾ 5 Jacob the blind man 2

28. al-Sūrānī 6 Abū Shaykha 2

29. 165

21. the daughter of al-Jady 2 the house of b. Yiḥye

22. the house of b. Saʿāda 4 b. al-Murahhiṭ (the son of the writer/singer of liturgical poetry) 8

23. Abū Khalīfa 6 the wife of the seller of fuqqāʿ (honey sherbet) 3

24. Ṣāliḥ 4 b. Daniel 8

25. Solomon the scribe 3 the wife of the tanner 4

26. Makhlūf the blind man 2 ʿAyyāsh 4

27. Simḥa the grave digger 4 Naḥum 2

28. b. Nafīʿ and his sister 8 Barakāt 3

29. the acquaintance of b. Ṭibān 4 and the in-law of the supervisor 4

217 [[. . .]]

Verso

**Col. IV**

1. the producer/seller of fine things and his mother-in-law 6 al-Makḥūl 4

2. Naʿīm 4 Jacob the dyer 3

3. the wife of Simon 4 Aaron of Jerusalem 4

4. the in-law of R. Joseph 8 the man from Malīj 6

5. the son of the afflicted man 8 b. al-Ḥilāl 8

6. the cantor from Baʿalbek 6 al-Jāzifīnī 8

7. Salmān 8 the daughter of Ḥasīka 4

**Col. I**

1. (the letter) h (= the number 5?)

2. the man from the Ḥijāz 3 b. Na[f]īʿ and his sister 8

3. Barakāt 3 Isaac and his sister 4

4. the producer/seller of fine things 4 and his mother-in-law 2

5. Jacob the dyer 3 Makḥūl 4

6. Naʿīm 4 Maʿlāʾ [. . .]

7. Kalāsiyya 3 Abū Hilāl 4

8. the wife of Maʿlāʾ [and] her in-law 10

9. Kalāsiyya 3 Abū Hilāl 4

10. the female teacher 3 the wife of Ḥadāda 3

11. the blind woman 5 the wife of b. al-ʿAnānī 4

12. the slave girl of Mukhtār 2 an orphan girl 4

13. Lubuwwa 4 Yaʿqūb 8

14. the wife of the silk worker 5 b. Abuʾl-Ḥayy 8

15. al-Sīlqūnī 8 the acquaintance of Ghālib 3

16. Umm ʿUbayd 4 Umm Kaḥlāʾ 5

17. the divorcée of the producer/seller of fine things 2 b. al-Kāmukhī (the son of the preparer of vinegar sauce and other appetizers) / 3 / [[2]]

18. b. al-Murahhiṭ (the son of the writer/singer of liturgical poetry) 3 [[the cook 2]]

19. transport 1 Maʿlī[38] 3

20. 170

21. five hundred fifty-two

8. Abraham the coo[k] 3 the blind woman 5

9. the female teacher 3 the wife of Hurāra 3

10. the wife of al-ʿAnānī 4 the mother of the orphan girl 4

11. Lubuwwa 3 the house of Simon 4

12. Sabīʿ and the orphan 6 the mother-in-law of Mukhtār 2

13. b. al-Ḥilāl 8 the mother-in-law of the woman from Palestine 3

14. Jacob 8 b. al-Kāmukhī (the son of the preparer of vinegar sauce and other appetizers) 4

15. [t]he preparer of litharge 8 b. Abuʾl-Ḥayy

16. Umm Ibrahim 2 the acquaintance of Ghālib 4

17. Abraham the supervisor 6 Naḥum 2

18. Ḥasan the glassmaker 4 [. . .] 3

19. the guide of the blind man 8 the man from [A]cre 6

20. the ḥaver R. Joseph 8 Salmān 8

21. the daughter of Ḥasīka 4 al-Jāzifīnī 8

22. Rebecca 4 Umm Matatya 2

23. the widow (written: wife) of the furrier 5 ʿAyyāsh 4

[38] This is the baker whose name is spelled elsewhere Maʿālī.

24. Umm Kaḥlā' 5 Maʿālī 3

25. Abū Shaykha 2 the Maghrebi woman 2

26. Umm Sālim 3 transport 2

27. a man from Rūm 1 the wife of the son of the Rav

28. an errand boy from Rūm 4 a man from Rūm 2

29. 233
five hundred sixty-seven loaves

64. TS Box J 1.4[39]

Two lists similar to nos. 60–63, copied by the same scribe and containing mostly the same names. One column is headed Friday, Marheshvan 14, another Tuesday the 18th of the same month. Since no. 62 above has the date Tuesday, 11 Marheshvan, this list must record the following two semiweekly distributions. There is a special section for the Rūm (forty-two persons, almost the same number as in no. 62). Umm Ẓarīfa has her allocation reduced from three to two loaves. Elsewhere in these lists she gets four (twice), three (six times), and two (one other time). One wonders why. But the same question can be posed for many other entries with varied allocations. The parnasim constantly revised rations on the basis of fluctuating family need and available food resources.

This list, as well as others, has an entry for an old woman or man (the Arabic word is *ʿajūz* and it can mean either a man or a woman). Consistent with what we know from documents concerning poverty elsewhere and in other times, old age appears in this community as a typical cause of indigence.[40]

At the end of the list of the Rūm four additional adults are postscripted, collecting a total of eight loaves, and the subtotal is thus revised upward from seventy-nine to eighty-seven.

**Col. II**

1. Also dis[p]ensed for them

2. on Tuesday the 18th

3. of that (month) five qinṭārs (500 pounds)

**Col. I**

1. Also dispensed for them

2. on Friday the 14th

3. of Marheshvan five qinṭārs (500 pounds)

[39] Cf. *Med. Soc.*, 2:443, App. B 23; 1:56–57, and 402n88.
[40] See for comparative purposes, Thomas Sokoll, "Old Age in Poverty."

4. b. Daniel 8 the slave girl of Mukhtār 2

5. the man from Baʿalbek 5 Umm Khalaf 3

6. the female washer of the dead for Fustat 2 b. Shekhanya 6

7. the cantor al-Quḍāʿī (healer of stomach ailments) 6 Sibāʿ 3

8. the wife of the man from Sicily 3 Abū Shaykha 2

9. the Maghrebi woman 2 Maʿlāʾ 3

10. the son of the deaf man 8 the man from Malīj 5

11. the son of Abū Saʿīd and his divorcée[41] 4 Sulaymān 2

12. Shamīʿa 4 b. Nathan 2

13. Ḥasan the glassmaker 3 Barakāt and his father-in-law 5

14. al-Sūrānī 4 Abū Mukhtār 7

15. Furayj 3 [[2]] Umm Hilāla 1

16. Zuhayr 3 the female washer of the dead and her daughter 2

17. the acquaintance of the dyer 4 the son of the ḥaver Menaḥem 3

18. Umm Furayj 1 Abraham of Tyre 3

19. the woman from Malīj 1 Salāma 3

4. the supervisor of milk and his in-law 4 the wife of the man from Sicily 3

5. Aaron and his wife 2 b. al-Kharazī (son of the maker of beads) 1

6. the son of the afflicted man 1 the female washer of the dead for Fustat 1

7. Samīḥ the Kohen 3 Makhlūf the blind man 2

8. the wife of the tanner 2 Abū Saʿīd the blind man 3

9. Sibāʿ 3 Umm Furayj 1

10. the divorcée of Bū Saʿīd 3 Umm Hilāla 1

11. Zuhayr 4 [[3]] Barakāt the supervisor 3

12. the cantor Saʿadya 2 Umm Ibrahim 2

13. Umm Sālim 2 Abraham of Tyre 3

14. Jacob the blind man 2 an orphan from Andalusia 2

15. Umm Khalīf 2 Joseph the night watchman 5

16. Ṣāliḥ 4 Abū Khalīf the blind man 3

17. Abū Khalīfa 4 Furayj the man with tremors 3

18. Barakāt the glassmaker 2 Sulaymān the supervisor 2

19. the man from the Ḥijāz 2 mother of the blind person 2

[41] The son of the divorcée of Abū Saʿīd, who is listed here with his mother, together collect four loaves, whereas she is listed separately on the other list, directly opposite on this bifolio, collecting three loaves, doubtless for herself and the same child.

20. Umm Ibrahim 2 b. [al-ʿA]mmānī [[3]] 5

21. Umm Ẓarīfa 3 [[2]] the [man from A]cre 6

22. Jacob the blind man 2 the m[other-in-la]w of Muṭālibī 2

23. b. al-Murahhiṭ (the son of the writer/singer of liturgical poetry) 2 b. al-Kāmukhī (the son of the preparer of vinegar sauce and other appetizers) 2

24. Joseph and his brothers 8 b. al-Kharazī (the son of the maker of beads) 1

25. Umm Sālim 2 the mother-in-law of the woman from Palestine 3

26. the silk worker 4 [[Aaron from Jerusalem]]

27. Ṣāliḥ 4 the man from the Ḥijāz 3
[[159]] 163

20. the wife of the seller of fuqqāʿ (honey sherbet) 2 the mother-in-law of Muṭālibī 2

21. the wife of the man from Qalahā 3 b. Daniel 6

22. b. al-Munajjim (the son of the astrologer) and his brother 6 the son of al-ʿAmmānī 3

23. al-Jāzifīnī 10 the man from Malīj 5

24. Salmān 6 the daughter of Ḥasīka 3

25. Abū Mukhtār 7 the mother-in-law of Mukhtār 2

26. Hilāl 2 Umm Shamʿa 4

27. the acquaintance of Abu'l-Munā 3 the acquaintance of b. Ṭībān 3

28. the man from Baʿalbek 5 the wife of Maʿlā' 4

29. Umm Ẓarīfa 2 Salāma 3

30. b. al-Ḥilāl 8 the ḥaver R. Solomon 6 165

Verso

**Col. IV**

1. b. [Sh]ekhanya 6 the wife of ʿAwāḍ 5

2. Moses the Kohen 2 the Kohen from Sudan 5

3. the orphans of Joseph 8 the wife of the silk worker 4

**Col. III**

4. Ṣadaqa and transport[42] 11 [[Wahīb]] al-Kalāsiyya 3

5. the acquaintance of Azhar 8 the acquaintance of the man from Damietta 6

6. Ṣadaqa[43] Ṣadaqa

7. the daughter of al-Thulayth 2 the sister of Isaac 2

8. the daughter of al-Jady 2 the house of Saʿāda 4

9. b. al-Murahhiṭ ( the son of the writer/singer of liturgical poetry) and the stricken man 8 b. Yiḥye 4

10. Abū Kathīr 4 Umm Ibrahim 2

11. the divorcée of the producer/seller of fine things 2 the wife of Maʿlāʾ and her in-law 10

12. the wife of Wahīb 3 Abū Hilāl 5

13. the wife of Ḥurāra 3 the blind woman 8

14. the wife of al-ʿAnānī 4 the mother of the orphan girl 4

15. Lubuwwa 4 a woman from Palestine 3

16. the producer/seller of fine things and his mother-in-law 6 b. Nafīʿ and his sister 10

17. b. al-Quḍāʿī (the son of the healer of stomach ailments) 6 Simḥa 4 [[3]]

18. al-Makḥūl 4 Naʿīm 4

19. Ḥasan the glassmaker 3 the deaf man 8

1. The Rūm

2. Elijah 2 an orphan 1 Mubāraka 2 Sittān 2

3. Zaʿfarān 6 Umm al-Khayyāṭ (the mother of the tailor) 1 the female proselyte (al-gera) 2

4. Shemarya 4 the mother-in-law of Elijah 2 the female washer of the dead 2

5. an orphan 1 Mordechai the blind man 3 a semiparalyzed woman 2

6. Jacob 1 Dīnī 2 the orphan of the Karaite [[1]] 2

[42] Ṣadaqa is the baker we have seen above.

[43] His name is at the top of each of the two parallel columns of names on this bifolio.

20. Sabīʿ the blind man 5 the in-law of Joseph 6

21. Simon 4 the man from Acre 6

22. ʿAyyāsh 4 Jacob the blind man 3

23. the wife of the furrier 5 Umm ʿUbayd 3

24. Abraham of Tiberias and his in-law 6 Abū Shaykha 2

25. Maʿālī 3 Umm Kaḥlā'

26. b. Abu'l-Ḥayy 10 Moses the preparer of litharge 10

27. for expenses 10 8

28. 251

7. the son of the Kohen 3 the old woman or man 3 Umm Matatya 2

8. Rebecca 2 Malīḥa 2 Umm ʿAynayn Ḥamd 3

9. the wife of Elijah 2 Elijah 2 Eliakim 1

10. the wife of the deceased man 4 Kināna 1 Umm Yūsuf 2

11. Judah 2 an orphan 1 Moses 1 a scribe 2

12. the mother-in-law of the parnas of the Rūm 2 the female teacher 3

13. an errand boy from Rūm 4 the wife of an elder from Rūm [[79]]

14. four from Rūm 8 87

15. the total: five hundred and three loaves

65. TS Misc. Box 8.25[44]

Another list in the same hand as nos. 60–64. This one is dated Friday the 28th, we may assume of Marheshvan of 1107. The figure of 555 loaves was later corrected to 559. The postscript: "Total dispensed in Marheshvan thirty-six qinṭārs (3,600 pounds) of bread costing eighteen dinars," again reveals the unit cost of 1/5 dirhem per loaf. It also gives us an average figure for each week (presuming the entire four weeks of the month is meant) of 900 loaves, the allocation for 225 adults. If we keep in mind that some of the bread went to children, at about half the weekly adult ration of four loaves, the number of adults on the dole that month might have been less than 200 per week.

Analyzing this list with regard to the women, Goitein came up with the following breakdown of the forty-two women heading households:[45]

women living alone 16
women living with one other person 19
women with more than one person 7

As in some other lists, the names of the bakers Ṣadaqa and Maʿālī appear inserted at various points between lines, indicating that they were to distribute

[44] Cf. *Med. Soc.*, 2:443–44, App. B 24; cf. ibid, 2:76; 3:64–65.
[45] *Med. Soc.*, 3:64.

their loaves to the names following on the list. Ṣadaqa's own allotment of ten loaves and Maʿālī's of five loaves are also recorded, more loaves than the average adult indigent received and doubtless meant as payment or partial payment for their services, not as charity. Perhaps they actually received the cash equivalent. Each five loaves was worth one dirhem.

Several entries record additions to individual allocations, more evidence of the parnasim at work.

The list is signed by the two parnasim ʿUlla b. Joseph ha-Levi and Eli b. Yaḥyā ha-Kohen, who often worked together, and by the scribe, Abraham b. Aaron ha-Mumḥe.

**Col. I**

1. (in Arabic characters, the beginning of a letter)

**Col. II**

1. Also dispensed for them
2. Friday the 28th of that (month)
3. five qinṭārs, numbering f(ive hundred) and 55 (loaves)
4. Ṣāliḥ 4 Shemaʿya 5
5. the silk worker 6 Abū Mukhtār 7
6. the orphans of the astrologer 8 the man from the Ḥijāz 3
7. Shemarya 4 al-ʿAmmānī 3
8. the son of the deaf man 6 the mother-in-law of Elijah and an orphan 2
9. Zaʿfarān 8 al-[. . .] 3
10. Sabīʿ and a blind man 5 Si[tt]ān 3
11. Umm Ibrahim 3 [the wife of] Abraham 2
12. b. al-Kharazī (the son of the maker of beads) 2 the [w]ife of B[ū] Saʿīd 6
13. a semiparalyzed woman 2 Khalīf the blind man 4
14. Umm Hilāla 2 Isaac and his in-law 6

15. the in-law of R. Joseph 8 [[al]] Judah 3

16. the acquaintance of the dyer 3 the man from Malīj 6

17. Umm Khalīf 3 the mother-in-law of the son of the woman from Palestine 3

18. the female washer of the dead for the Rūm 2 the cantor and his in-law 6

19. the mother-in-law of the parnas of the Rūm 8 Elijah 2

20. the mother-in-law of al-Muṭālibī 2 Samīḥ the Kohen 4

21. Wahīb 3 the mother-in-law of the elder 2

22. the man from Sicily 4 Sabīʿ 4

23. Eliakim 2 his brother [. . .]

24. Aaron from Jerusalem 4 the Kohen and the brother of his mother and his grandmother 4[46]

25. [[his mother and grandmother 4]] the orphans of Joseph 6

26. Raḥamim 3 Umm al-Khayyāṭ (the mother of the tailor) 3 [[2]]

27. Nathan 2 Jacob [. . .]

28. 86 91

[46] Four loaves for three adults is a substandard ration. In the next line his mother and grandmother are allotted four loaves, the standard adult ration, but the entry is crossed out.

Verso

**Col. III**

1. b. Shekhanya 6 Kināna 1
2. the cantor b. al-Quḍāʿī 6 Maʿlāʾ 4
3. the acquaintance of Azhar 8 the ac(quaintance of) the man from Damietta 6 Ṣadaqa
4. Jacob al-Burj[47] 8 the daughter of al-Thulayth 2
5. the sister of Isaac 2 the daughter of al-Jady 2
6. the house of Saʿāda 4 the house of b. Yiḥye 3
7. b. al-Murahhiṭ (the son of the writer/singer of liturgical poetry) 8 the man from Sudan 6
8. the female washer of the dead 2 b. al-Jāzifīnī [. . .] Maʿālī
9. Simon 4 the son of the man from Andalusia 2
10. the man from Baʿalbek 6 Joseph the night watchman 5
11. Sulaymān 3 Jacob the blind man 3
12. Umm Yūsuf 6 orphans 2
13. the wife of the deceased man 4 Abraham and his sister and her husband 3
14. Solomon the scribe 3 Hilāl 2

**Col. IV**

1. the man from Acre 6 Abū Shaykha 2 Ṣadaqa
2. [the] woman from the [M]aghreb 2 Abu [. . .] 6
3. Simḥa 4 the wife of the furrier 5
4. Ṣadaqa 10 the wife of Maʿlāʾ 10 Ṣadaqa
5. Abū Hilāl 4 Wahīb 3
6. the blind woman 5 the mother of the orphan girl 4
7. Lubuwwa 3 the acquaintance of Ṣāʿid 3
8. the wife of Ḥadāda 3 Ṣadaqa? 4
9. the wife of al-ʿAnānī 4 Umm Matatya 2
10. added: the female washer of the dead for the Rūm 1 Umm Kaḥlāʾ 5 Maʿālī
11. b. al-Murahhiṭ (the son of the writer/singer of liturgical poetry) 4 the wife of the tanner 4
12. b. [. . .] Yūsuf 8 Maʿālī 5
13. a man from [R]ūm 2 added to Umm Hilāla 1
14. added to the sons of the deaf man 2 Umm ʿUbayd 3

[47] I am uncertain about the spelling of this name.

| | |
|---|---|
| 15. Furayj 3 Zuhayr 4 | 15. Jacob 2 [[b. al-Kāmukhī]] |
| 16. the wife of the seller of fuqqāʿ (honey sherbet) 3 Umm Ẓarīfa 3 | 16. Umm ʿAynayn 5 b. al-Kāmukhī (son of the preparer of vinegar sauce and other appetizers) 3 Ṣadaqa |
| 17. the wife of the man from Qalahā 3 Salāma 4 | 17. the acquaintance of Gh[ā]lib 4 Umm Ibrahim 2 |
| 18. an orphan 1 a or[p]han 2 | 18. b. Abu'l-Ḥayy 8 the slave girl of Mukhtār 3 |
| 19. Abraham of Tyre 4 the wife of his brother 2 | 19. the Kohen from Rūm 2 Ḥasan the glassmaker 3 |
| 20. b. Nafīʿ and his sister 8 Barakāt 3 Ṣadaqa | 20. b. al-Ḥilāl 8 a man from Rūm 1 [[41]] |
| 21. the ac(quaintance of) b. Ṭībān 4 the producer/seller of fine things and his mother-in-law 6 | 21. an errand boy from Rūm 4 69 91 |
| 22. al-Makḥūl 4 Naʿīm 4 | 22. five hundred and 59 (loaves) |
| 23. the wife of Jacob 3 Abraham the supervisor and his in-law 6 | 23. The total dispensed in Marheshvan |
| 24. the divorcée of the producer/ seller of fine things 2 Elijah 3 | 24. thirty-six qinṭārs (3,600 pounds) of bread |
| 25. b. Daniel 8 Sulaymān 8 Maʿālī | 25. costing eighteen dinars |
| 26. b. Ḥasīka 4 Makhlūf the blind man 2 | 26. ʿUlla ha-Levi b. Joseph (may his) e(nd be) g(ood) |
| 27. the wife of ʿAwāḍ 5 ʿAyyāsh 4 | 27. Eli Ha-Kohen b. Yaḥyā (may his) s(oul be at) r(est) |
| 28. 119 [1]103 | 28. Abraham b. Aaron the Mumḥe (may his) m(emory be) b(lessed) |

66. TS Box K 15.113[48]

Unlike the preceding lists, this one records a distribution of wheat (1 wayba = about 15 liters), not loaves of bread. Wheat was dispensed to the poor in addition to loaves of bread so they could make their own flour and then dough for baking in a neighborhood oven. This was either a bow to personal taste or

[48] Cf. *Med. Soc.*, 2:444, App. B 26.

a way of providing bread indirectly, at a lower unit cost, to supplement the nutritionally insufficient weekly bread ration. Indeed, several of the names on this list appear above as recipients of bread. Possibly, too, the local bakers could not keep up with the bread needs of the poor.

The list is copied in the same hand as nos. 58 and 59. The recipients are Rūm, altogether 49 households including households consisting of only one person. It is unusual to find a goldsmith on an alms list. The vast majority of goldsmiths were donors, not recipients of charity. The fact that this goldsmith was one of the Rūm newcomers—an immigrant and not yet economically established in Fustat—probably explains this exception to the rule.

1. In the n(ame of the Merciful)
2. List of the Rūm[49] [. . .] and 3/4 wayba[s]
3. the proselyte 3 waybas his slave girl Mubāraka 1/2 wayb(a)
4. Menaḥem 1/2 wayba Ma[ḥ]āsina 1/2 wayba
5. the wife of Abraham the [. . .] [1/]2 wayba [. . .] 1[/]2 [way]ba
6. the wife of the blind man 1/2 wayba Nathan 1/2 wayb[a]
7. Eliakim 1/2 wayba Shemarya 1/2 wayba
8. Umm Matatya 1/2 Shelomit 1/4 wayba
9. [al-]Farisīnī 1/2 wayba the goldsmith 1/2 wayba
10. [. . .] 3/4 wayba Qalīna 3/4 wayba
11. [al-]Qāl.qūrī 3/4 wayba Umm Senior 1/2 wayba
12. Shilḥiyā one wayba Sara 1/2 wayba // and her husband // [[Mūsh]][50] Moses 1/4
13. Judah 1/4 wayba Shemarya 1/2 wayba
14. Judah 3/4 wayba Abū Mīkhā'īl one wayba
15. [. . .] 1/4 the mother of the captive 1/4 wayba
16. [. . .] 1/2 wayba [[Elia]] b. Isrā'īl 1/2 wayba
17. Ni[s]an 1/2 wayba Umm Khūlia 1/2 wayba
18. [[Umm Abu'l-Munā 1/4 wayba]] Judah one wayba
19. Ibrahim 1/4 wayba
20. [Is]aac one wayba Shemarya 1/2 wayba
21. al-[. . .] 1/4 wayba [[Ḥasūna 1/4 wayba]]
22. Moses the lame 1/2 wayba Qarʿa 1/4 wayba
23. [[the Maghrebi elder 1/4 wayba]] Solomon the scribe 1/2 wayba
24. Yaʿqūb of Rūm 1/4 wayba
25. the mother-in-law of Nathan 1/4 wayba the uncle of Nathan 1/4
26. the mother-in-law of Eli[j]ah 1/2 wayba Simon of Rūm 1/4
27. [[Elijah 1/2 wayba]] Elijah 1/2 wayba
28. a dyer from Rūm 1/2 wayba the errand boy of "the Segullat" (a Hebrew title) 1/4

[49] Arabic: *thabat al-rūm*. The fractions are written in Arabic words, e.g., *niṣf* = 1/2.

[50] The scribe evidently began misspelling the name Moshe (= Moses), crossed it out, then added *wa-zawjuhā*, "and her husband," above the deletion.

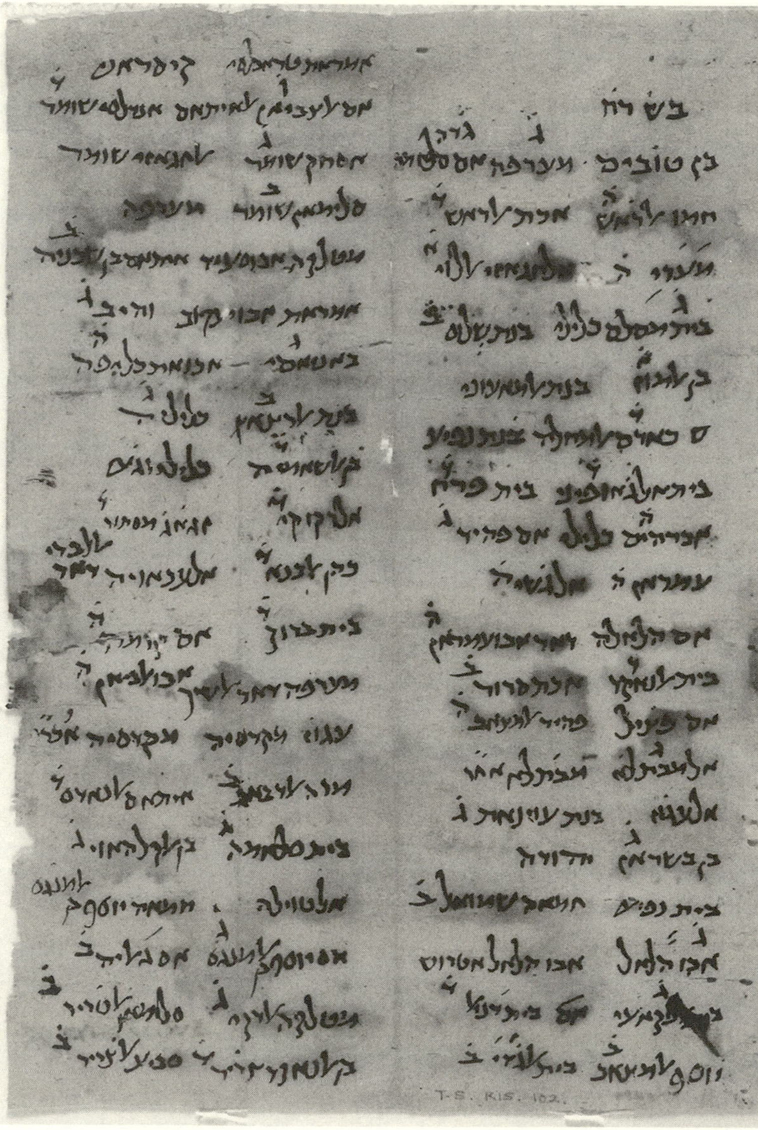

Fig. 4. Page from list of eligible beneficiaries;
(no. 67) TS Box K 15.102

67. 10. TS Box K 15.102[51]

This exceptionally large-sized, calligraphically written alms list dates from the first half of the twelfth century. It was apparently "prepared to form the basis for the allocation of communal assistance" (Goitein). What kind of assistance was meant cannot be determined (cash?), but Goitein suggests that the numbers squeezed in between the lines represent the number of persons in each household (there are about eighty-five households) and that the entries bearing no numbers consist of households with only one person. In most of the alms lists recording the ration of loaves of bread distributed Tuesday and Friday the numbers occur *next to* the names of the recipients. On the reverse side, room was left for the Rūm, but instead, there is a telling note: "The Rūm cannot be counted."

The list is headed by a *ben ṭovim*, a man from a good family, who, Goitein observes, "would not lose face even if personal misfortune deprived him of the material well-being normally enjoyed by respectable families."[52] As we have seen in several letters in part 1, these people experienced shame, like the "shamefaced poor" of medieval and early modern Latin Europe. To counteract embarrassment, this "man from a good family" was listed anonymously, though in first position on the list, a position of prestige, just before the relatives of two other persons of stature. The persons of stature are called "the head," perhaps a government clerk or a physician, so called because they often headed hospital departments.[53]

Later in the list we come upon an unusual entry, the "concealed" glassmaker, *zajjāj mastūr*, nestled among a (poorly paid) parchment maker, a mason (another low-paid wage-earner), and an immigrant woman (a widow, apparently) from Acre who was living in the home of one of the prominent merchants of Fustat, al-Lebdī.[54] This glassmaker, a representative of the "working poor" and ashamed to appear on an alms list, had himself listed (or was listed by the charity overseers) both anonymously and as mastūr, indicating that he normally did not seek charity.

Note should be taken in this list of the many menial occupations, including a teacher, several synagogue beadles, and several kashrut supervisors. Hovering just above the "poverty line," they frequently needed supplementation from the community chest. Plenty of widows and orphans crop up here, as well as a couple of divorcées. Other "weak" persons are the ill or afflicted. The incidence of blindness and eye disease in this and other lists reminds one of the prevalence of poor people with eye disease on the streets of many contemporary Middle Eastern cities.

[51] Cf. *Med. Soc.*, 2:446, App. B 31. Some unrelated writing in Arabic script is found on one side of the verso.

[52] *Med. Soc.*, 1:77 and 409n7.

[53] See Cohen, *Jewish Self-Government*, 167–68.

[54] Parchment makers and masons rank in the underclass in the taxonomy of the poor compiled in Cohen, *Poverty and Charity*, chapter 1.

Several categories of persons are clustered together, for instance, blind, afflicted, supervisor (of kosher food), persons from Jerusalem. This is probably how the notary remembered them when compiling the list.

**Col. I**

1. In (your) n(ame) O Me(rciful)

2. man from a good family someone's aquaintance 3 Umm Salāma 3 4 5[55]

3. the father-in-law of "the head" 5 the sister of "the head" 4

4. Maʿarrī 5 the Levite from the Ḥijāz 1

5. the house of Musallam from Hebron 3 the daughter of Shalom 2

6. b. al-Mawwaz (son of the banana grower or vendor) 1 the daughter of al-Māʿūnī

7. the beadle of al-Maḥalla[56] 4 the daughter of Nafīʿ

8. the house of Jāzifīnī 4 the house of Faraḥ 4

9. Ibrahīm from Hebron 5 Umm Fuhayd 3

10. ʿImrān 5 the man with fainting spells 5

11. Umm Hilāla the house[57] of Abū ʿImrān 5

**Col. II**

1. the wife of the man from Tripoli the man from Caesarea

2. the mother of the orphan errand boys 6 a supervisor from Andalusia 4

3. Isḥaq the supervisor 3 the supervisor from the Ḥijāz

4. Sulaymān the supervisor 2 someone's acquaintance

5. the divorcée of Abū Saʿīd the orphans of b. Shekhanya 2

6. the wife of Abū Yaʿqūb Wahīb 3

7. the man from Bānyās 3 the brothers of Khilāfa 5

8. the daughter of the worker and/or dealer in lead 2 a woman from Hebron 3

9. the son of the woman from Palestine 4 an ailing man from Hebron

10. the parchment maker 4 the "concealed" (i.e., normally not needy) glassmaker 4

11. the Kohen the mason 4 the woman from Acre, living in the courtyard-house of // al-Lebdī //

12. the house of Barukh 4 the mother of his people[58] 5

[55] There is a *gimel*, followed by a *dalet* and a *heh*, perhaps indicating a change in the number (twice).

[56] There is a mark preceding the word "beadle," evidently a false start.

[57] Here, unlike elsewhere in this list, the word for "house" is *dār*.

[58] Arabic: *qawmihi*. I am unsure of the meaning.

12. the house of the money assayer 4 the sister of Surūr 2

13. Umm Fuḍayl Fuhayd the stricken man 5

14. the afflicted person 3 another afflicted person

15. the old woman or man bint ʿAnaynāt 3

16. b. Bishrān 3 Judah

17. the house of Nafīʿ the mother-in-law of Samuel 2

18. Abū Hilāl 3 Abū Hilāl the deaf man

19. b[int al-]fuqqāʿī (the d[aughter of the] seller of fuqqāʿ, (honey sherbet) 3 the mother of the house of Daniel 4

20. Joseph the stricken man 2 the house of al-Jady 2

13. the acquaintance of the house[59] of the elder Abuʾl-Bayān 5

14. an old man or woman from Jerusalem another woman from Jerusalem

15. the wife of the tanner 2 the orphans of the beadle 4

16. the house of Salāma 3 son of the man from Qalahā 3

17. the tall woman the mother-in-law of Joseph b. al-Munajjim (son of the astrologer)

18. Umm Joseph b. al-Munajjim (son of the astrologer) 3 Umm Jāliya 2

19. the divorcée of the producer/ seller of fine things 3 Sulaymān the blind man 2

20. b. al-Nāqid (the son of the money assayer) the blind man 4 Sabīʿ the blind man 2

Verso

1. the sister of Isḥaq the wife of Musāfir

2. Umm Hilāla the orphans of Simḥa 4

3. b. Simḥa 2 the person with ophthalmia

4. Simon 3 a stricken man from Alexandria

5. Abū Saʿīd the teacher 3 Umm Maʿālī

6. b. [. . .] 3 the woman from Aleppo and her children

(Arabic writing upside down)

[59] This instance of "house" seems to mean "wife." See note 29.

The Rūm cannot be counted

the beadles of the synagogues the orphans in the house of the cantor

68. TS Box K 15.48[60]

Also from the first half of the twelfth century, this list (actually two lists, in different handwritings) of recipients of clothing contains half women, many of them called "house" (on this expression, see no. 60) The disproportionate presence of women is not surprising given the mores of society, in which the modesty of women wearing appropriate clothing was highly valued. The *jūkāniyya* is evidently a short robe, worn by both men and women. The *thawb* is a regular robe, covering the whole body. The *muqaddar*, a word not found outside the Geniza in any pertinent meaning, was apparently a type of male clothing of some value (hence the word, "valued"). *Shuqqa*, originally used to designate a textile manufactured in Tunisia, means here the name of a garment.[61]

The repetition of several names indicates that two different collections are recorded here. Column I is headed "third leaf," which suggests that the total number of names originally listed might have been three times as many as the eighty or so counted here (Goitein). The second distribution was in the charge of the parnas Abu'l-Faraj, whereas he is listed as a recipient of an item of clothing himself in the first distribution, and other parnasim also receive clothing. This reminds us of the Qur'ānic zakāt (Sura 9:60) that includes administrators of the poor tax as one of the eight classes of people eligible to receive this form of charity. Over half of the names are accompanied by the Hebrew letter *m*, which Goitein takes to be the abbreviation of *tasallam*, "received." There are many foreigners here, as elsewhere, representing the class of the "foreign poor," on whom see Cohen, *Poverty and Charity*, chapter 2 and above, chapter 3.

Some entries are crossed out, represented here by double square brackets. There are a few words in Arabic characters in some of the lines. I do not know if they are related to the list itself.

[60] Cf. *Med. Soc.*, 2:444, App. B 25; ibid, 1:94 and 414n14; 1:99 and 416n2; 1:108; 1:109 and 421n62; 1:124 and 428n60; 1:128; 2:79; part of column I is translated *Med. Soc.*, 4:155.
[61] On clothing distributions see *Med. Soc.*, 2:130–32, and on *shuqqa* see ibid., 4:409–10n223.

**Col. IV**

1. the wife of the brother

2. of the parnas Hiba a jūkān(iyya) (receive)d

3. the acquaintance of Abu'l-Faraj a jukān(iyya)

4. Rabbi Isaac of Rūm a muqaddar

5. Ibrahīm the parnas a shuqqa (receive)d

6. and through Abu'l-Fa[r]aj

7. the parnas also a jūkān(iyya)

8. the wife of Abū Naṣr

9. the maker of spindles (al-maghāzilī) [. . .]

10. the house of the man from Malīj

11. Abu'l-Faraj a jūkāni(yya) (receive)d

12. Umm Sibāʿ

13. b. Ṣaʿīd a jūkā(niyya)

14. the Kohen the blind man

15. in the house of the man from Mal[ī]j a jukān(iyya) (receive)d

16. a relative of al-Lebdī a jukān(iyya) (receive)d

17. the sister of the wife of

18. Menasse a jūkān(iyya) (receive)d

**Col. I**

1. 3 ("third leaf")

2. Sulaymān the astrologer a jūkān(iyya) (receive)d

3. the boy (servant) of Hoshaʿna a jūkān(iyya) (receive)d

4. [[mother of the fat woman (Umm Shaḥīma) a jūkān(iyya) ]]

5. the wife of ʿImrān of Tripoli a jūkā(niyya)

6. the wife of b. al-Ḥallā' (the son of the jeweler) a jūkā(niyya) (receive)d

7. [[b. al-Baghdādī (the son of the man from Baghdad) a jūkā(niyya)]]

8. the mother-in-law of the Kohen a jūkā(niyya) (receive)d

9. Joseph b. Ḥasan a robe (thawb) (receive)d

10. [[Abu'l-Faraj the parnas a robe]]

11. the maidservant (waṣifa) [[jū]] a jūkāniyya

12. b. al-Munajjima (the son of the female astrologer) a jūkā(niyya)

13. the son of Abū Ghālib the goldsmith a jūkā(niyya)

14. [[the wife of Karīm of Ti[b]erias a jūkā(niyya)]]

15. Abū ʿAlī the blind man a jūkā(niyya)

16. the daughters of Abū Ghālib the goldsmith a jūkā(niyya)

19. the wife

20. of b. Manīdū a jūkān(iyya) (receive)d

21. the wife of b. ʿAfdān a jūkān(iyya)

17. [Y]aḥyā of Banyās in the house of al-ʿIbra[. . .] a jūkā(niyya)

18. the sister of the parnas from Jerusalem a jūkā(niyya) (receive)d

19. the Kohen the blind man in the house of the man from Malīj a jūkā(niyya)

20. a relative of al-Lebdī a jūkāniyya (receive)d

21. [[the acquaintance of Abu'l-Ḥasan b. al-Sharābī (son of the potion preparer/ seller)]] a jūkā(niyya) (receive)d

22. Umm Ḥabīb a jūkā(niyya) (receive)d

23. the sister of the wife of Menasse a jūkā(niyya) (receive)d

24. the wife of b. Manīdū a jūkā(niyya) (receive)d

25. the house of b. Sutayt a jūkā(niyya) (receive)d

26. b. Shimlāṣ a jūkā(niyya) (receive)d

27. the man from al-Maḥalla in [. . .] a jūkā(niyya) (receive)d

28. the house of b. Shekhanya a shuqqa (receive)d

29. [[b. al-Shawīzānī]]

30. the elder, the acquaintance of Kathīr a jūkā(niyya) (receive)d

31. the parnas of Damietta a jūkā(niyya) (receive)d

32. the wife of the man from Haifa a jūkā(niyya) (receive)d

Verso

**Col. II**

1. the wife of Ṣemaḥ the parnas a jūkā(niyya) (receive)d

2. the house of Nuṣayr b. Thābit a jūkā(niyya) (receive)d

3. the son of al-Rifā', the relative of the maker of vinegar sauce and other appetizers a jūkā(niyya) (receive)d

4. Khalūf of Jerba a jūkā(niyya) (receive)d

5. Barakāt RD al-GH (or J)-Ḥ-SH[62] a jūkā(niyya) (receive)d

6. [[the parnas from Crete muqaddar]]

7. [[the Aleppan who is (living) in (the synagogue of) the Iraqis a jūkā(niyya)]]

8. Khalaf of Aleppo a jūkā(niyya) (receive)d

9. [[the proselyte (living) in the synagogue of the Iraqis a jūkā(niyya)]]

10. [[b.]] Nathan the astrologer a jūkā(niyya)

11. Abraham the acquaintance of "The Diadem" a jūkā(niyya)

12. the wife of b. Ḥashīsh a jūkā(niyya)

13. bint al-Baghdādī (the daughter of the man from Baghdad) a jūkā(niyya) (receive)d

14. the wife of al-Nās[63] jūkāniyya (receive)d

**Col. III**

1. Ibrahīm the Maghrebi a jūkān(iyya)

2. the house of ibn al-Qalʿī a jūkān(iyya)

3. the Persian spoon maker (al-malāʿiqī) a jūkān(iyya) (receive)d

4. Mūsā the brother of Menaḥem a jūkān(iyya) (receive)d

5. Qālūs the grave digger a jūkān(iyya) (receive)d

6. the house of ibn al-[Mu]jīr? a jūkān(iyya) (receive)d

7. Umm Fakhīra a jūkān(iyya) (receive)d

8. the house of ʿAzrūn a shuqqa (receive)d

9. the house of Makhlūf

10. who serves "the Diadem" a jūkān(iyya) (receive)d

11. the wife of Ibrahīm

12. the milkman a jūkān(iyya)

13. Umm Dā'ūd ibn al-Muṭālibī a jūkān(iyya) (receive)d

14. Yaḥyā the in-law of the man from Acre a jūkān(iyya) (receive)d

[62] I am uncertain what to make of this name.

[63] Al-Nās means "the people." I am uncertain what this name means.

15. through Abu'l-Faraj the parnas

16. bint Simḥa (the daughter of Simḥa) the semiparalyzed woman a jūkān(iyya)

17. the wife of ibn

18. al-Kharrūbiyya a jūkān(iyya) (receive)d

19. the daughter of ibn al-ʿAni a jūkān(iyya)

20. Umm Ḥasan in the house

21. of Ḥabīsh a jūkān(iyya)

22. the wife of Mufarrij the amputee a jūkān(iyya)

23. the house of ibn Marwān a jūkān(iyya) (receive)d

24. the house of ibn ʿAzīra a jūkān(iyya)

15. Umm Abu'l-Ḥasan

16. in the house of the sugar producer a jūkān(iyya) (receive)d

17. Umm Nujūm a jūkān(iyya) (receive)d

18. the woman from Malīj a jūk[ān](iyya)

19. the wife of Niʿma a jūkān(iyya) (receive)d

69. ENA NS 77.291

Small as it is, this fragment of a list of beneficiaries relates importantly to the administration of public charity in the community. It includes a woman (or two different women), followed by the words "she should be investigated" (*yukshaf ʿanhā*). I believe that this notation, which I have found only here and on one other tiny fragment, which seems to go together with this one,[64] reflects the system for verifying the deservedness of the poor. This system is marked elsewhere (and in the second tiny fragment) by the identification of recipients of alms as "acquaintance of X," where X vouches that the applicant is needy enough to deserve public assistance.

1. [in the synago]gue of the Palestin[i]ans
2. Umm Ibrahim, who lives
3. in the house of the arch of trees and plants[65] and her mother
4. [the wi]fe of Shabbat
5. she [should be investigated]

[64] The other fragment, mentioning two names of men who should be investigated, is ENA NS 77.242.

[65] Dār al-Ḥunduj. For the meaning, see A. de-Biberstein Kazimirski, *Dictionnaire arabe-français* (Paris, 1869), 1:502, which gives another meaning as well: small hill of sand.

Verso

1. [the wif]e of Barakāt
2. she should be investigated
3. Abraham b. Barakāt the [m]aker of spindles
4. the wife of b. Ḥunayn in the house of al-Ghazzāl?[66]
5. Umm Nujaym
6. the Alexa[ndrian][67]

70. TS 6 J 1.12v

List of expenditures on the reverse side of a marriage-match agreement, including for both communal officials (a cantor, two teachers) and needy persons. The former, typically underpaid, hovered close to the poverty line themselves, and monies collected for charity were regularly used for other communal purposes, such as to pay the salaries of communal officials like cantors and teachers. See above no. 39 and below nos. 72 and 73. The man living in the Iraqi synagogue is but one of many who found shelter in a communal building. Others lived in a funduq, an inn.

1. Dispensed from the revenues[68] of Muḥarram
2. "the Beloved" 3
3. b. al-Maṭarī 1 1/2
4. the teacher from Malīj 1 1/2
5. ʿAbd Allāh who (lives) in the (synagogue of the) Iraqis 2
6. Abu'l-Ḥasan ibn Abu'l-Rukub 1 1/2
7. Abū Saʿd the cantor, son of the female teacher 3
8. R. Shemarya the teacher 3
9. [Abū] Naṣr of Malīj, through "the Chosen" 3
10. [. . .] the blind man 2

71. TS Arabic Box 30.67[69]

This list has particular importance because it illustrates that the community was not always able to raise all the cash necessary for immediate needs, and so had to dispense some of its charity via payment orders. Goitein describes: "Two lists in an unusually large cursive script with a postscript in another, small and neat script. *a*) The superscription 'I[n Your] N[ame]' shows that this is the first list. It is followed by: 'Those who have not yet received their share'

[66] Pronunciation uncertain. Written *al-gh-z-l*. An al-Ghazzāl appears in the Geniza documents. See Moshe Gil, *Documents of the Jewish Pious Foundations from the Cairo Geniza* (Leiden, 1976), Index p. 551.

[67] Or: the Alex[andrians].

[68] Arabic: *mustakhraj*.

[69] Cf. *Med. Soc.*, 2:456–57, App. B 65 (1100–40).

(and are receiving it now, as is proved by the second list [*b*]." The second list is headed "'Expended on . . .' (illegible, perhaps referring to the holiday concerned) . . . The numerals in the postscript are Coptic but conform with the Hebrew numerals in the main list, as far as preserved . . ." Goitein surmises that the document records "a distribution of money, probably before a holiday, in a time of severe hardship, when the community had not enough means, and about fifty families had to wait for their shares. Even then about one-third received their allocations in orders of payments—and we do not know how much the ruqaʿ*i* charged for converting them into cash."

The document comes from the first half of the twelfth century. Many names are deleted by overlining, probably indicating they had received their allowance. The most interesting entry is that of "Muʾammala the 'concealed' (mastūra) widow who has never, ever taken anything." Like the *zajjāj mastūr* in no. 67, she was normally self-sufficient, taking care of herself, without need for charity.

1. I(n Your) n(ame)

2. Those who have not received their share

3. [[Maʿlāʾ]] 10 the producer/seller of fine things 5

4. [bint al-Thulayth (the daughter of al-Thulayth)]] 3

5. [[the aunt of Ṣadaqa]] 3

6. [[Samīḥ]] 4

7. Jonah and his brother 6

8. [[Lubuwwa]] 3 [[the stricken one]] 2

9. [[b. al-Murahhiṭ (the son of the writer/singer of liturgical poetry)]] 10

10. [[b. Jarmān]] 5

11. [[b. Faraḥ and his sister]] 5

12–13. [[b. al-Abār]] 2 the glassmakers from Tyre 8 [[Malika]] 1

1. [[al-Makḥūl]] 5 [[b. Nuṣay[r]]] [. . .]

2. [[the decorator]] 3 [[the woman from the Maghreb]] 2

3. Umm Mikhāʾīl 5

4. [[bint Mukhtār (the da[u]ghter of Mukhtār)]] 3

5. [[U[mm I]sḥaq]] 3

6. b. al-[M]BWSH 5 [[the lame woman]] 5

7. [[[the dau]ghter of "[t]he [s]py"]] 5

8. [[the w[ater carrier] from Baghdad]] 4

9. Quṭayṭ 4 the afflicted one 7

10. Umm Jāliya 4

44[70]

[70] This Coptic number does not equal the computed total in the column above it.

14. [[the mother of the errand boys]] 4

15. [[the wife of the deaf man]] 6

Verso

1. Expended

2. on [. . .]

3. [the] elder [. . .]

4. [[a Euro[pe]an (living) in the synagogue]] 2

5. [[the children of the wif[e of . . .]]

6. five

7. [.]b[. . .]

8. [. . .]

9. [[[the] orphan via a payment order (*ruqʿa*)]]

10. [[my master]] 6 [[Ḥasūna]] 2

11. [[a scribe from Rūm]] 2

12. [[the female agent]] 2

13. [[a poor (lit. "weak") errand boy who arrived]] in

14. the evening and whose overcoat was taken from him

15. as collateral for 5 dir(hems);

16. his name is Abu'l-Munā

17. and he is sick [[Maʿālī 4]]

1. an acquaintance of the parnas

2. [[b. Sabarā]] 4

3. Maʿālī the porter in Cairo

4. Yaʿqūb the Maghrebi four dir(hems) five

5. Mu'ammala, a widow

6. "[c]oncealed"[71] (i.e., normally self-sufficient) who has never, ever

7. taken anything 5

8. the elder from Jerusalem 10

9. the brother of b. ʿAlī ten dir(hems)

10. b. Yaḥyā 2 (+) ten dirh(ems)

11. the female beadle of the Palestinian synagogue and her mother four dir(hems)

12. [[Farāḥ]] 6

13. Also through orders of payment

14. Jacob the Maghrebi 5 Mu'ammala 5

15. [. . .] 2 the man from J[eru]salem 10

16. Umm Shalom 4 [the b]r[other] of b. ʿAlī [10]

17. [. . .] orphan 6 [b. Ya]ḥyā 12

[71] Arabic: *[m]astūra.*

18. Ḥasūna 2 [the female] beadle of the Palestinian synagogue [4]

19. a scribe 2

20. the female agent 2

21. the poor errand boy 5

22. b. Sabarā 4

23. Maʿālī 4

72. ENA 2727.54[72]

This is an account of receipts and disbursements, one of many of its type from the first decades of the thirteenth century written by the court clerk, elementary school teacher, and cantor Solomon b. Elijah the judge (see also no. 76).[73] It nicely illustrates the porous boundary between charity and other payments. The disbursements in these accounts include salaries for communal servants (called *rusūm*) as well as a global figure for bread for the poor (*khubz*) and alms for needy private individuals. Here the needy include a wayfarer with his traveling companion, who are given some money to travel to their next destination. One of the expenses is for transporting the bread (*ḥumūla*) to the central pick-up point, presumed to be the synagogue. We have seen this also in the alms lists.

The word *mezonot* (line 9) is an old rabbinic term, literally "maintenance" (the root of the word means "to feed"), that is, maintenance for wives, children, orphans, widows, wives with absentee husbands, laborers, and work animals. In the Geniza it encompasses a seemingly new and wider range of distributions, from food for the poor to contributions toward the salaries of the generally poorly paid communal officials, such as cantors, teachers of poor children, and kosher meat inspectors. Here the word designates revenues to be used for several of those purposes.[74] The association in this account and in others like it (see no. 73) of seemingly disparate categories of expenditure, collectively termed mezonot, shows that charity and payment of communal officials were closely linked in Jewish thinking of the time. In this regard, it resembles Islamic waqfs that include scholars and other "servants" of the community, along with the poor, among their beneficiaries.[75]

[72] Cf. *Med. Soc.*, 2:462, App. B 82.

[73] Cf. *Med. Soc.*, 2:93–94 and 542n3.

[74] Further discussion of this term in Cohen, *Poverty and Charity*, chapter 8.

[75] The letter TS 8 J 17.27, a petition complaining about transfer of proceeds from a charitable collection to another communal need (apparently, salary for a cantor), obliquely reflects this practice of the Jewish community of Fustat. See further discussion in nos. 39 and 70 above and in Cohen, *Poverty and Charity*, chapter 8. On the broadened compass of the Islamic waqf with reference to the Ottoman soup kitchen, see Amy Singer, *Constructing Ottoman Beneficence: An Imperial Soup Kitchen in Jerusalem* (Albany, 2002).

The communal officials appearing here, as they do in other such lists, as recipients of payments include a cantor named Yedutun. Under his full name—Yedutun ha-Levi Abu'l-Ḥasan b. Abū Sahl, the cantor of the synagogue of the Palestinians—he wrote a letter of appeal, which we have. He was suffering from hunger from one Sabbath to the next, he says there.[76] Instead of the usual seven dirhems he receives in similar ledgers, which Goitein thinks represents his weekly salary, a "pittance" for a man with a family, here he gets only one.[77] The dirhem must be a balance owed him from the previous week. R. Jephthah, who also appears in the other accounts, was a judge. The "beadles of the synagogues" listed here (Arabic, *khādim*; Hebrew, *shamash*) are given their names in the other accounts: Abu'l-Ṭāhir, Abu'l-Maḥāsin, and Abu'l-Faraj. With two rabbanite synagogues in the community, at least two beadles needed to be in service at any given time. The third might be the beadle of the Karaite congregation. The ritual "cleaner," the *munaqqī*, a specialist who removed the sciatic nerve from an animal to make it kosher, is named Joseph elsewhere. Who the "master and teacher" might be I do not know, but he was evidently a scholar. Goitein seems to think he is the judge Elijah, the father of Solomon, the clerk who copied the document.[78] Algebraically, his salary, which is effaced, computes to be six. One very small expenditure is for copper, perhaps needed to make a repair in the synagogue or in one of the houses or other buildings maintained by the community as pious foundations.

The heading "The Fast" means that the twenty-nine dirhems were collected on a fast day in the synagogue. Usually the heading contains the weekly Torah portion in the liturgical cycle (see no. 73), designating the specific week in which the collection was made. The collection recorded here may have been extra.

1. The Fast 29
2–3. Expended: bread and transport 11 3/4
4–5. Bu'l-Majd 4 his (maternal) uncle Joseph M[. . .] 1
6–7. Yūsuf ben ʿAwāḍ and his traveling companion[79] for travel 2 1/6[80]
8. balance: 9 3/4[81]
9. mezonot 39
10–11. Total 48 3/4
12–13. bread 17 3/4 R. Yedutun 1 R. Jephthah 6 1/2
14–15. the ritual cleaner 6 beadles of the synagogue 6 ritual cleaners 3

[76] TS NS J 323, cf. *Med. Soc.*, 5:89; Goitein writes "b. Abu' l-Faraj."
[77] *Med. Soc.*, 5:89.
[78] "Fragment mentioning (the local) judge Elijah and his elder son Abu Zikri." *Med. Soc.*, 2:462. It is not clear to me why he says Abū Zikrī, who was another son of the judge, a physician.
[79] Arabic: *rafīq*.
[80] 2 plus 1/2 (the Coptic fraction) minus "one third" (*thulth*).
[81] Mathematically this should be ten, but their sums were not always exact.

16–17. (our) ma(ster) and t(eacher) [6] copper 1/2
18–19. balance 2

73. TS Box K 15.25[82]

An account of weekly income and expenditures from December 1241, supervised by the "collector of the mezonot." The first item of expenditure here, as usual, is for bread for the poor, one hundred pounds making one hundred loaves. Per loaf, the cost was considerably higher than the five loaves per dirhem seen elsewhere. The other disbursements are for salaries of a beadle, a kashrut supervisor, a teacher, and a nasi, one of those ubiquitous descendants of the royal house of King David who circulated in the Arab world and received assistance from communities and individuals. Some of the people mentioned without title might simply be poor persons.

1. (Week of) Torah portion "Then (Jacob) went up (to him)" (Genesis 44:18–47:31) 1553 (December 1241)
2. Collector of the mezonot: the precious elder (our) ma(ster)
3. Muḥarraz (may his) e(nd be) g(ood). Collected: 52 dirh(ems)
4. Expended: Cost of a qinṭār of bread
5. 31 1/4 dirh(ems). Balance:
6. 21 dirhem(s).[83] Expended:
7. for the Nasi [5] Nissim 3
8. Joseph the supervisor 3 the elder Hiba the beadle
9. 3 the teacher // Nethanel // 2 the Kohen 2 Munajjā 3

[82] Cf. *Med. Soc.*, 2:453, App. B 50.
[83] The figure is rounded off.

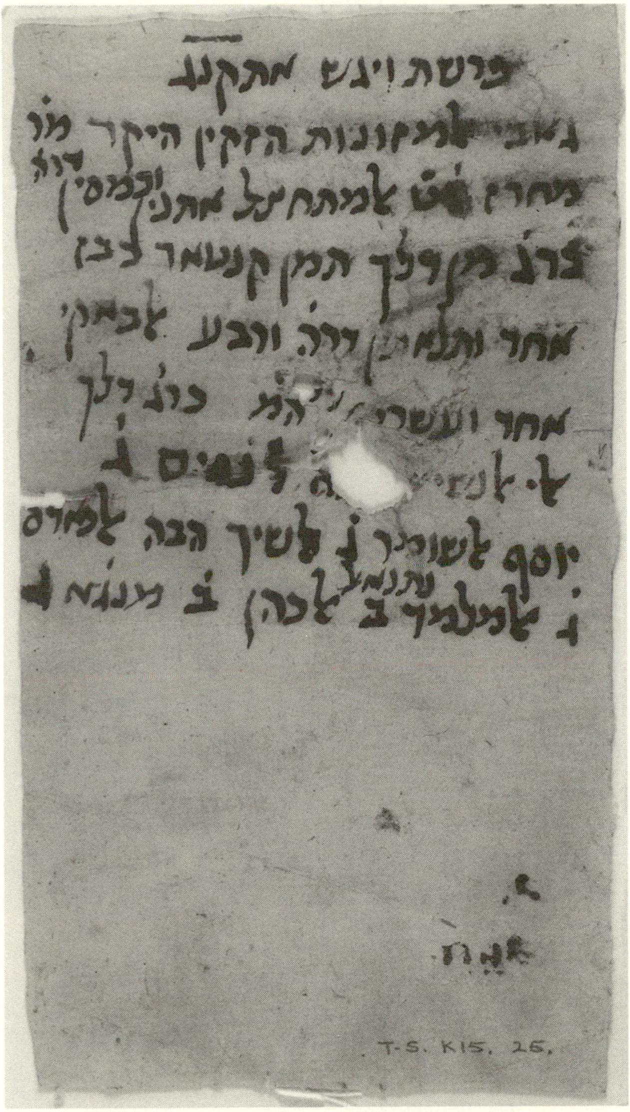


Fig. 5. Account of weekly expenditures;
(no. 73) TS Box K 15.25

# Chapter Nine

## DONOR LISTS

74. TS Box K 15.60v[74]

Dating from the first part of the thirteenth century, this is a typical record of collections (Arabic: *jibāya*) for public charity. Like accounts of income and distribution (see no. 73), it gives the name of the collector and the week according to the liturgical cycle (the Torah portion). Twenty-seven contributors give a total of 36 1/2 (waraq dirhems). Collections were normally based on pledges. A huge list of 127 individual, household, and business pledges including eleven of the names found on this register shows that some people gave exactly what they pledged there, while others gave more.[2] Goitein attributes this to the general scarcity of fractional coins (quarter dirhems). Actual payments, Goitein explains, were made once for several weeks. The list of names was made out beforehand and the sums were entered when the pledges were collected. The word "Thursday" is inserted between lines 18 and 19, indicating, Goitein surmises, that the collector R. Baruch completed his collection in the synagogue on that day, a weekday when the Torah was read and more men came to the synagogue than usual.

Donations by businesses, that is, Jews in partnership, were common. Pledges would be gathered by the parnasim in the marketplace, whether from partners or from individuals at their place of work, as was done in antiquity, according to stories in the Talmud.

As elsewhere in the donor lists, this one includes people of economic means: bankers, gold/silversmiths, people in the food trades (people always have to buy food), persons working in the clothing trades (people always have to be clothed), and persons in medically related professions. There are also members of the social and religious elite (for example, the "elders" in the list and those who themselves or whose relative held a prestigious title). We imagine that the two sons of captives on the list felt particularly charitable in light of the help the community must have given their parents. In subsequent lists we shall encounter others who belonged to the "nonpoor" contributing to public charity.[3] A legal document concerning a "collector" is translated below (no. 85).

[1] Cf. *Med. Soc.*, 2:490–91, App. C 49.

[2] Bodl. MS Heb. c 28.47, ed. Ashtor, *Zion* 7 (1942), 140–45; cf. *Med. Soc.*, 2:488–90, App. C 46.

[3] See the discussion of the taxonomy of the poor and the nonpoor above, 107–9, and in Cohen, *Poverty and Charity*, chapter 1.

1. Collection by R. Baruch, w(eek of) "In the Beginning" (Genesis 1:1)[4]
2. R. Joseph and his partner in waraq 5
3. the Elder Mufaḍḍal the goldsmith (or silversmith) in waraq 1
4. the Elder Abū Isḥaq of Palestine in waraq 1
5. al-Thiqa Hiba, street of the greengrocers 1
6. al-Rashīd Abu'l-Faḍl b. al-Ahuv (son of "the Beloved [of the Yeshiva]") 1/2
7. Joseph the cook 1/2
8. Bu'l-ʿIzz the dyer 1/2
9. Joseph the gold/silversmith Khiḍābi (seller of dyestuff) 1/4
10. [Bu]'l-Faraj the Kohen 1/2
11. Bishr the dyer 1
12. Abū Saʿd son of the captive 1
13. b. al-Ribāṭ 1/2
14. Bu'l-ʿIzz father of the Rayyis 1/2
15. the Elder Abu'l-Maʿālī b. al-Dayyān (the son of the judge), (may his) m(emory be) b(lessed) 2
16. Abū Naṣr the son of Karam the banker 1 2
17. the ḥaver Abu'l-ʿAlā' the banker 9
18. al-Levi b. al-Makīn the druggist 1/2 Thursday
19. Bu'l-ʿAlā', in the Great Market 1/2
20. the Kohen Muʿammar 1/2
21. Mufaḍḍal, in the Great Market 1
22. Makārim the oculist 1 1/8 and some copper coins 1/4
23. Abu'l-Ḥasan the greengroce[r] [. . .]
24. the son of [. . .] 1/2
25. Abu'l-Faraj the son of al-Raṣuy ("Desired [by the Yeshiva]") 1
26. al-Makīn Mufaḍḍal the sugar maker/seller 3
27. Bū Manṣūr son of the captive 1/2
28. Bū Shabīb 1 1/2

36 1/2

75. ENA 2727.22[5]

This collection is in kind, not cash, namely, bread for the poor, ranging from one hundred pounds (loaves) down to one half a pound. One person gives cash instead (three dirhems, which would normally buy about fifteen loaves). Goitein tentatively places the list in Alexandria rather than Fustat, and dates it about 1230. He speculates that this is an inventory of loaves contributed to the breadbasket (quppa), the talmudic "institution" mentioned only in connection with Alexandria (the quppa is not mentioned for Fustat), and that it was submitted to the Nagid (Abraham Maimonides) while he was investi-

[4] Usually in September.
[5] Cf. *Med. Soc.*, 2:491–92, App. C 53.

gating a complaint about the quppa administrator's handling of bread distributions around that time.[6] Abū Zikrī in the first line, taken to be the son of the Alexandrian judge and physician Elijah, was involved in that complaint, as were others recorded in this list.

Not surprisingly, we find many "Elders" and people with titles as contributors.

| | |
|---|---|
| 1. my master the Elder Abū Zik[rī] | 1. b. Az[ha]r 1/4 qinṭār (25 pounds) |
| 2. one half qinṭār (50 pounds) of bread | 2. my master "the Generous" a qinṭār |
| 3. R. Yesh[u]ʿa 10 p[o]unds | 3. my master "the Tre[as]ure" 5 pounds |
| 4. the Elder Abuʾ-F[ara]j [. . .] | 4. my master the ḥaver 1/2 Abuʾl-Faḍ[l] |
| 5. Yaʿqūb 1/2 Munajjā 1 [. . .] | 5. Ba[r]hūn 5 [. . .] |
| 6. and his brother 1/2 Ibrahīm b. al-Mawāzīnī (son of the maker of scales) 1/2 | 6. [. . .] a qinṭār [. . .] |
| 7. my mast[er t]he Elder Abū Saʿd 4 dir(hems) | 7. [. . .] our lord [. . .] qinta[r . . .] |
| 8. Sa[sso]n 10 the teacher [. . .] 1/2 | 8. 1/4 qinṭār |
| 9. b. Mardūk 1 b. al-Ḥazzan (the son of the cantor) 1/2 the Kohen Ṣadaqa 1 | |
| 10. my uncle 3 pounds | |
| 11. Musallam 1/2 two sons 1 Maḥfūẓ 1/2 | |
| 12. the [oi]l-makers 1 the Elder Abū ʿAlī 2 | |
| 13. the Karaite 1/2 the Elder Ab[ū . . .] RB 1 | |
| 14. R. Yeshuʿa [t]he [. . .] 10 the Elde[r] | |
| 15. Abuʾ-[. . .] 1/2 the Elder | |
| 16. [t]he [Elder . . . from the M]aghreb | |
| 17. [. . . A]braham 1 | |

[6] For an explanation, see Cohen, *Poverty and Charity*, chapter 8.

76. TS NS J 76v[7]

A record of pledges collected. This list also logs names of donors who had not yet made good on their pledges. The heading is "Still owed by the people." The bottom of the list is torn away. The handwriting is that of Solomon b. Elijah, from whom we have many administrative documents dealing with communal funds and expenditures (see no. 72), and many persons are known from contemporary documents, making it datable to circa 1220. The other side contains a list of expenditures on clothing for communal officials.

Note, again, the generally high economic status of the givers. The fraction 1/2 is a symbol, found commonly in the Geniza, that looks like the right half of an *alef*, the Hebrew letter designating the number 1. On the right-hand page (below rendered on the left) the numbers are inscribed underneath the names; hence I have combined line numbers.

| | |
|---|---|
| 1. Still owed by the people.[8] | 1. Bu'l-Fakhr the Kohen b. al-Makīn the banker 2 |
| 2. Arrears of [Abu]'l-Riḍā ʿAlī al-As[ʿa]d 1/8 | 2. al-Rashīd Levi the lute player 3 |
| 3–4. b. al-Naḥḥāl arrears 5 Bu'l-Khayr b. Mun[ajj]ā [. . .] | 3. Levi b. al-Bahā the maker/seller of sugar 3 |
| 5–6. al-Asʿad the physician 1 b. al-Siqillī Q'YRY[9] 5 | 4. Joseph the sugar cook[10] 2 |
| 7–8. Hiba b. Dā'ūd and his brother 2 Bu'l-Fakhr [. . .]ānī 1 | 5. Asad b. al-Naḥḥās [. . .] |
| 9–10. Ibrahīm the money assayer 2 Tamīm b. M[ūsā] 1/2 | 6. Ibn al-Ribāṭ [. . .] 1 |
| 11–12. Sulaymān b. al-Ṣanīʿa[11] 1/2 Bū Khalaf the silk weaver 1 | 7. Bu'l-Baqā b. Naʿaman Bu'l-Faḍl and his partner |
| 13–14. Bayān b. al-Kohen R. Ṭuvia 1/2 Mufaḍḍal the gold/silversmith 1 | 8. Bu'l-Majd b. al-[. . .] 5 |
| 15–16. b. Nājī Bu'l-Khayr 1/2 Bu'l-Faraj the purveyor 1 | 9. Bū [Man]ṣūr b. al-Nushādirī (son of the dealer in sal ammoniac) 1 |

[7] Cf. *Med. Soc.*, 2:499, App. C 87.

[8] Arabic: *al-bāqī ʿind al-nās*.

[9] I am uncertain what to make of this name.

[10] Arabic: *ṭabbākh al-sukkar*, as opposed to *sukkarī* in the previous entry, which is much more common and also ambiguous.

[11] The Arabic word means "client," short for "Trusted Client," a title attached to people in government circles; *Med. Soc.*, 5:81

17–18. Naḥum the seller 1/2 (or 1)[12]
[B]u'l-Ḥasan the physician 1

19–20. Abū ʿImrān the son of the brother of the judge (may his) m(emory be) b(lessed) 1

21–22. Hiba the saffron miller 1
Ḥasūn the saff[ron] miller 1/2 (or 1)

23. Maḥāsin the brother of MN[. . .]

24. LY[. . .]

10. [and] his brother Abu'l-ʿAlā' 1

11. and his younger brother 1

12. Bu'l-ʿAlā' b. Daniel 1

13. Bayān Levi b. al-[. . .] 1

14. Jose[ph the s]ilk weaver 1

15. Maʿānī the money assayer 2

16. Sālim b. [. . .]l the silk weaver 1

17. Joseph the silk [worker. . .]z 1

18. [. . .]

77. TS 8 J 17.18[13]

Chapter 4 in this book features letters regarding ransom of captives. Here is an account of contributions toward the same charitable cause by ten Egyptian provincial towns in the countryside (Rīf). Together with two notables listed separately, they contributed the hefty sum of 225 3/8 dinars. Like ad hoc pledge drives for individual indigents, it is called a pesiqa.

The copyist of this calligraphic document (of four pages), who was also one of the two persons in charge of the collection, was the "distinguished" member of the academy Abu'l-Surūr b. Ṭarīf. We know that he lived in a small town, which would explain why he was entrusted with the collection in the Rīf. The time is during the administration of Samuel Nagid b. Ḥananya as head of the Jews (1140–59). Of the ten towns or villages, six were visited by the famous traveler Benjamin of Tudela, who passed through Egypt around 1168. Five of these were middle-sized communities (three had two hundred and two had five hundred Jewish inhabitants according to Benjamin). These are the kinds of communities that could be expected to contribute more than trifling amounts.[14] Of

[12] The paper is torn where the left side of the letter (making it an *alef*) might have appeared.

[13] Ed. Mann, *Jews*, 2:289–90; translated Starr, *Jews in Byzantine Empire*, 220–21; *Med. Soc.*, 2:481 App. C 29.

[14] Benjamin of Tudela, *The Itinerary*, ed. and trans. Marcus Nathan Adler (London, 1907), 66, 69 (Hebrew), 74, 77 (English). On community sizes, see *Med. Soc.*, 2:43–51. Jews are known to have lived in about ninety towns and villages in Islamic Egypt when Benjamin of Tudela passed through. Norman Golb, "The Topography of the Jews of Medieval Egypt: Inductive Studies Based Primarily upon Documents from the Cairo Geniza, *Journal of Near Eastern Studies* 24 (1965), 251–70; 33 (1974), 116–49.

course, when ransom of captives was necessary, agents were sent even to the smaller villages. A couple of these also appear on the list.

Worthy of note, some of the pledge money—ninety-three dinars—was collected by the captives themselves ("collected by the *captives* as per his request, with the letter of *his excellency the Nagid, may his rule continue forever*"). This practice is known from letters. The community paid the captors in cash as soon as possible in order to release their unfortunate brethren and then expected the captives, in gratitude (and they *were* grateful!), to help collect pledges to repay their redeemers. Here the captives were armed also with a letter of recommendation from the nagid. A small amount of money was transferred to Fustat to the head of the Jews and paid directly to captives from Rūm.

Page 1 recto
Account of what was collected from the pledge drive for the *captives, may God release them*, in the Rīf.

Page 1 verso
*In (your) name, O Merc(iful)*

Amount collected from the Rīf in the pledge drive for the *captives, may God release them*, that was ordered by *his excellency, honor, greatness, holiness, the wreath, the glory, our master and teacher, our lord Sa[m]uel the Great Nagid, Chief of the Dignitaries, Nagid of the Nagids, Master of Masters, Right-hand of the Government, Diadem of the Nesiut, may his glory be exalted and his greatness increase*, whose collection was in the charge of his servant Abu'l-Surūr b. Ṭarīf, *(who) r(ests in) E(den)*, and the elder Abu'l-Maʿālī, *(his) ho(nor) o(ur) ma(ster) and te(acher) Samuel the precious elder, son of o(ur) te(acher) Judah the honored elder, (who) r(ests in) E(den)*

in gold and waraq (silver coins) at the exchange rate of 40 dirhems to the dinar—225
3/8 dinars.

| | |
|---|---|
| 24. Itemization: al-Maḥalla | 40 1/4 dinars |
| 25. Minyat Ziftā | 37 dinars |

Page 2 recto

| | |
|---|---|
| 1. Sambuṭiya | 26 dinars |
| 2. Damsīs | 12 dinars |
| 3. Sammanūd | 11 dinars |
| 4. Malīj | 28 dinars |
| 5. Damīra | 14 dinars |
| 6. Tinnīs | 3 dinars |
| 7. the Elder Abū Saʿd | |

| | | |
|---|---|---|
| 8. and the Elder Abu'l-Maʿālī | | 20 dinars |
| 9. Benhā al-ʿAsl | | 14 1/8 dinars |
| 10. Damietta | | 20 dinars |
| 11–12. | Total: | 225 3/8 dinars |

Transferred by the Elder Abu'l-Maʿālī to Fustat to the trust of the Elder Abū Saʿd—37 dinars—(page 2 verso) and also from him what he and his partner the elder Abū Saʿd, *(may the) Mer(ciful) wa(tch over him)*, were in charge of, to the elder Abu'l-Munā

in gold coin—20 dinars

Collected by the *captives* as per his request, with the letter of *his excellency the Nagid, may his rule continue forever*

in gold coin—93 dinars

Remaining with the Elder Abū Manṣūr "The Designate" in Damietta, *(may the) Mer(ciful) wa(tch over him)*

in gold coin—20 dinars

Transferred by Abu'l-Surūr b. Ṭarīf, *(who) r(ests in) E(den)*, to the trust of the Elder Abū Saʿd—55 dinars.

Transferred by Muʿammar, "*The Treasure of his Community*," to the seat of our lord, *may he live forever*, paid to the *captives* from Rūm, in waraq valued at 45 dirhems (per dinar): one dinar and 1/8.

Grand total—226 1/8 dinars.[15]

78. TS Box K 15.61[16]

This list of sixty-seven contributors is headed by "our lord, may his glory be enhanced," namely, the nagid Abraham Maimonides (d. 1237). A second accounting, headed by abbreviation *sh* = *sheni*, "second," contains thirteen names mentioned before who made additional contributions. The figures are given in Coptic numerals and fractions.

As on other donor lists, we note the preponderance of people of economic means and from the social elite (many with Arabic titles indicating their connection with government circles; most explicit is Abu'l-Ḥasan the kātib). The clustering of people with the same profession (e.g., druggists, brokers, physicians, etc.) indicates that the collections were made in the marketplace, where stores were typically concentrated according to category. This, too, explains the entries for businesses (a store; partners).

[15] When the sums were transferred, slightly more money was counted than in the itemization of the collection.

[16] Cf. *Med. Soc.*, 2:486–87, App. C 40; 1:83–84; 1:427n40.

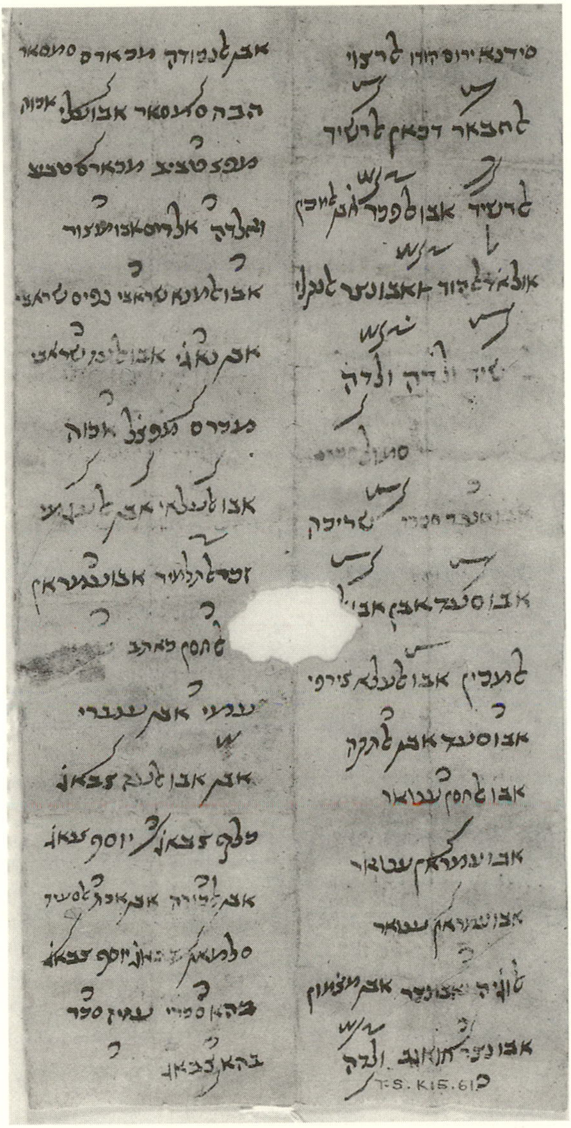

Fig. 6. Page from list of donors; (no. 78) TS Box K 15.61

1–2. Our lord, *may his glory be exalted* 3 1/2 al-Raṣuy 3 1/2

1–2. Ibn al-Nakhūda (son of the ship owner) 1/2 Makārim the broker[17] 1/2

3–4. the ḥabbār[18] 1 1/2 store[19] of al-Rashīd 2 1/2 and 1/4

3–4. Hiba the broker 1 Abū ʿAlī his brother 1/2

5–6. al-Rashīd 10 Abu'l-Fakhr ibn al-Makīn 2 1/2 and 1/4

5–6. Mufaḍḍ(al) the physician 1 Makārim the physician 1

7–8. the children of "the Hod" 3 1/2 Abū Naṣr the seller of dried fruit[20] 2 1/2 and 1/4

7–8. his father 1 the Rayyis Abū Manṣūr 1

9–10. [al-R]ashīd    his son    his son 1/2

9–10. Abu'l-Munā the potion preparer/seller 1 Nafīs the potion preparer/seller 1

11–12. [. . .] 1 Samawwal [. . .] 3 1/2

11–12. Ibn Nājī 1/2 Abu'l-ʿIzz the potion preparer/seller 1

13–14. Abu Saʿd the sugar maker/ seller 3 1/2 his partner 3 1/2

13–14. Mukarram 1/2 Mufaḍḍal 1/2 his brother 1/2

15–16. Abū Saʿd ibn Abu'l-[. . .] 3

15–16. Abu'l-ʿAlāʾ 1/4 Ibn al-ʿAjamī 1

17–18. al-Makīn 1 Abu'l-ʿAlāʾ the banker 1

17–18. Zikrī the scholar 1 Abū ʿImrān 1

19–20. Abū Saʿd ibn al-Thiqa 1

19–20. [Abu]'l-Ḥasan the kātib 1 [[. . .]]

21–22. Abu'l-Ḥasan the druggist 1/2

21–22. my uncle 2 Ibn ʿAnbarī 1/2

23–24. Abū ʿImrān the druggist 1/2

23–24. Ibn Abu'l-ʿIzz the dyer 1 1/2

25–26. Abū ʿImrān the druggist 1

25–26. Khalaf the dyer 1 Joseph the dyer 1

27–28. al-Wajīh and Abū Naṣr 1 1/2 Ibn Maḍmūn 2 1/2 and 1/4

27–28. Ibn al-Būra[21] 1/2 the son of the sister of al-Saʿīd 1/2

29–30. Abū Naṣr Ḥawājib 1 his son 1/2

29–30. Salmān the dyer 1 Joseph the dyer 1

---

[17] Arabic: *simsār*.

[18] Unusually, the Arabic form of the common Hebrew title *haver*.

[19] Arabic: *dukkān*. Means that the money came from the donor's place of business. In the next line we have his personal contribution, which was much greater than that from "the store."

[20] Arabic: *al-nuqalī*.

[21] I am uncertain about this name.

31–32. Bahā the sugar maker/seller 1
ʿAzī[z] the sugar maker/seller 1

33–34. Bahā the dyer 1/2

Verso, left-hand page only
1–2. al-Saʿīd 10 Abū ʿImran the druggist 1

3–4. Abu'l-Majd the broker 1
al-Sadīd 1/2

5–6. Makīn ibn Munajjā 1 Abu'l-Faḍl 1/2

7–8. Abu'l-ʿIzz the physician 1 1/4 and 1/6 Hiba the potion preparer/seller 1

9–10. Abū Manṣūr 1/2 the son of al-Sadīd and his partner 2 1/2 and 1/4

11–12. Abū Saʿd ibn al-[. . .] 2 1/2 and 1/4

13. S(econd, i.e., list of gifts)

14–15. al-Raṣuy the b(anker) 4[22] the dyer 1/2

16–17. Hiba 1/2 Abu'l-Khayr 1/2

18–19. Abu'l-ʿIzz 1 Mufaḍḍal 1/2 his brother 1/2

20–21. Muʿammar 1/2 Abu'l-ʿImrān 1

22–23. Abū ʿImrān 1/2 Abu'l-Ḥasan 1/2

24–25. Abū Saʿd 1/2 the store of al-Rashīd 2 1/2 and 1/4

(Margin: figure not clear, perhaps a total)

[22] Here he donates half more than above, where, Goitein notes, his contribution could not exceed that of the nagid, who immediately preceded him.

79. ENA 2591.6[23]

We have seen in the letters[24] that the poll tax constituted a heavy burden for the poor or nearly poor and that, in addition to private charity, the community collected money to subsidize their annual poll tax debt. There are lists of beneficiaries indicating what the recipients' share should be, the rest being made up by public charity. The "Collection for the Poll Tax" below is a donor list, as proved by the economic and social status of the persons. It gives the sums each contributed toward the poll-tax subsidy for the poor. The total, Goitein notes, was less than the poll tax for one man, so he suggests these are installments on larger, or more frequent, pledges.

The symbol I have rendered 1/3 is represented by a "v" on its side with a dot in the middle and another on top. The text also has a fraction represented by a "v" on its side without a dot in the middle, representing 1/2. The common Coptic S-shaped slash for 1/2 is also used.

1. Collection for the poll tax,[25] w(eek of) "This is the story of Is(aac)" (Genesis 25:19) (the sixth weekly reading of the Jewish liturgical year, usually in November).

| | |
|---|---|
| 2. Abu'l-Fakhr[26] Levi the druggist one waraq | 2. the sons of the dealer in odoriferous wood [[1]] nuqra // 1 1/2 waraq //[27] |
| 3. his son Abu'l-Faḍl 1/2 and 1/3 waraq | 3. Fakhr al-Dawla Kohen 1 |
| 4. the sons of the dealer in odoriferous wood 1/2 and 1/3 | 4. the ḥaver Abu'l-ʿAlā' 1/2 |
| 5. Abū ʿImrān Levi the druggist | 5. al-Rashīd Abu'l-Faḍl 1/2 |
| 6. Abū ʿImran Kohen the druggist 1/3 | 6. al-[Sa]dīd Abū Naṣr ʿAlī 1/2 |
| 7. [al]-Mevin b. Munajjā the banker 1/3 | 7. [[Bū Manṣūr b.]] Ṣafī 1/2 |
| 8. [al-Sa]dīd Abū Naṣr his neighbor 1 | 8. Shabīb 1/2 |
| 9. al-Makīn b. al-Nafīs *(who) r(ests in) E(den)* 1 | 9. the sons of Nafīʿ 1 |
| 10. Abu'l-Ḥasan the money assayer 1/2 and 1/3 | 10. the sons of al-Lebdī 1 |

[23] Cf. *Med. Soc.*, 2:505, App. C 128.
[24] Chapter 5 above. See also Cohen, *Poverty and Charity*, chapter 4.
[25] Arabic: *jibāyat al-jawālī.*
[26] The name is written as if in the genitive, Abi'l-Fakhr, reflecting the conflation of the nominative and genitive cases in the spoken Arabic of the time.
[27] The pure silver nuqra dirhem was worth about three times as much as the waraq dirhem, so it seems that the contribution here was halved and written above the line, in place of one nuqra.

11. R. Samuel son of the judge (*may his) m(emory be) b(lessed)* 1/2 and 1/3

12. al-[. . .] b. Nājī 1

13. Abū Manṣūr b. Nafīʿ 1/3

14. Abū ʿAlī b. Karam 1

15. Bū Manṣūr the distributor of seeds 1/2 and 1/3

16. Bu'l-ʿIzz the oculist 1

17. Abū Manṣūr son of the captive 1/2 and 1/3
18. the Kohen b. al-Najīb the banker 1/4
19. al-Thiqa Hiba, street of the greengrocers 1/3
20. Bu'l-ʿAlā' and his partner 1/3
21. Mufaḍḍal the gold/silversmith and his son 1
22. Yaʿqūb the seller [of food stuff] 1/4
23. 3 1/2
24. Friday
25. b. al-Najī[b] the herald[29] 1
26. al-Raṣu[y] b. al-Kohen 1

11. al-M[. . .] Samawwal 1/2

12. Walī al-Dawla 1

13. Bishr from RSTYH[28] 1/2

14. paid one waraq

15. Sulaymān the dyer 1/2

16. [. . .]

17. al-T[. . .] 1

Recto

1. Manṣūr [. . .] 1/3 waraq

2. ʿAzīz 1 1/2

3. Abu'l-Manāshir Abu'l-HDHB[30] [. . .]

4. Abū ʿImrān b. al-[. . .]

5. his brother Ab[ū] S[urūr] 1/2

6. Ibrahīm [. . .] 1/3

7. Maḥfūẓ b. al-[. . .] 1/3

8. Abū ʿAlī b. Baqā [. . .]

1. Bū'l-ʿIzz the dyer

2. Abu'l-[ʿAl]ā' the [ba]nker 1/3

3. [. . .].n the banker

4. Abū'l–Majd Kohen 1/3

5. Abū] Saʿīd 1/3

6. [. . .]

7. [. . .]

8. [. . .] 1/3

[28] I am uncertain about the vocalization or identification of this place-name.
[29] Hebrew: *al-mashmīʿa*. Goitein speculates that this functionary might have been a person who announced pledges publicly in the synagogue. *Med. Soc.*, 2:87.
[30] I am uncertain about the vocalization of this name.

9. Abu'l-Faḍl Kohen b. al-[. . .] 1/3

10. al-Thiqa Hiba Ḥamām the banker 1/3

11. his neighbor Baqā 1/3

12. Abu'l-ʿIzz his neighbor 1/3

13. Abu'l-ʿAlā' Levi the druggist 1/3

14. Abu'l-Faḍl 1/3

15. Mufaḍḍal [. . .] 1/3

16. [his] son 1/4

17. Joseph the dyer 1/3

18. the Kohen Muʿammar 1/3

19. b. al-Qūṣī (the son of the man from Qūṣ) 1/3

20. Makārim the oculist 1/3

21. al-Sadīd Bū Naṣr the money assayer 1/3

22. al-Thiqa al-Raḥbī 1/3

23. Abu'l-Fakhr Levi the banker 1/3

24. al-Rashīd the money assayer 1/3

25. Nafīs the potion maker/seller 1/3

26. Sulaymān b. Bū ʿAlī 1/3

27. [. . .] his brother [. . .]

9. al-M[. . .] Tamīm 1/3

10. (undecipherable name in Arabic letters) 1/3

(Left side, written diagonally, beginning opposite line 16) expenditure in the hand of Hiba // the beadle // —8. Collected at the store of the banker // Bū Saʿd // from his loan—2 1/2. b. al-Taʿhīʿ Bu'l-Ḥasan the price of sugar—1 [. . .] the [d]ruggist—1

80. TS Box K 15.58[31]

The main text here is a list of donors, relatively late, from the fourteenth century, as is indicated by the appearance of the ḥ[aver], the nagid Mūsā, as a donor. He was the eldest son of the nagid Abraham II b. David b. Abraham I Maimonides and was born in November 1290. Twenty-six people pledge gifts from

[31] Cf. *Med. Soc.*, 2:495, App. C 67.

five to sixty (dirhems, again using Coptic numerals). What is particularly interesting is that ten donors remain anonymous, designated *mattan*, from the beginning of the biblical verse, "a gift (*mattan*) in secret averts anger" (Prov. 21:14), meaning the anger of God. Taking seriously the praise for anonymous giving in Jewish tradition, these Jews asked that their names be excluded from the donor lists, which were sometimes tacked up on the wall of the synagogue.

Anonymous giving was surely practiced and highly valued in the earlier period, and suppliants often quoted the verse from Proverbs in letters of appeal to exhort would-be benefactors—whom they did not know or who did not know them—to give. But the specific emphasis on mattan as a category is found so far on no list from the earlier period. It is tempting to think that this apparent innovation, evident from the fourteenth century, had something to do with the influence of Maimonides, who died in 1204 and who described the relative worthiness of different modes of charitable giving at the end of his laws of charity in the Mishneh Torah. Second on the "ladder" to providing the needy with a gift, a job, or a loan, Maimonides praised anonymous charity, which could be double (neither party knowing the other—most highly praised by Maimonides) or one-sided.[32]

The other side of the page, written in a different hand, contains entries of donations made over three consecutive weeks (the first week is incomplete), and again in yet a third hand, notes on pledges during a later week. Here, too, a number of pledges are anonymous.

Notice that a couple of items are pledges for other than direct charity, namely, for nails and for wood. These are doubtless for the upkeep of the synagogue, a meritorious benefaction akin to charity.

1. the E(lder) Faraj Allāh al-Kharazī (the maker of beads) 5 1/2

2. anonymous gift 7 1/2

3. Ibrahīm known as the YTWN[33] 14

4. anonymous gift 25

5. the ḥ(aver) Fakhr al-Kāfī 2

6. the Kohen Yaʿqūb i(bn) ʿAnnāb 9

7. the ḥ(aver) ʿAfīf al-Nushādirī (the dealer in sal ammoniac) 19

8. [Ab]ū Yūsuf his father 9 1/2

[32] See Cohen, *Poverty and Charity*, chapter 8.

[33] I am uncertain about the vocalization or meaning of this word. The possibility that it is a spelling mistake for *ha-yatom*, "the orphan," does not seem likely.

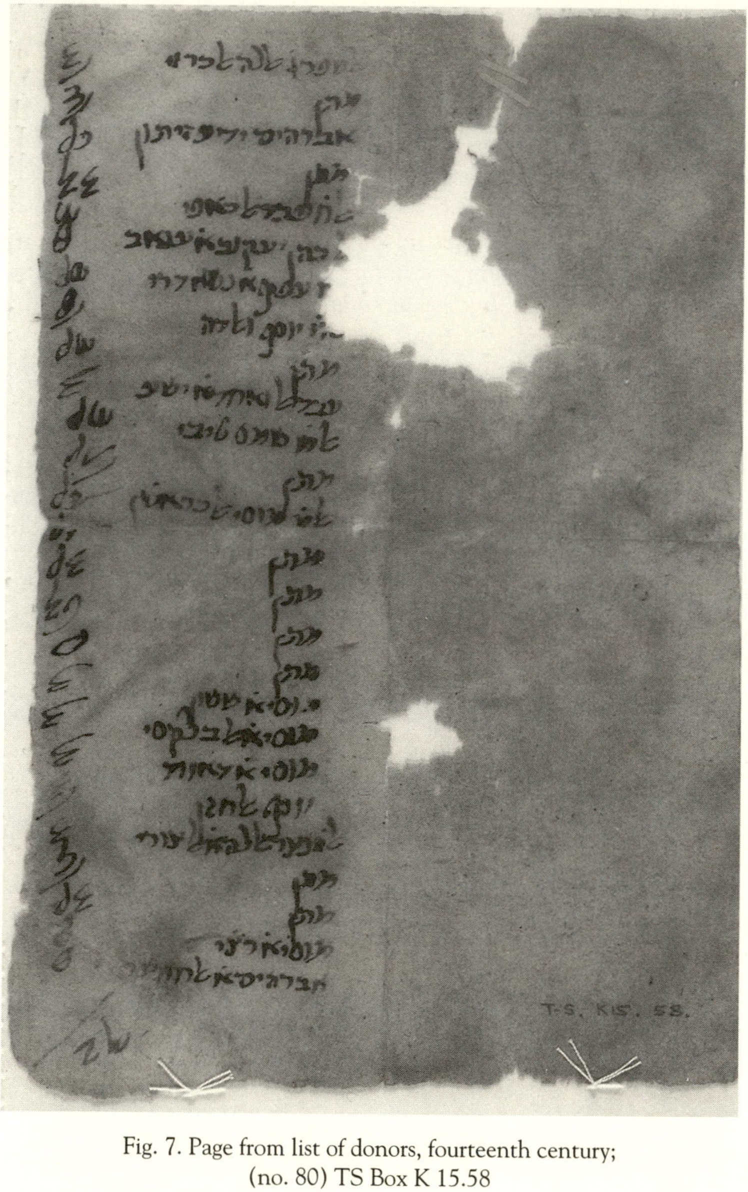

Fig. 7. Page from list of donors, fourteenth century;
(no. 80) TS Box K 15.58

9. anonymous gift 12

10. ʿAbd al-Wāḥid i(bn) Yeshaʿ 6

11. the ḥ(aver) Shams Ṭībī 12

12. anonymous gift 13 1/2

13. the E(lder) Mūsā, (street of) the turners

14. anonymous gift 13

15. anonymous gift 15

16. anonymous gift 24

17. anonymous gift 70

18. Mūsā i(bn) Sasson 6

19. Mūsā i(bn) al-Balaqsī 6

20. Mūsā i(bn) Dā'ūd 6

21. Joseph the cantor 5 1/2

22. the ḥ(aver) Naṣr Allāh i(bn) al-Ṣūrī 5

23. anonymous gift 8 1/2

24. anonymous gift 15

25. Mūsā i(bn) Riḍā 10

26. Ibrahīm i(bn) al-Ḥāshir (son of the tax-payment rallier) 9
27. 320

Verso

1. Joseph Abū Nāshī 5

2. Yehoshuʿa 7 1/2

3. Ibrahīm Muskā 7 1/2

4. anonymous gift 10

5. anonymous gift 7

6. anonymous gift 39

1. 530 1/2 225 1/2 389?

2. [. . .]9 378 1/2 508

3. [. . .] 330 1/2 320

7. anonymous gift 30

8. Week of "(The Lord spoke to Moses) on Mt. (Sinai)" and "(If you follow) my laws" (Leviticus 25–27)

9. the ḥ(aver) Mūsā the Nagid[34] 44

10. Ibrahīm Ḥ(or DH)RH[35] 15

11. anonymous gift 12

12. anonymous gift 12

13. ʿAfīf al-Nushādirī (the dealer in sal ammoniac)

14. anonymous gift 15

15. Yaʿqūb b. Ṭabbākh (son of the cook) the preparer/seller of potions 10

16. anonymous gift 7 1/2

17. [Hi]ba b. [. . .] 8

18. Ibrahīm [. . .] 20

19. ʿAbd al-Wāḥid the seller of chickens (Dajājī) 8

20. Ibrahim the maker of towels (Munāshifī) 20

21. Week of ". . . in the wilderness (of Sinai)" (Numbers 1:1)

22. anonymous gift 8

23. anonymous gift 10

24. Dāʾūd the fishmonger (Sammāk) 13

25. ʿAbdūn Sharaf al-Dunyā 5 1/2

26. Riḍā 4 1/2

4. [. . .] 1/2 6302?

5. Week of ". . . Send men (to scout)" (Numbers 13:2)

6–7. Hibat Allāh 5 1/2 and Hiba the man from the Rīf 11 anonymous gift 23

8–9. the cost of assaying money? 20 1/2 a man from the Rīf 15 Mūsā 24 S[. . .] 4

[34] See in the Introduction.
[35] I am uncertain about this word.

27. the cost of some nails 20

28. the cost of clean (unpainted?) wood 45

29. anonymous gift 7 1/2

30. Menaḥem the seller of chickens (Dajājī) 7 1/2

31. 274 1/2?

margin: ʿAbd al-. . .

(Additional numbers on opposite page)

81. TS Box K15.16[36]

As in the Islamic surroundings, holidays and other festivities were occasions for giving (and expecting) charity. This document lists pledges made at a wedding. In the first line, the name of the bridegroom appears in larger letters than those of the others. Verso contains random names and scribblings, which I have omitted in the translation.

1. the Elder the scholar Abu'l-Bahā the bridegroom pledged[37] // 1/2 dirhem //
2. the Elder Abu'l-Fakhr the scholar the banker 1/2 dirhem
3. the Elder al-Rashīd the scho[lar] al-ʿŪdī 1/2 dirhem
4. the most illustrious Elder the sch[olar Abu]'l-Faḍl the druggist 1/2 dirhem
5. the Elder the scholar the [. . .] 1/2 dirhem

82. TS NS J 404[38]

Written in the hand of Solomon b. Elijah (beginning of the thirteenth century), the author of many administrative documents dealing with communal funds and expenditures (see nos. 72 and 76), this list of sums promised or paid, ranging from 1/8 to 6 1/2, mostly in fractions, probably represents school fees for needy children (Goitein). Note that a few of the sums are revised by deletions and/or additions above the line. Others are simply crossed out, meaning apparently that they had been paid in full. The list gives the appearance of having initially been prepared on the basis of sums pledged or expected, then adjusted to conform with actuality (changed pledges or pledges paid).

On verso, the same scribe noted prices obtained for four books, e.g., thirty dirhems plus two dirhems broker's fee for a copy of Maimonides' *Guide of the Perplexed*.

[36] *Med. Soc.*, 2:495, App. C 65.
[37] Arabic: *asmā*, lit., "put his name" (on the donor list).
[38] Cf. *Med. Soc.*, 2:495, App. C 66.

1. the Elder Abu'l-Munā b. ʿImrān (*may his) R(ock) pr(otect him)* [[eight]] // six //[39] 1/2
2. Abu'l-Ḥasan the preparer/seller of potions three dirhems
3. the Elder Abū Isḥaq the preparer/seller of potions 1 1/2 dirhems
4. the Elder Abraham the teacher from al-Maḥallā 1 3/4 dirhems
5. the Kohen Abu'l-Faraj the clothier six [[less 1/4]]
6. the father, (*may God) make his honor permanent* [[2 dirhems exactly]]
7. the tailor Faḍl (Al)lāh[40] [[1 dirhem exactly]]
8. the seller of chickens Faḍl (Al)lāh [[1 1/2 dirhems]]
9. another Faḍl (Al)lāh 1/2 dirhem
10. Abū Naṣr b. al-Dajājī (son of the seller of chickens) 3/8
11. Manṣūr b. Bishār [[1/4]] 1/8 dirhem
12. Yaʿqūb the seller (of food stuff) 3/8
13. Mufaḍḍal in the Great Market [[3/4]]
14. total
15. 26
16. paid up on Friday
17. Munā the seller of chickens [. . .]

(Torn off)

83. TS Box K 15.64[41]

List of around sixty "houses" (*bayt*) and of eight male individuals, each followed by Coptic numerals. As Goitein observes, the appearance of the entry "the house of the Rayyis, the house of our lord R. Abraham," namely, the head of Jews Abraham Maimonides (d. 1237), proves that this is a donor list, not an alms list. Goitein speculates that this might be "[a] collection arranged by women to which also a few gentlemen contributed." I think, however, that "house" here means, not "wife," but "household." Once in the list a wife *is* mentioned explicitly, but by the term imra'a (col. II, line 17), and *bayt* can only mean "household" in the entry "the *bayt* of ʿAziza," a woman's name (col. III, line 12). Many entries are crossed out, meaning these people had paid their pledges.

**Col. IV**

1–2. [[the house of Rashīd ibn al-Dajājī]] 1/4

**Col. I**

1–3. [[the house of Dā'ūd the son of]] the daughter of my uncle 1/4 [[the house of Abu'l-Faraj

[39] Usually, whole numbers are given in Hebrew letters, but here and elsewhere in this account some of the numbers are given as Arabic words, here *sitta* for six.

[40] The word *allāh* in the popular, compound, theophoric name is truncated, reflecting the elided pronunciation, not an abbreviation meant to avoid writing out the divine name.

[41] Cf. *Med. Soc.*, 2:493, App. C 57; cf. 1:124–25.

3–4. [[the house of Ibrahīm the preparer/maker of potions]] 1/4

5–7. the house of the Rayyis, the house of our lord R. Abraham 1/4 [[the house of the gold/silversmith Abu'l-ʿAlā']] 1/4

8–9. [[the house of his brother Ibrahīm]] 1/4 and 1/8

10–11. the house of Tamīm 1/8 [[the house of Masʿūd]] 1/8

12. [[the house of Dā'ūd]] 1/4 another one of them 1/4

13. Ibn al-ʿAwwām

14–15. [[the house of Hiba ibn Mardūk]] 1/4 the house of Fāḍil 1/4

16–17. [[the house of Makīn]] 1/4 [[the house of Umm ʿAwāḍ]] 1/4
Abu'l-Riḍā

18–19. the house of the doctor (al-ḥakīm) 1/4 [[the house of Hiba]] [[. . .]]

20–21. [[Ibn al-Dayyān (the son of the judge)]] 1/4

22–23. [[the house of Ibrahīm his brother]] 1/4

24–25. [[the house of Muwaffaqa]] 1/4

26–27. [[the house of the daughter of my uncle]] 1/4

28. the house of Surūr ibn ʿAwā[ḍ] 1/4

4–5. the Kohen]] 3/8 [[the house of Abū Saʿīd]] 1/4 and 1/8

6–7. [[the house of the butcher]] 1/4 [[Abu'l-Riḍā]] 1/2

8–9. [[Ibn al-Ḥāshir (the son of the tax-payment rallier)]] 1/4 the house of ʿAfīf 1/4

10–11. the house of Barakāt 1/4 [[the house of Joseph the brother of Taqiyya]] 1/4

12–14. [[the house of Mufaḍḍal ibn Ibrahīm]] 1/4

15–16. [[the house of "the Pious" (al-ḥasīd) Abu'l-ʿAlā']] 1/4 and 1/8

17–18. [[the house of ʿAbd al-Wāḥid]] 1/4

19–20. [[the house of Hiba the baker]] 1/4

21–22. the house of Abū ʿImrān 1/8

23–24. [[the house of Muwaffaq ibn Ṭāhir]] 1/8

Verso

**Col. II**
1–2. [[the house of Hiba ibn Mufaḍḍal]] 1/4 and 1/8

**Col. III**
1–2. [[the house of al-ʿŪdī]] 1/4 [[the house of Joseph ibn al-ʿŪdī]] 1/4

| | |
|---|---|
| 3–4. the house of Makīn 1/8 [[Mūsā]] 1/8 | 3–4. [[the house of the merchant]] 1/2 and 1/4 [[[the hous]e of Abū ʿImrān]] 1/4 |
| 5–6. the house of Abū Isḥaq 1/8 | 5–6. [[the house of al-Muwaffaq 1 1/2 and 1/4 [[a mother from Rūm]][42] 1/8 [[1/4]] |
| 7–8. the house of Ibrahīm of Raḥba 1/4 | 7–8. [[the house of Maḥāsin]] 1/4 [[the house of Abu'l-Majd]] |
| 9–10. the house of Karīm 1/8 the house of Sulaymān the Kohen 1/8 | 9–10. [[Ibn al-Nushādirī (son of the dealer in sal ammoniac)]] 1/4 the house of Hiba |
| 11–12. Samuel ibn Bahā 1/4 | 11–12. [[the son of the captive]] 1/8 [[the house of ʿAzīza]] 1/8 |
| 13–14. Abū Isḥaq ibn Judah 1/4 | 13–14. [[the house of Mak[ār]im]] 1/4 the house of Abū Saʿd 1/2 |
| 15–16. the house of Makīn the merchandiser (al-musawwiq) 1/4 | 15–16. the beadle 1/2 and 1/4 [[the house of Abu'l-Faraj]] [. . .] |
| 17–18. [[the wife of Isḥaq ʿAkāra[43]]] 1/8 | 17–18. [[Ibn Ṭayyib]] 1/4 and 1/8 [[the house of Joseph the fruit dealer (al-fākihānī)]] 1/8 [[1/4]] |
| 19. the house of | 19–20. [[Abu'l-Faraj ibn Nuʿmān]] 1/4 |
| | 21–22. [[Umm Nāṣir ibn Qarīḥ]] 1/4 |
| | 23–24. the house of Abū Saʿd the Maghrebi 1/4 |
| | 25–26. the house of the daughter of Ibrahīm 1/4 |
| | 27–28. [[the [hous]e of Sulaymān son of the midwife (al-qābila)]] 1/4 |
| | 29–30. [[the house of Abū Naṣr]] 1/4 Abu'l-Munā 1/4 |
| | 31–32. [[the house of ʿAz[ī]z the banker]] 1/4 [[the house of the Kohen]][44] |

[42] Written Umm mi-Rūm, a hybrid of Hebrew and Arabic (min Rūm).
[43] I am uncertain about the spelling of this name.
[44] The word "house of," begun in line 31, is repeated in line 32 owing to lack of room.

33–34. [[Abu'l-Fakhr the banker]] 1/4 [[Abu'l-Fakhr]]

35–36. [[the house of Abu'l-ʿAlā' the seller (of foodstuffs)]] 1/4 [[the house of Abu'l-Faraj]] 1/4

84. TS 8 J 13.14v[45]

We have seen alms lists for distribution of wheat and letters requesting a gift of wheat. Here we have a list of contributors of wheat from the early thirteenth century. On the other side we find a letter of condolence to a physician Samuel, leading Goitein to speculate that the wheat was contributed in connection with the mourning rites, which required special acts of charity. It should be recalled that one irdabb equaled six waybas and that one wayba contained about fifteen liters or about four gallons. The average middle-class household, where both parents were present, needed twelve irdabbs of wheat per year, or one per month.

1–2. son of the midwife one wayba Menasse b. al-Dajājī (son of the chicken seller) 3 waybas Joseph the baker/seller of bagels (al-kaʿkī) 1 1/2 waybas
3–4. Menaḥem b. al-Muzaghlil one wayba Fāḍil b. al-ʿAfīf one wayba Faḍl b. Ḥadīd 1/2 irdabb
5–6. Abū Naṣr b. al-Fāḍil one [i]rdabb Abu'l-Riḍā the doctor one wayba
7–8. David b. [. . .]n 1/2 irdabb

85. BM Or 5542.3[46] (Judaeo-Arabic)

This legal document, drawn up in the Fustat court serving under the authority of the head of the Jews the gaon Nethanel ha-Levi b. Moses, certifies that a certain perfumer named Abu'l-Fakhr b. Abraham Ibn al-Amshāṭī (son of the comb maker) had acted as collector of mezonot, or alms money, in December 1161. It is copied in the hand of the judge Mevorakh b. Nathan, from whom many legal documents during this period have survived in the Geniza, and is signed by two witnesses. The collectors (Arabic: *jābī*) of these charitable contributions to finance the semiweekly bread distribution and other needs of the community served for short periods of time and worked with the parnasim, who sometimes held the title "collector" themselves and performed that function as well.[47] We possess many lists of donors to the mezonot collection, one of which is translated above (no. 73). It is not clear why the court had to confirm this matter. Perhaps someone accused the collector of having evaded his turn in this public duty.

We witnesses whose signatures are placed at the end of this document state that we know and attest that the elder Abu'l-Fakhr the perfumer, *who is known as Ibn*

[45] Cf. *Med. Soc.*, 2:490, App. C 48.
[46] Not folio 34, as in *Med. Soc.*, 2:498, App. C 81.
[47] See Cohen, *Poverty and Charity*, chapter 8.

*al-Amshāṭī, (our ) ma(ster) and t(eacher)* Saadya *the elder son of (our) m(aster) and t(eacher)* Abraham *the precious elder (who) r(ests in) E(den)* served as collector of the *mezonot* during the middle third *of the month of Kislev of the year 1473 of (the Era of) Contracts in Fustat, Egypt, which sits on the Nile River, under the a[uthority] of his excellency, the precious, the garland, the splendor, his honor, greatnes[s], and hol[iness] our (master) and teacher, the uniqu[e] in his generation, our prince, prince of God in our midst, our lord Nethanel ha-Levi, "Israel's chariots and horsemen" (2 Kings 2:12), may his name live forever.* Accordingly we wrote our signatures on the abovementioned date. *All confirmed.* Solomon ha-Kohen b. Judah ha-Kohen *of b(lessed) m(emory)*

Tiqva b. Shemarya b. Mevasser

*the ḥaver (who) r(ests in) E(den)*

86. TS 10 J 7.10c[48] (Judaeo-Arabic)

Completing our selection of documents relating to donors to public charity is a will (actually, a copy of a will) of a woman, Khulla bint Shabbat. Among other bequests she stipulates that, from the sale of her *ghulām*, a slave-agent, half the proceeds should go for repairs to the pilgrimage synagogue at Dammūh, located up the Nile from Cairo.[49] This in itself constitutes a kind of charitable bequest, serving the same purpose of maintaining religious institutions that the waqf, or pious foundation, did in Islam and in Judaism (in Hebrew it was usually called the *qodesh*, "holy [trust]"). The other half of her estate was to remain in the hands of the Jewish court of Fustat to be used for needy people unable to leave behind funds for their funeral expenses or for those detained on account of the poll tax without financial means to extricate themselves. As we have seen, difficulty paying the annual poll tax looms large in the Geniza documents relating to the poor, both in letters of appeal and in charitable donations.[50] Here charity for burial of the poor is the province of a bequest. In late medieval and early modern European communities, this service was usually the province of confraternities. The Geniza records show no evidence of the existence of confraternities.[51]

As in wills in general, Khulla itemizes her debts and the manner of repayment. A leader in the community, Nathan b. Samuel the ḥaver, suggested she devote some money to the repair of a Bible codex, but she declined. "Books," comments Goitein, "were not part of her life experience."

The court notes the presence of "plene and defectiva spelling" in the text of the will they were copying. They did not want to be held accountable for what seem like mistakes.

[48] Ed. Yosef Rivlin, *Ha-yerusha veha-ṣeva'a ba-mishpaṭ ha-ʿivri* (Inheritance and Wills in Jewish Law) (Ramat-Gan, 1999), 371–73; cf. *Med. Soc.*, 5:139–40 and 544n61.

[49] See Joel Kraemer, "A Jewish Cult of the Saints in Fāṭimid Egypt," in *L'Egypte Fatimide: son art et son histoire*, ed. Marianne Barrucand (Paris, 1999), 579–601.

[50] See Cohen, *Poverty and Charity*, chapter 4.

[51] See *Poverty and Charity*, chapter 8.

Verso contains another, unrelated document, dated 1135. Rivlin's edition has been checked against the original manuscript at Cambridge University Library and some corrections have been made.

This is a copy of the will of Khulla bint Shabbat which was brought before *the court*, with everything contained therein, written in the hand of Judah son of the *scribe*. We copied it with its plene and defectiva spelling and its witnesses, *letter by letter, word by word. Testimony that took place in our presence, we the under[s]igned, as follows*: We came into the presence of Khulla bint Shabbat and she said to us, bear witness for me with all the (necessary) firm words and types of testimony that I affirm before you that I possess one-third of a house in the Fortress of the Candles (Qaṣr al-Shamaʿ)[52] in partnership with my brothers,[53] and one-third of a house near the funduq (inn) of al-Dhahabī in partnership with the son of her sister and 2 2/3 qirāṭs of the house of the Ikhshādiyya[54] in partnership with her brothers. She also has a ghulām (slave, business agent) who is to be sold, the proceeds to be divided equally, one-half for the upkeep of Dammūh and the other half to remain with *the court*, designated for someone who d[i]es impoverished or to a person who gets detained on account of the poll tax and has not the wherewithal to extricate himself. We made to her the suggestion of "the Diadem" *may the Rock protect him*, "the Diadem of the Scholars"[55] namely, that in the synagogue of the Iraqis and in that of the Palestinians there is a Bible codex wort[h] a certain sum. We suggested that (the money) be designated for its restoration, but she said "No." She acquitted her brothers of all claims and demands, they being *as trustworthy as two reputable witnesses*. She stated that she owes the son of her sister 7 1/2 dinars, and (another) 4 dinars. The 7 1/2 should be repaid from the sum received by her heirs, [and the] 4 [di]nars from the sum (received by) her two sisters. She also stated that she owes her slave[56] 2 dinars, and 6 dinars to the daughter of her brother Abū ʿAlī al-Kohen. We performed the qinyan with her brothers that they would stand surety for the 12 dinars . . . from the sum that will be apportioned to them in the inheritance, *and peace*.[57] Yeshuʿa ha-Kohen b. Eli, *m(ay his) s(oul) (be) b(ound up) with (the bundle) of (life)*. Judah b. Solomon *the scribe, (may his) s(oul) d(well) in (prosperity) and (his descendants) i(nherit the) e(arth)*. This constitutes everything contained in the abovementioned will. We compared it, and it was confirmed in the co[m]pa[r]ison, letter . . . (end of page).

[52] The old Roman fortress in Fustat.

[53] Rivlin misread this word. It is *(i)khwatī* with the *alif* elided and written *plene* as a long vowel.

[54] This sounds like a property named after the Ikshīdids, who ruled Egypt at the beginning of the tenth century.

[55] The title of Nathan b. Samuel he-ḥaver, a court clerk and judge, dated documents 1128–53. See *Med. Soc.*, 2:513.

[56] Rivlin misunderstood this word. It is *mamlakathā*. See Kazimirski, *Dictionnaire arabe français*, 2:1152.

[57] This phrase, found at the end of letters, signifies the end of the copy of the will.

# PART THREE

## EPILOGUE

## Chapter Ten

# POVERTY AND CHARITY IN THE FOURTEENTH CENTURY

DISPERSED AMONG the Geniza collections is a cache of letters emanating from the office of the nagid Joshua Maimonides, the great-great grandson of Moses Maimonides and head of the Jews of Egypt in the first half of the fourteenth century (he died in 1355).[1] He lived in (New) Cairo and his letters are addressed to the community of Fustat. About twenty of them deal with charity, illustrating aspects of poor relief and the role of the leadership of the community in this enterprise especially in the late period, when the community was economically and otherwise much reduced in significance and displayed a concomitant increase in poverty.

The letters are nearly all written in the same handwriting, that of the nagid's secretary. They betray some linguistic features of the correspondence of Islamic rulers seen in Arabic epistolographic manuals and a firmness seemingly reflecting both the decline of the community and the stern, centralized rule of the Mamluk sultans of Joshua's time.[2] The language is formulaic, because, like the secretaries or clerks (*kātibs*) in Islamic administration, Joshua's secretary used a formulary, or at least had one in his head. The biblical verse from Isaiah used as the epigraph had become the signature epigraph of the Maimonidean dynasty long before Joshua's time and, along with the Arabic phrase (see the explanation below in the notes), functioned exactly like the *ʿalāma*, the authenticating marker of Islamic rulers, well known in its most beautiful form in the Ottoman tughra. Like Islamic examples, the ʿalāma of Joshua Nagid, particularly the Hebrew part, takes the form of a cipher.

Following is a selection of the nagid's missives regarding poverty and charity, illustrating the situation after the end of the classical Geniza period.

[1] These letters are discussed, and some of them are transcribed and/or translated into Hebrew in the important article by S. D. Goitein, "The Twilight of the House of Maimonides: Joshua Nagid (1310–1355)" (Hebrew), *Tarbiz* 54 (1984–85), 67–104.

[2] See Mark R. Cohen, "Correspondence and Social Control in the Jewish Communities of the Islamic World: A Letter of the Nagid Joshua Maimonides," *Jewish History* vol. 1, no. 2 (Fall 1986), 39–48.

## 87. "The bearer of this is the orphan boy Mūsā"

The first letter is addressed to a cantor, whom the nagid asks to arrange shelter for an orphan, on pain of stern repercussions (one of the themes of social control in the nagid's letters). This same cantor turns up elsewhere in charge of the weekly collection in September 1387.[3] The comment "ask the elder Isaac about him" reflects a system of verification long in use in the community to confirm the deservedness of the poor and mirrored in many of the alms lists.

TS 6 J 6.21[4] (Judaeo-Arabic)

In the name [of the Compassionate][5]

"*Behold God is my salvation,*" *etc.*[6]
The *cantor* Faraj Allāh, (*may the) R(ock) p(rotect you*), shall take note [that] the bearer of this is the *orphan boy* Mūsā. Ask the e(lder) Isaac [about him]. If they refuse to give [him she]lter, please send a messenger and let me know immediately, so that [I can do] what is necessary to them. Beware of [being disobedient].[7] And may God,[8] the ex(alted), be your succor.

## 88. "Do not make it neccesary [for us] to reprove you"

Here, Joshua Nagid commands the release of funds due to a certain person to defray his poll tax payment—for centuries, one of the most important ongoing charitable activities of the community.

[3] *Med. Soc.*, 3:494n126.
[4] Translated into Hebrew in Goitein, *Tarbiz* 54 (1984–85), 81–82, and into English in *Med. Soc.*, 3:303–304. I have made minor changes to Goitein's translation.
[5] Written in Arabic characters, part of the authenticating motto, *ʿalāma*, of the nagid Joshua. Completed on the basis of other letters (see below). It is a form of the Islamic *basmala*. In his article "The Twilight of the House of Maimonides," Goitein misread this caption as the full *basmala* (*bism allāh al-raḥman al-raḥīm*; ibid., 81n43), and the present writer accepted that interpretation in "Four Judaeo-Arabic Petitions of the Poor," 450n13. In fact (see the facsimile of no. 89 below), as my student Nancy Khalek suggested, the Arabic characters are to be deciphered *bism al-raḥīm*, "In the name of the Compassionate." This is precisely a translation of the Aramaic *bi-shmakh raḥmana*ʾ, the normal Jewish "basmala." Jews did sometimes write out the complete Islamic formula. See part 1, chapter 1, note 18.
[6] The biblical motto verse is from Isaiah 12:2, "Behold God is my salvation, in Him do I trust, hence have no fear." The first two words, *hinei el*, are written in the form of a cipher, readily recognizable as the signature of this nagid.
[7] Arabic: *al-ḥadhar min al-[mukhālafa]*, an Arabic expression prescribed for the correspondence of Arabic official letters from the court of the ruler; see Cohen, "Correspondence and Social Control," 45.
[8] Arabic: *al-ḥaqq*, literally, "the Truth," a common expression for God in classical Arabic.

TS 8 J 17.12[9] (Judaeo-Arabic)

In the name of the Compassionate

*"Behold, God is my salvation," et[c.]*
The most illustrious master the *c(antor)*, the e[lder] *(may) God b(e your succor)*, is hereby informed that we [. . .] since [the tim]e of the poll-tax payments [. . .] in you [. . .] with him [. . .] that the bearer of this has with him. [Sta]nd by [him and a]ssist him and release them to him [imm]ediately, and do not make it neccesary [for us] to reprove you. Appear with [him] at once, with the money in hand. Beware of being disobedient. May God the ex(alted) be [your succor] and may He watch over you. *And peace.*

## 89. "This is the time for virtuous generosity."

Here, the nagid instructs the two Rabbanite congregations of Fustat, the Palestinian and the Babylonian, to arrange a collection for an old man who wished to travel to Jerusalem. Goitein comments that the old Arabic term for "manliness" or "gentlemanly nature," *muruwwa* (literally, "virtue," in its old sense, from Latin, *vir*, "man") is used here and elsewhere in the Geniza letters, especially in later times, to denote the virtue of generosity. The motif of "embarrassment" ascribed here to the needy person might mean real embarrassment, rather than the "shame" of the "shamefaced poor" discussed earlier and in Cohen, *Poverty and Charity*, chapter 1. The Arabic expression "open up your hands wide in giving to him" recalls the biblical command "open your hand and lend him sufficient for whatever he needs" (Deuteronomy 15:8), one of the crux passages about charity in the Torah. Aid for needy travelers to Jerusalem ranked high in the eyes of the community.

TS 8 J 9.15[10]

In the name of the Compassionate

*"Behold, God is my salvation," etc.*
The noble community in Fustat, *may their Rock bless them, a(men) f(orever) s(ela)*, knows that the duty of charity brings a great reward in His, the ex(alted's), pr[esence]. This is especially so when the person is *poor and embarrassed and old*, such as the bearer, Yeshuʿa, *(may he have a) g(ood) e(nd)*.[11] It is in your beneficent nature to help and assist him because he wishes to travel to his

[9] Hebrew summary in Goitein, *Tarbiz* 54 (1984–85), 92.
[10] Briefly summarized in Goitein, ibid., 85; cf. *Med. Soc.*, 5:192; 561n38.
[11] Aramaic: *s-ṭ* = *safeh ṭav*, according to Goitein, an expression applied to the living and reinterpreted in later times to mean *sefaradi ṭahor*, "pure-bred Spaniard," to distinguish Jews with authenticated Iberian lineage from other Middle Eastern Jews going by the name "sefaradi."

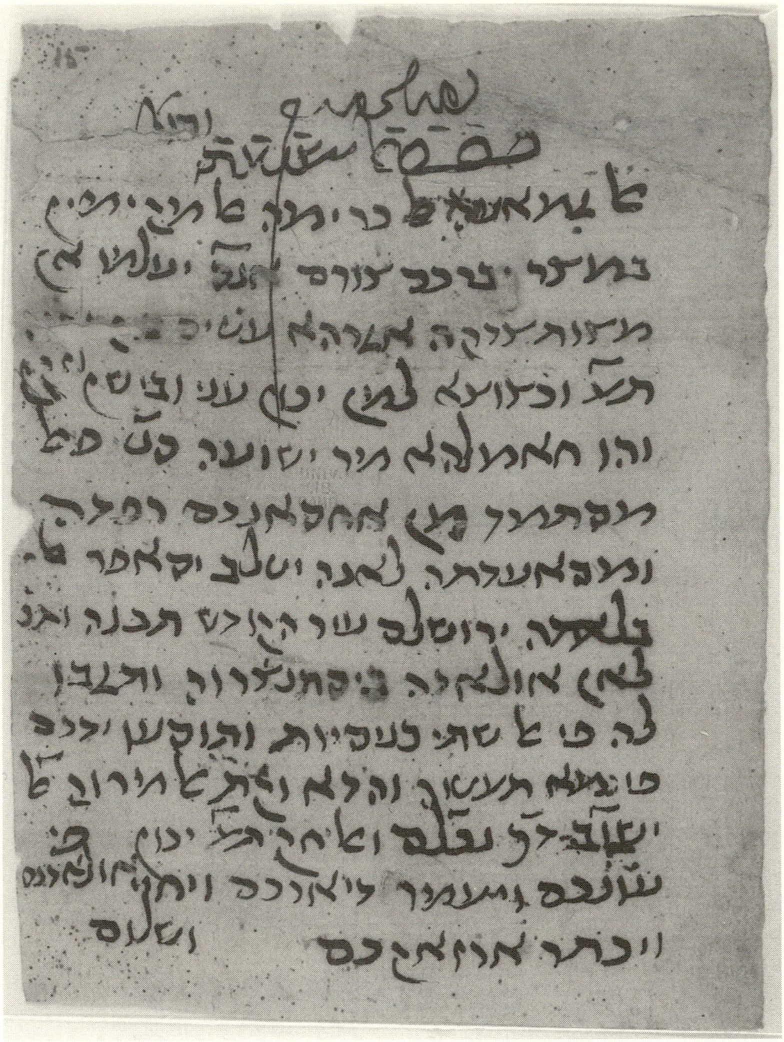

Fig. 8. Letter from the nagid Joshua Maimonides, fourteenth century; (no. 89) TS 8 J 9.15

city, *Jerusalem, the Holy City, may it be rebuilt and est(ablished)*, for his children are waiting for him. Therefore, take up a collection for him in the *two congregations* and open your hands wide in giving to him, for this is the time for virtuous generosity. "Let not the downtrodden turn away disappointed" (Psalm 74:21). May God the ex(alted) be your succor, make your habitations prosper, grant long life to your children, and increase your sustenance. *And peace.*

## 90. "The duty of charity brings a great reward in His, the ex(alted's), presence"

Another letter from the office of Joshua Nagid to the community of Fustat, asking them to give charitable assistance to a needy person, a certain Moses, described as "poor, old and embarrassed."

TS NS J 258[12] (Judaeo-Arabic)

[In the name of the Compassionate][13]

["*Behold, God is] my s[alvation,*" *e]tc.*
"[*Thus] says the Lord: [Do] justice and deeds of charity,*" *etc.* (Isaiah 56:1).
The noble [commun]ity in Fustat, *may their Rock [ble]ss them and their [Cre]ator help them, a(men) n(eṣah) s(ela)*, knows that the duty of charity brings a great reward in His, the ex(alted's), presence. This is especially so when the person is *poor and old [and] embarrassed*, such as the bearer, Mr. Moses, *(may he have a) g(ood) e(nd)*. It is i[n] your beneficent nature to help him [. . . *and] lacking everything*. So open [your hands] wide in [giving to him . . .] mercy [of God] and the mercy of *Israel*, and do not turn him away empty-handed [and "*Let not the] downtrodden [turn] away disappointed*" (Psalm 74:21). *You, O vineyard of the Lord of hosts*, [are d]oers of *charitable acts and good deeds*, so keep that [up]. May God the ex(alted) be your succor and increase your [s]ustenance, and never separate you from your homeland.[14] *And peace.*

## 91. "Collect from the *women*"

Here Joshua Nagid commands that a collection be taken up by two women, one of them the wife of the beadle Sulaymān. They are called "house," following the rabbinic idiom, "his house means his wife."[15]

[12] Summarized in Goitein, *Tarbiz* 54 (1984–85), 84.
[13] The Arabic *ʿalāma* is torn off.
[14] Arabic: *lā yushattitukum min awṭānikum*. I have found this motif elsewhere in letters of the foreign poor; see Cohen, *Poverty and Charity*, chapter 2. See also Goitein, "The Twilight of the House of Maimonides," 84.
[15] See above part 2, no. 60.

Women appear but rarely on the donor lists.[16] Public charity was mainly a male endeavor since only the male members of the community frequented the synagogue, which was the main venue for charitable vows and collections. Sometimes donations were solicited at people's places of work (see below) in the marketplace, similarly a male preserve. Here we see that a special arrangement was made to allow women to participate in the religious duty of giving charity. Other women, of course, gave charity privately, and they are praised for their generosity in letters.

The letter was penned at the time of the Jewish New Year (usually late September), the season when Jews, men and women alike, think especially earnestly about repentance. Charity could earn divine favor in this respect.

TS 8 J 17.30[17] (Judaeo-Arabic)

[. . .] let your "*house*" (i.e., wife) and the "*house*" (wife) of the *beadle* Sulaymān collect from the *women*. In addition, you alone should make the collection. Exert yourself in this. Whatever is obt[ained] from everyone, keep with you until we inform you what to do. We know about this matter only from you. Do not make it necessary for us to reprove you. Beware of being disobedient. May God the ex(alted) be your succor, *and may you be inscribed in the book of [lif]e, the book of remembrance. And peace.*

## 92. "Collect from the *women* and exert themselves in collecting"

Like the preceding letter, this one regards a collection by women at holiday time, and the two letters likely refer to the same thing. The margin takes up another matter.

TS 13 J 28.13[18] (Judaeo-Arabic)

[. . .] the collection, and exert yourself in this so you receive it. We notified you also that your "*house*" (wife) and the "*house*" (wife) of the *beadle* the e(lder) Sulaymān are the ones who shall collect from the *women* and exert themselves in collecting. [Do] not e[x]clude us from your noble thoughts and [yo]ur prayers which will be accepted (by God) in this esteemed holiday period. God the ex(alted) in his mercy will not forget you nor will He turn [y]ou back disappointed [. . .] (margin, in another hand) [. . .] the *ḥ(aver)* R. Joseph b. Samuel *(of) b(lessed) m(emory), who stands in the breach* presented himself before the most illustrious Emir, th[e] Emir [Sayf] al-Dīn [. . .] they redeemed the items held

[16] See Cohen, *Poverty and Charity*, chapter 8.

[17] Hebrew translation in Goitein, *Tarbiz* 54 (1984–85), 83.

[18] Ibid.

in partnership [. . .] Go[d . . .] victory and may He make your habitations prosper [. . .] and sustain you [. . .] and pure intention [. . .] which he did, shall do.[19] (verso) Abraham b. [. . .].

## 93. "The members of his household are poverty stricken"

This letter bears enough similarities of language and form to the previous ones to assign it to the office of Joshua Nagid, even though the handwriting is dissimilar, evidently the work of a stand-in clerk (who forgot the Hebrew epigraph from Isaiah). This letter recommends a man who is "poor but from a good family." On the "good family" motif, see above, chapter 2.[20] His family is described as "weak," a synonym for poor. The community of Fustat is asked to help him by taking up a collection in the synagogues. This would have been a pesiqa.

TS 8 J 13.23[21] (Judaeo-Arabic)

In the name of the Compassionate

The noble community in Fustat, *may their Rock bless them and their Creator help them, a(men) n(eṣaḥ) s(ela)*, is hereby informed that the person just arriving in your midst, the elder R. Yom Ṭov, is *a poor man from a good family*, and the members of his household are poverty stricken (Arabic: "weak"). Through the beneficence of the community, *may you be bl[ess]ed*, I h[o]pe you will collect something for him in the *synagogues* to help him in his hour of need. *It will [b]e to your merit as an act of righteousness (charity)* (cf. Deuteronomy 24:13). May God the ex(alted) make you "*givers rather than givers*" [*sic*],[22] [m]ake [yo]ur habitations prosper, increase your sustenance, *[b]less you, men, women, children and young men. May he fulfill through you the verse "May the Lord, the G(od) of your fathers, increase your numbers a thousandfold," etc.* (Deuteronomy 1:11). *And peac[e]*.

## 94. "Do not deprive him of something"

This letter, in the same hand as the preceding one (no. 93) and similarly addressed to the community of Fustat, asks them to help a financially strapped traveler so he can proceed to his next destination by caravan, which was about to depart. This is called ṣedaqa. The Arabic part of the ʿalāma found on Joshua

[19]Translation very uncertain, owing to lacunae.

[20]More on this in Cohen, *Poverty and Charity*, chapter 1.

[21]Summarized briefly in Goitein, *Tarbiẓ* 54 (1984–85), 85.

[22]He meant to write "takers." See the next letter. On this phrase, see chapter 1, at note 11.

Nagid's official correspondence is present but the normal Hebrew cipher verse is absent. I cannot decipher the writing that comes in its place.

TS 8 J 17.13[23] (Judaeo-Arabic)

In the name of the Compassionate

[. . .]
The noble community in Fustat, *may their Rock bless them, and their Creator help them, a(men) n(eṣaḥ) s(ela)*, knows that the duty of charity is a great thing in the eyes of Him, the ex(alted). This is especially so when the person is scholarly (lit., possesses the fragrance of Torah) and is on his way to *Jerusalem the Holy City, (may it be) r(ebuilt) and (established) during your lifetime and the lifetime of all Israel.* Through the beneficence of the community, *may they be blessed*, I hope they will strive to take up a collection in the *synagogues* for the bearer of this letter, the elder R. David, *(may) God b(e his succor)*. Do not deprive him of something since he prays in thanks for your charitableness. May God the ex(alted) not put you in need, but rather make you "*givers rather than takers.*"[24] I hope you expedite this and g[iv]e him what you collect so that he can set out with the caravan. [*It will be] to your merit [as an act of righteousness (charity*)] (cf. Deuteronomy 24:13). May God the ex(alted) affirm through you the verse ["*May the Lord, the God of] your fathers increase your [numbers a thousandfold," etc.*] (Deut. 1:11). *And peace.*

(Margin:) Do not hold him back for he is all ready for the journey.

[23] Summarized in Goitein, *Tarbiz* 54 (1984–85), 85; cf. *Med. Soc.*, 2:37, 136; 5:35.
[24] Here quoted correctly. See the previous letter, no. 93.

# LIST OF GENIZA TEXTS

**British Museum (now: British Library), London**

| | |
|---|---|
| BM Or 5542.3 | (no. 85) |

**Bibliotheque Nationale, University of Strasbourg**

| | |
|---|---|
| BNUS 4038.9 | (no. 12) |

**Cambridge University Library Collection (historically cited by Goitein as ULC), Cambridge, England**

| | |
|---|---|
| CUL Or 1080 J 31 | (no. 18) |
| CUL Or 1080 J 48 | (no. 57) |
| CUL Add. 3423 | (no. 40) |

**Elkan Nathan Adler Collection, Jewish Theological Seminary of America, New York**

| | |
|---|---|
| ENA 2591.6 | (no. 79) |
| ENA 2727.22 | (no. 75) |
| ENA 2727.54 | (no. 72) |
| ENA 2738.37 | (no. 37) |
| ENA 4011.17 | (no. 49) |
| ENA 4020.62 | (no. 32) |
| ENA NS 77.36 | (no. 7) |
| ENA NS 77.291 | (no. 69) |

**Jewish Theological Seminary of America, MS Krengel**

| | |
|---|---|
| JTS Krengel 5.123 | (no. 8) |

**Jewish Theological Seminary of America, New York**

| | |
|---|---|
| JTS MS 8254.7 | (no. 33) |

**Mosseri Collection, Paris (photographs in Institute of Microfilmed Hebrew Manuscripts, Jerusalem)**

| | |
|---|---|
| Mosseri L 129.1 | (no. 42) |
| Mosseri L 291 | (no. 55) |

**Taylor Schechter Collection, University Library, Cambridge, England**

**Fragments originally in boxes and now in binders and marked TS H, J, K etc.**

| | |
|---|---|
| TS Box J 1.4 | (no. 64) |
| TS Box K 15.5 | (no. 60) |
| TS Box K 15.15 | (no. 61) |
| TS Box K 15.16 | (no. 81) |

| | |
|---|---|
| TS Box K 15.25 | (no. 73) |
| TS Box K 15.39 | (no. 62) |
| TS Box K 15.48 | (no. 68) |
| TS Box K 15.50 | (no. 63) |
| TS Box K 15.58 | (no. 80) |
| TS Box K 15.60v | (no. 74) |
| TS Box K 15.61 | (no. 78) |
| TS Box K 15.64 | (no. 83) |
| TS Box K 15.102 | (no. 67) |
| TS Box K 15.113 | (no. 66) |

**Bound volumes, arranged according to size**

| | |
|---|---|
| TS 6 J 1.8 | (no. 36) |
| TS 6 J 1.12v | (no. 70) |
| TS 6 J 3.1 | (no. 30) |
| TS 6 J 3.10v | (no. 52) |
| TS 6 J 3.28 | (no. 13) |
| TS 6 J 4.16 | (no. 51) |
| TS 6 J 6.21 | (no. 87) |
| TS 6 J 8.4 | (no. 56) |
| TS 8 J 9.15 | (no. 89) |
| TS 8 J 13.5 | (no. 20) |
| TS 8 J 13.14 | (no. 84) |
| TS 8 J 13.23 | (no. 93) |
| TS 8 J 16.7 | (no. 25) |
| TS 8 J 16.29 | (no. 53) |
| TS 8 J 17.12 | (no. 88) |
| TS 8 J 17.13 | (no. 94) |
| TS 8 J 17.18 | (no. 77) |
| TS 8 J 17.27 | (no. 39) |
| TS 8 J 17.30 | (no. 91) |
| TS 8 J 18.19 | (no. 46) |
| TS 8 J 18.25 | (no. 35) |
| TS 8 J 18.28 | (no. 2) |
| TS 8 J 20.24 | (no. 34) |
| TS 8 J 21.6 | (no. 28) |
| TS 8 J 21.20 | (no. 4) |
| TS 8 J 24.6 | (no. 23) |
| TS 8 J 37.11 | (no. 3) |
| TS 8 J 41.1 | (no. 5) |
| TS 10 J 6.17 | (no. 38) |
| TS 10 J 7.10c | (no. 86) |
| TS 10 J 10.4 | (no. 31) |

| | |
|---|---|
| TS 10 J 10.9 | (no. 22) |
| TS 10 J 13.13 | (no. 16) |
| TS 10 J 16.4 | (no. 47) |
| TS 10 J 17.4 | (no. 17) |
| TS 13 J 9.11r | (no. 41) |
| TS 13 J 9.11v | (no. 41) |
| TS 13 J 13.6 | (no. 48) |
| TS 13 J 13.16 | (no. 44) |
| TS 13 J 18.10 | (no. 43) |
| TS 13 J 18.14 | (no. 1) |
| TS 13 J 18.18 | (no. 45) |
| TS 13 J 20.4 | (no. 6) |
| TS 13 J 20.20 | (no. 11) |
| TS 13 J 20.28 | (no. 27) |
| TS 13 J 28.13 | (no. 92) |
| TS 18 J 4.4 | (no. 14) |

**Fragments mostly in Arabic and Judaeo-Arabic, originally kept in boxes and now in binders and marked TS Arabic**

| | |
|---|---|
| TS Arabic Box 18 (1).33 | (no. 9) |
| TS Arabic Box 30.67 | (no. 71) |
| TS Arabic Box 46.253 | (no. 24) |

**Fragments originally kept in boxes and now in binders and marked TS Misc.**

| | |
|---|---|
| TS Misc. Box 8.9 | (no. 59) |
| TS Misc. Box 8.25 | (no. 65) |

**Fragments originally kept under glass, arranged according to size, and now in binders**

| | |
|---|---|
| TS 12.122 | (no. 29) |
| TS 12.192 | (no. 50) |
| TS 12.303 | (no. 26) |
| TS 24.46 | (no. 19) |

**New Series (fragments sorted since 1954, now in binders)**

| | |
|---|---|
| TS NS J 41 | (no. 58) |
| TS NS J 76v | (no. 76) |
| TS NS J 258 | (no. 90) |
| TS NS J 389 | (no. 54) |
| TS NS J 399 | (no. 15) |
| TS NS J 404 | (no. 82) |

**Westminster College, Cambridge, England**

| | |
|---|---|
| Westminster College, Misc. 34 | (no. 10) |

# BIBLIOGRAPHY


Abramson, Shraga. "Judah ha-Levi's Letter on His Emigration to the Land of Israel" (Hebrew). *Kiryat Sefer* 29 (1953–54), 133–44.

Alshech, Eli. "Islamic Law, Practice, and Legal Doctrine: Exempting the Poor from the Jizya under the Ayyubids (1171–1250)." *Islamic Law and Society* 10 (2003), 1–28.

Ashtor, Eliyahu. "The Number of the Jews in Medieval Egypt." *Journal of Jewish Studies* 18 (1967), 9–42; 19 (1968), 1–22.

———. "Some Features of the Jewish Communities in Medieval Egypt" (Hebrew). *Zion* 30 (1965), 61–78, 128–57.

Assaf, Simha. *Meqorot u-meḥqarim be-toledot yisrael* (Texts and Studies in Jewish History). Jerusalem: Mosad Ha-Rav Kook, 1946.

Assaf, Simha, and L. A. Mayer, eds. *Sefer ha-yishuv*. Volume 2. Jerusalem: Israel Society for History and Ethnography, 1944.

Avot de-Rabbi Nathan. Ed. Solomon Schechter. English translation, Judah Goldin, *The Fathers According to Rabbi Nathan*. New Haven: Yale University Press, 1955.

Babylonian Talmud.

Bagnall, Roger S. *Egypt in Late Antiquity*. Princeton: Princeton University Press, 1993.

Bareket, Elinoar. *Fustat on the Nile: The Jewish Elite in Medieval Egypt*. Leiden: Brill, 1999.

———. *Shafrir miṣrayim: ha-hanhaga ha-yehudit be-Fustat ba-maḥaṣit ha-rishona shel ha-me'a ha-aḥat-ʿesreh* (Jewish Leadership in Fustat). Tel Aviv: Tel Aviv University, 1995.

Bar-Ilan, Naftali Tzvi Yehudah ben Ṭuvyah. *Niqdash bi-ṣedaqa*. Rehovot: n.p., 1990.

Benjamin of Tudela. *Itinerary*. Ed. and trans. Marcus Nathan Adler. London: H. Frowde, 1907.

Bentwich, Norman. *Solomon Schechter: A Biography*. Philadelphia: Jewish Publication Society, 1940.

Bereshit Rabba. Ed. J. Theodor and Ch. Albeck. 2nd printing. 3 vols. Jerusalem: Wahrmann Books, 1965.

Boksenboim, Yacob, ed. *Iggerot melammedim* (Letters of Jewish Teachers). Tel Aviv: Tel Aviv University, 1985.

———. *Iggerot R. Yehuda Aryeh mi-Modena* (Letters of Rabbi Leon Modena). Tel Aviv: Tel Aviv University, 1984.

Boojamara, John J. "Christian *Philanthropia*: A Study of Justinian's Welfare Policy and the Church." *Byzantina* 7 (1975), 345–73.

Bosworth, Clifford Edmund. *The Mediaeval Islamic Underworld: The Banū Sāsān in Arabic Society and Literature*. Leiden: E. J. Brill, 1976.

Brown, Peter. *Poverty and Leadership in the Later Roman Empire*. Hanover, NH, and London: University Press of New England, 2002.

Cohen, Mark R. "Correspondence and Social Control in the Jewish Communities of the Islamic World: A Letter of the Nagid Joshua Maimonides." *Jewish History* 1, no. 2 (Fall 1986), 39–48.

———. "The Foreign Jewish Poor in Medieval Egypt." In *Poverty and Charity in Middle Eastern Contexts*. Eds. Michael Bonner, Mine Ener, and Amy Singer. Albany: SUNY Press, 2003, 53–72.

———. "Four Judaeo-Arabic Petitions of the Poor from the Cairo Geniza." *Jerusalem Studies in Arabic and Islam* 24 (2000), 446–71.

———. "Geniza for Islamicists, Islamic Geniza, and the 'New Cairo Geniza.'" Lecture given at Harvard University's Center for Middle Eastern Studies February 12, 2004, to be published in *Harvard Middle Eastern and Islamic Review*.

———. "Halakha and Reality in Matters of Charity during the Geniza Period" (Hebrew). In *Ha-islam ve-ʿolamot ha-shezurim bo* (Intertwined Worlds of Islam: Essays in Memory of Hava Lazarus-Yafeh). Ed. Nahem Ilan. Jerusalem: Yad Ben-Zvi, 2002, 315–33.

———. "Jewish and Islamic Life in the Middle Ages: Through the Window of the Cairo Geniza." To appear in a book edited by Joseph Montville.

———. *Jewish Self-Government in Medieval Egypt: The Origins of the Office of Head of the Jews, ca. 1065–1126*. Princeton: Princeton University Press, 1980.

———. "A Partnership Gone Bad: A Letter and a Power of Attorney from the Cairo Geniza, 1085." To appear in a Festschrift for Sasson Somekh. Eds. David Wasserstein and Mahmud Ghanaim, forthcoming.

———. *Poverty and Charity in the Jewish Community of Medieval Egypt*. Princeton: Princeton University Press, 2005.

———. "Poverty as Reflected in the Cairo Geniza Documents." To appear in the *Proceedings of the Seventh International Conference of the Society for Judaeo-Arabic Studies*. Ed. Paul Fenton.

———. *Under Crescent and Cross: The Jews in the Middle Ages*. Princeton: Princeton University Press, 1994.

———. "The Voice of the Jewish Poor in the Cairo Genizah." In *Semitic Papyrology in Context*. Ed. Lawrence Schiffman. Leiden and Boston: Brill, 2003, 239–55.

Cohen, Mark R., and Yedida K. Stillman. "The Cairo Geniza and the Custom of Geniza among Oriental Jewry: A Historical and Ethnographic Study" (Hebrew). *Peʿamim*, no. 24 (1985), 3–35.

Cowley, A., ed. and trans. *Aramaic Papyri of the Fifth Century* B.C. 1923. Reprint Osnabrück: Otto Zeller, 1967.

Crossman, Sylvie, and Michel Gabrysiak, *La guéniza: roman*. Paris: Éditions du Seuill, 1987.

Cuffel, Alexandra. "Call and Response: European Jewish Emigration to Egypt and Palestine in the Middle Ages." *Jewish Quarterly Review* 90 (1999–2000), 61–102.

Davis, Natalie Zemon. "Conclusion." In *Poverty and Charity in Middle Eastern Contexts*. Eds. Michael Bonner, Mine Ener, and Amy Singer. Albany: SUNY Press, 2003, 325–24.

———. *Fiction in the Archives: Pardon Tales and Their Tellers in Sixteenth-Century France*. Stanford: Stanford University Press, 1987.

Diem, Werner. *Arabische Briefe auf Papyrus und Papier aus der Heidelberger Papyrus-Sammlung*. Wiesbaden: Otto Harrassowitz, 1991.

———. *Arabische Briefe des 7. bis 13. Jahrhunderts aus den Staatlichen Museen Berlin*. Wiesbaden: Otto Harrassowitz, 1997.

———. *Arabische Privatbriefe des 9. bis 15. Jahrhunderts aus der Österreichischen Nationalbibliothek in Wien*. Wiesbaden: Otto Harrassowitz, 1996.

Dozy, R. *Supplément aux dictionnaires arabes*. 3rd ed. 2 vols. Leiden and Paris: E.-J. Brill and G.-P. Maisonneuve et Larose, 1967.

Farmer, Sharon. *Surviving Poverty in Medieval Paris: Gender, Ideology and the Daily Lives of the Poor.* Ithaca and London: Cornell University Press, 2002.

Fouquet, Yannick. *Pauvreté et assistance au XVIIe siècle: le cas exemplaire de Chambéry.* Chambéry: Société Savoisienne d'Histoire et d'Archéologie, 1986.

Friedman, Mordechai A. "New Sources from the *Geniza* for the Crusader Period and for Maimonides and His Descendants" (Hebrew). *Cathedra* 40 (1986), 63–82.

———. "Responsa of Abraham Maimonides on a Debtor's Travails." In *Genizah Research after Ninety Years: The Case of Judaeo-Arabic. Papers Read at the Third Congress of the Society for Judaeo-Arabic Studies.* Eds. Joshua Blau and Stefan C. Reif. Cambridge: Cambridge University Press, 1992, 82–92.

Galinsky, Judah. "'I Am Donating to Heaven for the Benefit of my Soul': Jewish Charitable Bequests and the *Hekdesh* Trust in the Rabbinic Responsa of 13th-Century Spain." *The Journal of Interdisciplinary History* 35:3 (Winter 2005), 423–40.

Geremek, Bronislaw. *Poverty: A History.* Trans. Agnieszka Kolakowska. Oxford: Blackwell, 1994.

Gil, Moshe. *Be-malkhut yishmael bi-tequfat ha-geonim* (In the Kingdom of Ishmael: Studies in Jewish History in Islamic Lands in the Early Middle Ages). 4 vols. Tel Aviv and Jerusalem: Tel Aviv University, Mosad Bialik, and the Ministry of Defense, 1997.

———. *Documents of the Jewish Pious Foundations from the Cairo Geniza.* Leiden: E. J. Brill, 1976.

———. *Ereṣ yisrael ba-tequfa ha-muslemit ha-rishona* (Palestine during the First Muslim Period [634–1099]). 3 vols. Tel Aviv: Tel Aviv University and Ministry of Defense, 1983.

———. *A History of Palestine, 634–1099.* Trans. Ethel Broido. Cambridge: Cambridge University Press, 1992.

Ginzburg, Carlo. *The Cheese and the Worms: The Cosmos of a Sixteenth-Century Miller.* Trans. John and Anne Tedeschi. Baltimore: Johns Hopkins Unversity Press, 1980.

Goitein, S. D. "Chief Judge R. Ḥananel b. Samuel, In-law of R. Moses Maimonides" (Hebrew). *Tarbiz* 50 (1980–81), 371–95.

———. "Elḥanan b. Shemarya as a Communal Leader" (Hebrew). In *Joshua Finkel Festschrift.* Eds. Sidney B. Hoenig and Leon D. Stitskin. New York: Yeshiva University Press, 1974, Hebrew section, 117–37.

———. *Ha-yishuv be-ereṣ yisrael be-reshit ha-islam uvi-tequfat ha-ṣalbanim* (Palestinian Jewry in Early Islamic and Crusader Times). Ed. Joseph Hacker. Jerusalem: Yad Izhak Ben Zvi, 1980.

———. *Letters of Medieval Jewish Traders.* Princeton: Princeton University Press, 1973.

———. "Maimonides, Man of Action: A Revision of the Master's Biography in Light of the Geniza Documents." In *Hommage à Georges Vajda.* Eds. G. Nahon and C. Touati. Louvain, Belgium: Peeters, 1980, 155–67.

———. *A Mediterranean Society: The Jewish Communities of the Arab World as Portrayed in the Documents of the Cairo Geniza.* 5 vols. plus Index volume by Paula Sanders. Berkeley and Los Angeles: University of California Press, 1967–93.

———. "New Sources on Palestine in Crusader Days" (Hebrew). *Eretz-Israel* 4 (1956), 147–59. Reprinted in Goitein, *Ha-yishuv be-ereṣ yisrael be-reshit ha-islam uvi-tequfat ha-ṣalbanim*, 283–305.

———. *Sidrei ḥinnukh bi-mei ha-geonim u-veit ha-Rambam* (Jewish Education in Muslim Countries, Based on Records from the Cairo Geniza). Jerusalem: Makhon Ben Zvi, 1962.

———. "The Synagogue Building and Its Furnishings according to the Records of the Cairo Geniza" (Hebrew). *Eretz-Israel* 7 (1964), 81–97.

———. "The Twilight of the House of Maimonides: Joshua Nagid (1310–1355)" (Hebrew). *Tarbiz* 54 (1984–85), 67–104.

Golb, Norman. *The Jews in Medieval Normandy: A Social and Intellectual History*. Cambridge: Cambridge University Press, 1998.

———. *Toledot ha-yehudim beʿir Rouen bi-mei ha-beinayim* (History and Culture of the Jews of Rouen in the Middle Ages). Tel Aviv: Devir, 1976.

———. "The Topography of the Jews of Medieval Egypt: Inductive Studies Based Primarily upon Documents from the Cairo Genizah." *Journal of Near Eastern Studies* 24 (1965), 251–70; 33 (1974), 116–49.

Golb, Norman and Omeljan Pritsak. *Khazarian Hebrew Documents of the Tenth Century*. Ithaca and London: Cornell University Press, 1982.

Gottheil, Richard. "Some Responsa of Maimonides." *In Occident and Orient . . . Gaster Anniversary Volume*. Eds. Bruno Schindler and A. Marmorstein. London: Taylor's Foreign Press, 1936, 173–80.

Grosse, Siegfried, et al., eds. *"Denn das Schrieben gehört nicht zu meiner täglichen Beschäftigung:" Der Alltag kleiner Leute in Bittschriften, Briefen und Berichten aus dem 19. Jahrhundert: Ein Lesebuch*. Bonn: Verlag J.H.W. Dietz Nachf., 1989.

Guo, Li. "Arabic Documents from the Red Sea Port of Quseir in the Seventh/Thirteenth Century, Part 1: Business Letters." *Journal of Near Eastern Studies* 58 (1999), 161–90.

Himmelfarb, Gertrude. *The Idea of Poverty: England in the Early Industrial Age*. New York: Alfred A. Knopf, 1984.

Hitchcock, Tim, Peter King, and Pamela Sharpe, eds. *Chronicling Poverty: The Voices and Strategies of the English Poor, 1640–1840*. New York: St. Martin's Press, 1997.

Humphreys, R. Stephen. *Islamic History: A Framework for Inquiry*. Rev. ed. Princeton: Princeton University Press, 1991.

Ibn Megas, Joseph. *Ḥiddushei Ha-RI Megas le-masekhet Bava Batra*. Ed. Moshe Shemuel Shapira, 2nd ed. Benei Berak: Lipa Friedman Press, 1979.

Ibn Shahin, Nissim ben Jacob. *An Elegant Composition concerning Relief after Adversity*. Trans. William M. Brinner. New Haven and London: Yale University Press, 1977.

Jacoby, David. "What Do We Learn about Byzantine Asia Minor from the Documents of the Cairo Genizah?" In Jacoby, *Byzantium, Latin Romania and the Mediterranean*. Aldershot: Variorum, 2001, 83–95.

Kazimirski, A. De Biberstein. *Dictionnaire arabe-français*. 2 vols. Paris: Maisonneuve, 1860.

Khan, Geoffrey. *Arabic Legal and Administrative Documents in the Cambridge Genizah Collections*. Cambridge: Cambridge University Press, 1993.

———. "The Historical Development of the Structure of Medieval Arabic Petitions." *Bulletin of the School of Oriental and African Studies* 53 (1990), 8–30.

Kraemer, Joel L. "A Jewish Cult of the Saints in Fāṭimid Egypt." In *L'Egypte Fatimide: son art et son histoire*. Ed. Marianne Barrucand. Paris: Presses de l'Université de Paris-Sorbonne, 1999, 579–601.

———. "Two Letters of Maimonides from the Cairo Genizah." *Maimonidean Studies*. Vol. 1. Ed. Arthur Hyman. New York: Yeshiva University Press, 1990, 87–98.

Lambert, Phyllis, ed. *Fortifications and the Synagogue: The Fortress of Babylon and the Ben Ezra Synagogue, Cairo*. London: Weidenfeld & Nicolson, 1994.

Lane, Edward W. *An Arabic-English Lexicon*. 8 vols. London: Williams and Norgate, 1863–93.

Loewenberg, Frank M. *From Charity to Social Justice: The Emergence of Communal Institutions for the Support of the Poor in Ancient Judaism*. New Brunswick and London: Transaction Publishers, 2001.

Mann, Jacob. *The Jews in Egypt and in Palestine under the Fāṭimid Caliphs*. 2 vols. 1920–22. Reprint 2 vols. in 1. New York: Ktav Publishing House, 1970.

———. *Texts and Studies in Jewish History and Literature*. 2 vols. 1931–35. Reprint New York: Ktav Publishing House, 1972.

Margulies, S. H. "Zwei autographische Urkunden von Moses und Abraham Maimuni." *Monatsschrift für Geschichte und Wissenschaft des Judenthums* 44 (1900), 8–13.

Martz, Linda. *Poverty and Welfare in Habsburg Spain: The Example of Toledo*. Cambridge: Cambridge University Press, 1983.

Mauss, Marcel. *The Gift: Forms and Functions of Exchange in Archaic Societies*. Trans. Ian Cunnison, with an Introduction by E. E. Evans-Pritchard. London: Cohen & West, 1954.

Midrash Mishlei. Ed. Salomon Buber. Vilna: Romm, 1893.

Midrash Vayiqra Rabba. Ed. Mordecai Margoliot (Margulies). 5 vols. Jerusalem: Ararat Publishing Society and American Academy for Jewish Research, 1953–60.

Midrash Zuṭa ʿal Shir ha-Shirim Ruth Eikha ve-Qohelet. Ed. Salomon Buber. Berlin: J. Kaufmann, 1894.

Mollat, Michel. *The Poor in the Middle Ages: An Essay in Social History*. Trans. Arthur Goldhammer. New Haven and London: Yale University Press, 1986.

Moses ben Maimon. Mishneh Torah. English translation in *The Code of Maimonides, Book Seven*. Trans. Isaac Klein. New Haven and London: Yale University Press, 1979.

Porten, Bezalel, et al., eds. *The Elephantine Papyri in English: Three Millennia of Cross-Cultural Continuity and Change*. Leiden: E. J. Brill, 1996.

Princeton Geniza Browser, www.princeton.edu/~geniza.

Pullan, Brian. "Support and Redeem: Charity and Poor Relief in Italian Cities from the Fourteenth to the Seventeenth Century." *Continuity and Change* 3 (1988), 177–208.

Rabie, Hassanein. *The Financial System of Egypt* A.H. *564–741* A.D. *1169–1341*. London: Oxford University Press, 1972.

Rāġib, Yūsuf. *Marchands d'étoffes du Fayyoum au IIIe/IXe siècle d'après leurs archives (actes et lettres), II. La correspondance administrative et privée des Banū ʿAbd al-Muʾmin*. Cairo: Institut français d'archéologie orientale, 1985.

Reif, Stefan C. *A Jewish Archive from Old Cairo: The History of Cambridge University's Genizah Collection*. Richmond, Surrey: Curzon, 2000.

Richards, D. S. "A Fāṭimid Petition and 'Small Decree' from Sinai." *Israel Oriental Studies* 3 (1973), 140–58.

Rivlin, Joseph. *He-yerusha veha-ṣevaʾa ba-mishpaṭ ha-ʿivri* (Inheritance and Wills in Jewish Law). Ramat Gan: Bar Ilan University Press, 1999.

Rodriguez, Jarbel. "Prisoners of Faith: Christian Captives in the Later Middle Ages." Ph.D. diss., Princeton University, 2001.

Rubin, Miri. *Charity and Community in Medieval Cambridge*. Cambridge: Cambridge University Press, 1987.

Sabra, Adam. *Poverty and Charity in Medieval Islam: Mamluk Egypt 1250–1517*. New York: Cambridge University Press, 2000.

Scheiber, Alexander. "Beggars' Letters from the Geniza" (Hebrew). In Scheiber, *Geniza Studies*. Hildesheim: Georg Olms Verlag, 1981, Hebrew section, 75–84.

Seder Eliyahu Zuṭa. Ed. M. Friedman (Ish-Shalom). 2nd ed. Jerusalem: Bamberger & Wahrmann, 1960.

Serjeant, R. B. *Islamic Textiles: Material for a History up to the Mongol Conquest*. Beirut, Librairie du Liban, 1972.

Shailat, Yitṣḥaq. *Iggerot ha-Rambam* (Epistles of Maimonides). *2 vols*. Maʿaleh Adumim: Hoṣaʾat Maʿaliyot le-yad Yeshivat "Birkat Mosheh," 1987.

Sharpe, Pamela. "'The Bowels of Compation:' A Labouring Family and the Law, c. 1790–1834." In Hitchcock, King, and Sharpe, eds. *Chronicling Poverty: The Voices and Strategies of the English Poor, 1640–1840*, 87–108.

———. "Survival Strategies and Stories: Poor Widows and Widowers in Early Industrial England." In *Widowhood in Medieval and Early Modern Europe*. Eds. Sandra Cavallo and Lyndan Warner. Essex: Longman, 1999, 220–39.

Singer, Amy. *Constructing Ottoman Beneficence: An Imperial Soup Kitchen in Jerusalem*. Albany: SUNY Press, 2002.

Slack, Paul. *Poverty and Policy in Tudor and Stuart England*. London and New York: Longman, 1988.

Sokoll, Thomas, ed. *Essex Pauper Letters 1731–1837*. Oxford: Oxford University Press, 2001.

———. "Negotiating a Living: Essex Pauper Letters from London, 1800–1834." *International Review of Social History* 45, supplement 8 (2000), 19–46.

———. "Old Age in Poverty: The Record of Essex Pauper Letters, 1780–1834." In Hitchcock, King, and Sharpe, eds. *Chronicling Poverty: The Voices and Strategies of the English Poor, 1640–1840*, 127–54.

Starr, Joshua. *The Jews in the Byzantine Empire 641–1204*. Athens: Verlag der Byzantinisch-Neugriechischen Jahrbücher, 1939.

Stillman, Yedida Kalfon. *Arab Dress: A Short History from the Dawn of Islam to Modern Times*. Leiden: Brill, 2000.

Taylor, James Stephen. *Poverty, Migration and Settlement in the Industrial Revolution*. Palo Alto: The Society for the Promotion of Science and Scholarship, 1989.

———. "Voices in the Crowd: The Kirkby Lonsdale Township Letters, 1809–36." In Hitchcock, King, and Sharpe, eds. *Chronicling Poverty: The Voices and Strategies of the English Poor, 1640–1840*, 109–26.

Tosefta. Vol. 1. Seder Zeraʿim. Ed. Saul Lieberman. New York: Jewish Theological Seminary of America, 1955.

Urbach, E. E. "Political and Social Tendencies in Talmudic Concepts of Charity" (Hebrew). *Zion* 16 (1951), 1–27.

Weinfeld, Moshe. *Social Justice in Ancient Israel and in the Ancient Near East*. Jerusalem and Minneapolis: Magnes Press and Fortress Press, 1995.

# INDEX

The spelling of names in the documents is often inconsistent with that of classical Arabic, sometimes reflecting actual pronunciation, e.g., Abū, Bū; Ibrahīm, Ibrāhīm, Ibrahim; Isḥāq, Isḥaq.